Napló

World War I Diary of Stolmár Géza
Period 1914 August 20 to 1918 May 14

S.Géza: 1878.03.10 - 1961.02.02

Paperback ISBN 978-1-80424-540-8
ePub ISBN 978-1-80424-541-5
PDF ISBN 978-1-80424-542-2

Published by MX Publishing
335 Princess Park Manor, Royal Drive,
London, N11 3GX
www.mxpublishing.com

Edited by Gene Nagy

Translations by Fekete Ágnes (Benyó), Kőszelyné Erzsébet (Benyó) Nagy Huba, Emeczné Zsófia (Nagy) and Gene Nagy (Nagy Jenci).

Cover design by Awan

Contents

FOREWORD

"Napló" means diary in English. This is the translation of Stolmár Géza, my maternal grandfather's diary, which he wrote in Hungarian, while serving during the First World War (WW1). My mother, Stolmár Ida, typed it out later as mentioned on the last page, making the translation easier. Mostly intact, but some pages of the diary did not make it through various wars. About 10 pages are missing. The translation was made from these typed pages, the actual Napló itself is lost. Five surviving grandchildren did the translation:

Sisters Fekete Ágnes (Benyó) and Kőszelyné Erzsébet (Benyó) daughters of Benyóné Flora, daughter of Stolmár Géza and siblings Nagy Huba, Emeczné Zsófia (Nagy) and Gene Nagy (Nagy Jenci), the three children of Nagyné Ida (Stolmár), daughter of Stolmár Géza and Dr. Nagy Jenő Ernő.

Place of residence in 2024 June:

Fekete Ágnes:	St. John's, Newfoundland.
Kőszelyné Erzsébet:	Budapest.
Dr. Huba Nagy:	Franklin, TN, USA.
Emeczné Zsófia:	Keszthely, Hungary.
Eugene Nagy (Nagy Jenci)	Vancouver, BC, Canada.

This diary is a daily account of a Hungarian soldier from the Austro-Hungarian era. There are also important differences between what was "correct", or generally accepted language and racial behaviour. No attempt was made to change the original.

The value of this diary is mostly for the descendants, (mostly the English-speaking ones), and for anybody interested in the history of the WW1. The names of the Officers and soldiers are real. Most of the names of towns and villages have changed during the last century. the borders have been redrawn soon after the end of WW1. (Through The Treaty of Trianon, 1920 June 4, the final result was to leave Hungary with only 35,893 of the 125,641 square miles or

92,962 of the 325,408 square km, that had constituted the lands of the Hungarian crown. Romania, Czechoslovakia, and Yugoslavia took large fragments, while others went to Austria and even Poland and Italy.) Even today, many Hungarians feel these areas were "stolen". Just two examples provide food for thought: almost all the towns in which Stolmár Géza fought in Galacia, sometimes spelt Galazia, (Now Ukraine) had Slavic names, and almost all the lowest ranking of the soldiers (which comprised the majority) were Romanian or Moldovan. Yet orders were given in German first, then Hungarian because after all, it was the Austro-Hungarian Empire. Needless to say, the Romanians understood neither language. Today the areas in which he fought, are part of Ukraine and Romania before he went to Italy in late 1917.

There was a picture of a guy in a typical Hungarian attire, who was born in Mohács. The subscript said: "I was born in Hungary, then lived in Czechoslovakia, then lived in Russia and studied at Moscow University. Now I live in Romania. Yet my home, where I have **always** lived, is still in the house and on the land where I was born." Another fact is that two of the most famous compositions of Zoltán Kodály were based on Hungarian folk tunes. One was "The Dances of Galánta", now in Slovakia, and "The Dances of Marosszék", now in Romania.

WW1 started with the assassination of Archduke Franz Ferdinand in Sarajevo. The assassination took place on 28th June 1914. In Hungary mobilization started in August 1914. Stolmár Géza, my grandfather, was 36, when he was called up to serve. He was not a career military person. In High School he studied commerce and upon graduating he was employed by Moktár, a Merchant Bank. For one year, he volunteered for Army training, before 1917. This, as well as his experience in commerce, meant an assignment as an officer. From my understanding, he oversaw about 100 to 200 men.

The Napló records the names of towns as of 1914-1918 but almost all those towns have a different name in today's Ukraine region (2024). The officers' names are real names. This Napló shows how many nationalities fought in that war. It is amazing that they could, for the most part, understand one another!

There was an obvious pecking order. The top layer of officers was mostly Austrian or German. The next layer of officers was mostly Hungarian. The soldiers at the lowest ranks were Romanians, Moldovans and other members of the Austro-Hungarian Empire. The soldiers under Stolmár Géza had predominantly Slavic names. At the same time several members of my grandfather's family lived their lives in these areas for generations. Even today, large areas of Hungarian speaking areas exist in Slovakia, Moldova, Romania and a fair part of the former Yugoslavia.

A glaring example of antisemitism is a time capsule of the times. There was no intent in denying this. It represented the prevalent attitude of the times during the WW1. We may wish that freedom of religion had been present, but it was not. My grandfather was an ardent Roman Catholic, which he did not mention in his diary.

Watching movies of WW1 does not present an accurate picture of what took place in the trenches. This diary was written contemporaneously, at the end of each day. Occasionally, some comments were added later when the *Napló* was typed up. It is one man's unvarnished account of his experiences, fears and joys. Obviously, he survived! When I read it, I found It fascinating! I hope you will also enjoy this rare account.

There are multiple examples of the true facets of the war. The weapons issued were substandard, the majority of my grandfather's unit was Romanian, the clothing substandard, officers ranged from dedicated and brave men to officers, who stayed in the safety of distant locations. In those days, as now, politics was a dirty word, but an ever-present fact.

Some war diaries talk about the excitement of war. This diary talks about the reality of disorganized fighting and periods of boredom. Whereas some commanders lost troops through incompetence, my grandfather was mindful of the troops under his command. He regularly reconnoitered areas he considered as the site of later fighting, prior to battle. This did put him in danger but avoided many injuries to troops under his command. The frequent disappointment about the lack of proper clothing, supply of food and arms, the suffering of soldiers with frostbite and inadequate medical care all speak of his intellectual acumen and true attention to the need of the troops. We are proud of him!

It is commonly accepted that history repeats itself. Napoleon was defeated in Russia. The triple alliance of Austria, Germany and Hungary was defeated in the WW1. The Axis lost in WW2. One mistake in each of these major events was the lack of recognition of the weather in different regions. It is hard to understand one of the most glaring examples, such as Stalingrad, which was predictable, but the lessons of the past were not heeded, and disaster followed. The Napló is a small mosaic of the much larger conflict, but it illustrates the story of one man's journey.

Throughout this English translation of the Napló, reference is noted as to what page the translation came from in the Hungarian version.

Huba Nagy
Franklin, Tennessee

2024 April

Diary log by date, military affiliation and location

	Regiment	Under Command	Log
1914 Aug. 20.			Call-up order to Beszterce. Departure.
Aug. 21 - 22.			Travelling via Nagyvárad.
Aug. 23.			Arrive in Beszterce.
Aug. 24 – Sept 3.		M.k. 32/II honv. hadt.zlj. I század parnok	Forming regiment (zászlóalj; zlj)
Sept 4. "			March to Borgó Prund
Sept 5. "			March to Tihucza
Sept. 6. "			March to Dorna Kandrény, Bukovina.
Sept. 7. "			March to Jakobény.
Sept. 8. "			March to Mestecanesti.
Sept. 9-29. "			Mestecanesti; fortification works, security service
Sept. 30. "			March to Jakobény.
Oct. 1. "			March to Lajosfalva.
Oct. 2 – 6. "			Lajosfalva: security service, trench digging.
Oct. 7. "			March to Jakobény
Oct. 8. "			Jakobény.
Oct. 9. "			March to Mestecanesti.
Oct. 10. – 18. "			Security service and trench digging in Mestecanesti.
Oct. 19. "			March to Jakobény.
Oct. 20. "			Jakobény.
Oct. 21.	M.K. 32/I hadt. zlj. parnok. 55Inf. Truppen Div. kötelékében		Take over 32/II dési hadtáp zlj. Taking over command.
Oct. 22. " "			March to Kirlibaba.
Oct. 23. "	"		March to Itwor.
Oct. 24. " "			March to Seleti.
Oct. 25 - 26. " "			March to Krsyworowna and rest day. On 26th, back to 32/II Battalion (zlj).
Oct. 27. 32/II hadt. zlj. I század parnok "			March to Kossow and readiness.
Oct. 28. " "			Security service around Kossow.
Oct. 29. " "			March to Lysa Gora and there in firing line formation.
Oct. 30. " "			Advancing to Snyatin.
Oct. 31. " "			Retreating to Roznow.

6

Regiment Under Command	Log
1914 Nov. 1. 32/III zlj parnoka 55 divisio	March to Kossow. Taking over the command of 32/III zlj.
Nov. 2. " "	Secure march to Lucki.
Nov. 3. " "	Advancing, met Russian scouts, battle lines setup at night just before Zarzecse.
Nov. 4 - 7. " Attens-Schreiter Div;	Advancing under shrapnel fire, taking up positions in Zarzecse.
Nov. 8. " "	Retreat to Lucki. Overnight the scattered troups made their way to Magura and Mikulyczin.
Nov. 9. " "	Gathering the battalion (zlj.) in Mikulyczin.
Nov. 10. " 55 gyalog dandár (footsoldiers)	55 soldiers on foot. March to Worochta.
Nov. 11. " "	March to Zabie.
Nov. 12. " "	March to Spetki.
Nov. 13. " "	March to Berwinkow.
Nov. 14. " "	Security service, same place.
Nov. 15. " "	Secure march to Kuty.
Nov. 16 -18. " "	Reinforcing service and other work in Kuty.
Nov. 19. " "	Advance march to Kossow and set up position.
Nov. 20. " "	Retreat to Wiznitz.
Nov. 21. " "	Rest day, same place.
Nov. 22. " Detachment leader: Schultheisz altábornagy (Lt. Gen.)	Night advance to Benilla Ruska.
Nov. 23. " "	Secure march to Karapceu.
Nov. 24. " "	Holding positions at same place.
Nov. 25. " "	Engagement, then retreat to Majdán.
Nov. 26. " "	March to Berhomet.
Nov. 27. " "	March to Sipot Privat.
Nov. 28. " "	March to Seletin.
Nov. 29 – 30. " "	Organization and rest in Seletin.
Dec. 1. " "	March to Storozintinec Putilla.
Dec. 2. " In Shuller tbn.'s Brigade	March to Rosticki.
Dec. 3. " "	Engagement near Rosticki. Retreat to Dolhopole.
Dec. 4. " "	Advance to Uscie Putilla.
Dec. 5. " "	Engagement there. March towards Sybeni to Hrynawa.

Regiment Under Command	Log
1914 Dec. 6. 32/III zlj parnoka Schuller Brigade	March to Sybeni.
Dec. 7. " "	March to Kopilás and back to Sybeni. Transferring battalion 32/III command.
Dec. 8. " "	March through Kopilás to Havasmező.
Dec. 9 – 10. " "	Rest days in Havasmező.
Dec. 11. " Independent	By train to Maramaros Island, then to Huszta. At night by road to Dolha.
Dec. 12. " "	By road to Bereznek.
Dec. 13. " "	Rest day in Bereznek.
Dec.14. " "	March to Stog to relieve the 2nd Company. Then return to Rika.
Dec. 15. " "	Security checks in Stog.
Dec. 16 – 19. " "	In Bereznek.
Dec. 20. " Polish Legion	Secure night march through Hrab to Bükköskő.
Dec. 21. " "	Attack followed by retreat to Bükköskő.
Dec. 22. " "	March to Bereznek.
Dec. 23. " "	March; then taking up position next to Bükköskő in the forest.
Dec. 24. " "	Fire exchange between patrols, march to Bereznek.
Dec. 25. " "	March to Hrab, security service.
Dec. 26 – 31. " "	In Hrab.
1915 Jan. 1 -16. " "	In Bereznek. Initializing the security service.
Jan. 17. " "	March to Hrab.
Jan. 18 -20. " "	Service in Hrab.
Jan. 21. " "	March to Bereznek
Jan. 22. " "	Withdraw from Bereznek to above the town; spent the night in the open.
Jan. 23 – Feb. 28 " Independent	In Bereznek.
Mar. 1. " "	March to Lipesér.
Mar. 2. " "	March to Vucskómező (Now Vechkove, Ukraine).
Mar. 3. " "	March to Majdánka. (Now Maidan, Ukraine)
Mar. 4. " "	March to Felső Sebes (Upper Sebes).
Mar. 5. " "	Resting day here.
Mar. 6. " "	(Illegible) in Titokvölgy. (Now Titkivtsi, Ukraine)

8

Date	Regiment Under Command	Log
1915 Mar. 7 – 20.	32/II zlj.1-ső sz.p. Independent	As reserve troops in Titokvölgy.
Mar. 21.	" "	March to elevation 1288m. Spending the night in underground shelters.
Mar. 22 -29	" "	Reserves, same place.
Mar. 30	" "	March towards Rozenka
Mar. 31 – Apr. 2	" "	As reserves same place.
Apr. 3	" "	Marching, camping at night in the forest.
Apr. 4 -5	" "	March towards Rozenka.
Apr. 6-7	32/II zlj. as workers. Guilhaume alezr.'s (Lt. Col.) group at Ostryn.	March to Slawsko. On Apr. 7March to Plawje. Reinforcement work at the front line.
Apr. 8 – May 13	" "	In Plawjek. Ostry, Makowka, Pliszka: road building.
May 14	" Independent	March to Rykow.
May 15 – 16	" " "	Organizing neglected battlefield.
May 17	" "	March to Augusztow.
May 18	" "	March to Kamionkár.
May 19	" "	March to Brzazár. Preparation of Prügelweg.
May 20	" "	March to Sukiel.
May 21 – June 6	" "	In Sukiel.
June 7	" "	March to Bolechow.
June 8	" "	March to Dolinár.
June 9	" "	March to Krechowiec.
June 10	" "	March to Kalusz.
June 11	" Hoffman hadtest (army corps)	March to Bendarow.
June 12-14	" "	Reenforcing work at the front lines at Bednarow.
June 15	" "	March to Pawelce.
June 16-18	Militär Arb. Abt. II/32 Deputy Officer Bolzano Brigade	Pawelce. Splitting up the zlj. Creation of two separate work groups.
June 19	" "	March to Wiktorow.
June 20-24	" "	Reinforcing work at the front line, same place.
June 25	" "	March to Halicz
June 26-27	" "	Work on the front line just before Halicz.
June 28	" "	March to Meducha

Regiment Under Command	Log
1915 June 29 Mil. Arb. Abt. II/32 Bolzano Brigade	March to Panowice.
June 30 – July 18 " "	Camping near Panowice, in the forest. Reinforcing work on the front at Zlota Lipa. June 17 to Halicz HQ.
July 19-22 " "	Lived in Panwicze and commuted to the front from there.
July 23 " Hoffman hadtest.	March to Toustababy.
July 24 – Aug. 24 " " "	Toustababy. Trench works.
Aug. 25 Mi. Arb.Abt. I/32 parnok Sapeurök (Sappers)	March to Nossow to my new assignment.
Aug. 26 – 27 " "	Nossow. Sapper work for the 28th attack.
Aug. 28 " "	After a dawn attack, we left for Jablonow after the troops left.
Aug. 29 " Independent	March to Wierzbow. Then to Podhajce for further orders.
Aug. 30 " Hoffman hadtest.	March and retreat from Folw. Debiki.
Aug. 31 – Sept. 3 " " "	Wierzbow. Building three bridges.
Sept. 4 " Sapeurök	March to Sosnow. Bridge building during the night.
Sept. 5 " 129 Brigade	March to Tiutkow.
Sept. 6 " Elsö honv. gy. ezr.	Tiutkow. Digging trenches.
Sept. 7 " Hoffman hadtest	Tiutkow completed, march to Sokolow where we dug trenches next to Strypa.
Sept. 8 " "	Camping in the open by Sokolow; trench digging.
Sept. 9 " "	March to Chatki. Trench digging.
Sept. 10 " "	March to Burkanow. Reinforcing work next to Strypa.
Sept. 11-13 " " "	Same work on the borders of Hajworonka and Wiezznowczyk.
Sept. 14 " "	Clash at Burkanowna, retreat to Podhajce.
Sept. 15-16 " "	Podhajce – rest. Handed over the divison to Galamb.
Sept. 17 " " "	Move with II/32 M.A.Abt into Bielokiernicza.
Sept. 18 Mil-Arb. Abt. II/32 beosztott (assigned). "	March to Chatki.
Sept. 19-20 " "	Chatki. Sapeur work at the front line.
Sept. 21 " " "	Sosnow. Take over sick Galamb's I/32 workers division – take leave of absence.
Sept. 22 " "	By car to Tassarorwka to Podhajc to Halicz and by train to Stanyslau
Sept. 23 " "	By train to Delatyn, change trains.
Sept. 24 " "	To Stryj then change trains, arrive in Budapest.
Sept. 25- Oct. 4 " " "	My first holiday: in Budapest.

10

Regiment Under Command	Log
1915 Oct. 5 M.A.A.II/32 beosztott (deputy) Hoffman hadtest	Return trip by railway. S.A. In Ujhely, change at Delatyn.
Oct. 6 " "	Stanyslau.
Oct. 7 " "	Potok Zloty-Halicz-Podhajce
Oct. 8-9 " "	In Podhajce.
Oct. 9 " "	By car to Sosnow, Est., on foot in the evening to Rakowiec; building "zsákállás" there in the hills.
Oct. 10-11 " "	Camping in the open: Studynka-Niederung. Digging trenches in the hills above Rakowiec.
Oct. 12-30 " " "	Camping beside Malowody in the open. Digging trenches at night, under fire.
Oct. 31 " " "	Break through Siemikowce. Overnight peperation.
Nov. 1 " "	March to Malowody. Building front positions. At the bridge in the evening, back to Malowodyb at night.
Nov. 2-26 Ldst.A.A. 68/u.V. "	In Malowody. Continuous work on the front line.
Nov. 27 " " "	March to Rakowiec.
Nov. 28 – Dec. 6 " " "	In Rakowiec. Work in the area of Siemikowce-Bienawa-Sosnow.
Dec. 7 " " "	By car to Stanislau. Meeting Flórus (wife).
Dec. 8-11 " " "	In Stanislau. Went to Stryjb by train.
Dec. 12 " " "	In Stryjb. Flórus returns to Pest.
Dec. 13 " " "	By train to Potutory-Podhajce.
Dec. 14 " " "	By car to Rakowiec.
Dec. 15 – 1916 Jan. 28 " " "	In Rakowiec. Building positions in Siemikowce-Bienawa-Sosnow area.
1916 Jan. 29 " " "	To Galamb's division in Sosnow.
Jan. 30 – Feb. 20 " " "	Railway building: Dolina-Podhajce-Sosnow-Studynka Niederung, in the hills above Rakowiec.
Feb. 21-23 " " "	Travel to Budapest, my second vacation.
Feb. 24 - Mar 13 " "	On vacation in Budapest.
Mar. 14 K.k. Baukomp. 103/14 "	By car to Burkanow: sub in the command of K.k. Baukomp. 103/14. Trench digging around Burkanow.
Mar. 15-28 " " "	Burkanow: Trench digging.
Mar. 29 " " "	By car to Rakowiec Steinbruch railway camp station. Railroad work.
Mar. 30 – Jun. 12 Ldst.A.A. 69/u.V. "	Railway camp work. Railway line construction to Rochosovacietz.
Jun. 13 " " "	March to Uwsier: trench digging.
Jun. 14-19 " " "	March and trench digging in Rigalicha.
Jun. 20-24 " " "	Return to Steinbruch. Railway camp service.

11

Regiment Under Command	Log
1916 Jun. 25 Ldst.A.A.C9/u.V Hoffman hadtest (army corps)	March to Rchosowacietz.
Jun. 26- Aug. 10 " "	Return to Steinbruch, railway camp service.
Aug. 11 " "	March to Sybalin-Posuchow. Trench digging in Lysoni.
Aug. 12 " "	In Posuchow. Reinforcing work.
Aug. 13 " "	Trenching at the rear guard. March to Adamowka.
Aug. 14 – Oct. 16 " "	During constant battles, sap work at the front line. We lived in Brzezany.
Oct. 17 " "	On my third vacation, by car to Wolkow, by train to Lemberg.
Oct. 18 – 19 " "	By train to Budapest.
Oct. 20 – Nov. 6 " "	On vacation in Budapest.
Nov. 7 " "	In the evening to Lemberg by train.
Nov. 8 – 12 Bahnbetrieb Hinowice parnok. "	By train to Wolkow, by car to Hinowic to sub in the Bahnbetrieb command.
Nov. 13 " "	By train to Lemberg.
Nov. 14 " "	Further, through Stryj and to Musterung.
Nov. 15 – 29 " "	Return to Hinowice; railway service.
Nov. 30 – Dec. 13 Ldst.A.A.69/u.V "	Return to Brzezany. Reinforcing and sap work at Lysoni, Potutory and Dziki-Láni.
Dec. 14 " "	March to Pawlow.
Dec.15 -26 " "	In Pawlow. Road building and rock-mine work.
Dec. 27 M.A.A. 253/Ldst.5. parnok. A.C.K. Szesztay group.	To Demnia to take over 253/Ldst15. Krickl hgy.
Dec. 28 – 1917 Jan.7 " " "	In Demnia. Road and rock-mine work.
Jan. 8 – 13 Ldst.A.A.69/u.V Hoffman hadtest	Return to Galamb in Pawlow.
Jan. 14 " "	By train to Podviszoky-Lemberg, meeting Flórus.
Jan. 15 – 19 " "	In Lemberg. Flórus travels to Budapest and me to Podwysok.
Jan. 20 – 21 " "	In Pawlow. Taking over K.k. 205/15 osztäg (division).
Jan. 22 K.k. Ldst.A.A.205/15 parnok. Deutsche Südarmee Szesztay group.	Moving to Demnia.
Jan. 23 – Feb. 13 " "	Building barracks, road building and rock mining. Demnia, Csesniky.
Feb. 14 " "	March to Pukow-Pezelasyk.
Feb. 15 – Mar. 9 " "	In Pezelasyk. Roadbuilding and rock mine work.
Mar. 10 " "	On my fourth vacation; by train to Chodrow-Stryj.
Mar. 11 " "	S.A.Ujhely-Budapest

Regiment Under Command	Log
1917 Mar. 12-31 K.k. Ldst.A.A.205/15 Duetsch Südarmee	On vacation in Budapest.
Szesztay group	
Apr. 1 "	By train to Stryj.
Apr. 2 "	By train to Chodorow-Pukow-Przelasky.
Apr. 3 – Jul. 22 " "	Przelasky. Road building. Rock mine.
Jul. 23 " Deutsche Südarmee.	By car to Urman.
Jul. 24 – 27 " "	In Urman. Harvesting power poles.
Jul. 28 "	By truck to Muzsilow with half my troops.
Jul. 29 " "	March to Muzsilow, while I went by car to Podhajce.
Jul. 30 " "	By car to Buczacz.
Jul. 31 " "	By car to Tribuchowce and from there to Pomorce.
Aug. 1 " "	Back to Buczacz where the division also arrives.
Aug. 2 " "	March to Pomorce.
Aug. 3 – 7 " "	Harvesting power poles.
Aug. 8 – 9 " "	By truck to Bialoboznic, then march to Simakowce.
Aug. 10 " "	March to Bialoboznica, camped in the open.
Aug. 11 " "	By truck to Kopiczynce.
Aug. 12 -15 " "	Camped in the forest by Kopiczince. Cutting poles.
Aug. 16 " Doutzoho Südarmee Szesztay group	By car: Czortokow-Zalesie-Bilce-Glenbouczek-Jezierzany-Zalesie-Czortkow-Uriszkowce-Kopiczynce
Aug. 17 "	March to Zalesie.
Aug. 18 – 27 " "	Camped in forest by Zalesei. Harvesting poles.
Aug. 28 " "	March to Bilcze.
Aug. 29 – Sept. 2 " "	Harvesting poles in the forest.
Sep. 3 " "	March to Pienky.
Sep. 4 " "	News about Nazi casualties. Starting my fifth vacation. By car to Czortkow.
Sep. 5 " "	By truck to Litiatyn, by car to Potutory, from there to Szaranczuky.
Sep. 6 " "	By car to Potutory railway station and by train to Podwiesoky-Stryj.
Sep. 7 " "	By train to Budapest.
Sep. 8 – 18 " " "	Vacation in Budapest.
Sep. 19 " "	By train: Vienna then Prague.

13

	Regiment Under Command	Log
1917 Sep. 20	K.k.Ldst. A.A. 205/15 Deutsche Südarmee Szesztay group.	Travel: Prague-Aussig-Brüx. Met my younger brother László. Back to Vienna by evening.
Sep. 21 " "		Vienna, starting for Lemberg.
Sep. 22 " "		Lemberg – Stanyslau.
Sep. 23 " "		Stanyslau – Wygnanka.
Sep. 24 " "		By car to Papierna to the division.
Sep. 25 " "		In Papierna. By car to Czortkow.
Sep. 26 " "		March to Popiszynce. By train to Jezierzany. March to Pienky.
Sep. 27 – Oct. 30 " "		In Pienky. Road building between Glenboczek and Ulaszkowce.
Oct. 31 " "		March to Probuzsna.
Nov. 1 " Muhr group.		By car to Hadynkowce railway station. By train to Stanyslau-Stryj.
Nov. 2 " "		In Stryj.
Nov. 3 – 4 " "		At Stryj feldgericht for my hearing.
Nov. 5 -7 " "		Met Flórus in Stryj; she is leaving in the evening.
Nov. 8 " "		Stanyslau.
Nov. 9 – 15 " "		By train to Hadynkowce. By car to Probuzna. Road building.
Nov. 16	Prisoner transport detachment Deutsche Süderarmee	By car to Hadynkowce, by train to Stanyslau-Stryj. Travelling for prisoners of war.
Nov. 17 " "		Stryj-Miskolcz.
Nov. 18 " "		Miskolcz-Budapest.
Nov. 19 " "		Budapest-Vienna.
Nov. 20 " "		Vienna-Sigmundsherberg.
Nov. 21 " "		Sigmundsherberg-Vienna.
Nov. 22 - 23 " "		Vienna. My appointment to Captain.
Nov. 24 " "		Vienna. Flórus arrives.
Nov. 25 " "		Vienna to Sigmundsherberg with Flórus.
Nov. 26 " "		Sigmundsherberg.
Nov. 27 " "		Sigmundsherberg to Vienna. Flórus goes home.
Nov. 28 " "		Vienna-Muthausen-Vienna.
Nov. 29 " "		Vienna-Budapest.
Nov. 30 – Dec. 8 " "		At home.

Regiment Under Command	Deutsche	Log
1917 Dec. 9 Prisoner transport detachment command	Südarmee	Budapest-Vienna-Budapest.
Dec. 10 – 15 " "		In Budapest.
Dec. 16 " "		Budapest-Vienna-Mauthasen.
Dec. 17 " "		Mauthasen-Vienna-Ostfyasszonyfa.
Dec. 18 " "		Ostfyasszonyfa-Budapest
Dec. 19-25 " " "		In Budapest.
Dec. 26 " " "		Budapest-Ostfyasszonyfa.
Dec. 27-29 " " "		Ostfyasszonyfa prisoner of war camp.
Dec. 30 " " "		Ostfyasszonyfa-Budapest.
Dec. 31-1918 Jan. 3 " " "		In Budapest.
1918 Jan. 4 " " "		Budapest-Ostfyasszonyfa.
Jan. 5-6 " " "		Ostfyasszonyfa prisoner of war camp.
Jan. 7 " " "		Start taking Italian prisoners of war to Budapest.
Jan. 8 " " "		Budapest-Miskolcz.
Jan. 9-11 " " "		Miskolcz-Stryj.
Jan. 12 " " "		Stryj-Zsidacsow-Stanyslau.
Jan. 13-14 K.k.Ldst. A.A. 205/15 "		Stanyslau-Borscow.
Jan. 15 " " "		By car to Sapahow.
Jan. 16 " " "		By car to Borscow, with prisoners to Tarosin.
Jan. 17-22 Baukomp.// 3/Sch.25 "		In Lanowce. Taking over A Baukomp. 6/Sch. 25.
Jan. 23-28 " " "		Preparing for march.
Jan. 29-Feb. 5 " " "		March to Jezierzany. Road building. Preparing for march.
Feb. 6-17 " " "		Same as above.
Feb. 18 " " "		March to Zalesie.
Feb. 19-22 " " "		Prepping for march to Zalesie.
Feb. 23 " " "		March to Czortkow.
Feb. 24 " " "		Registering (bewaggonirozás) in Czortkow.
Feb. 25 " 11 Armee. Kmdo.		Starting out for Italy. Körösmező.
Feb. 26 " " "		Körösmező-Királyháza.

15

Regiment Under Command	Log
1918 Feb. 27 Baukomp.3/Sch.25 11 Armee Kmdo.	In Budapest.
Feb. 28 " "	Budapest – Rákospalota and to Pozsony with the transport.
Mar. 1 " " "	Pozsony – St. Pölten.
Mar. 2 " " "	St. Pölten – Amstetten – Linz.
Mar. 3 " " "	Linz – Saalfeld.
Mar. 4 " " "	Saalfeld – Innsbruck – Trient – Caldonazzo.
Mar. 5 " " "	Caldonazzo.
Mar. 6 " " "	March to Ceuta. Working at the collapsed tunnel.
Mar. 7 " " "	Ceuta tunnel.
Mar. 8 " 52 Dion.	March to Carbonare. At cable cars in Pusterle.
Mar. 9-30 Munkás osztág csoport parnok. "	In Val d'Assa.
Mar. 31 "	By car to Monte Roverre.
Apr. 1 " "	On foot to Caldonazzo. By train to Innsbruck.
Apr. 2 " "	Innsbruck – Vienna – Budapest.
Apr. 3 – May 1 " "	In Budapest.
May 2 " "	Budapest – Pragerhof, back to the Italian front.
May 3 " "	Pragerhof – Trient.
May 4 " "	Trient – Caldonazzo. On foot to Monte Roverre.
May 5 " "	On foot to Pusterle
May 6 Sick leave "	On foot to Termine Hospital.
May 7 " "	By truck to Vezzena, on foot to Monte Roverre.
May 8 " "	On foot to Caldonazzo, by train to Innsbruck.
May 9-11 " "	In Innsbruck Hospital.
May 12 " "	On Red Cross train Hospital in St. Pölten.
May 13 " "	St. Pölten – Vienna.
1918 May 14 " "	Vienna – Budapest.

Part 1

IN BUKOVINA

1914 September 6 to 1914 December 11

Page 3 of the Napló.

My family enjoyed their summer holiday at Domonyvölgy, where I had a house in the country. It was located near Gödöllő, about 20 miles East of Budapest. It served as our residence during the summer holidays or whenever we needed a break from the crowded, hectic life in Budapest. My holiday from work by this time was exhausted, so I worked in the Capital from Monday to Friday and spent the weekends relaxing in Domonyvölgy. Towards the end of 1914 June, my boss, Dr. Joseph Schmidt, the Bank's CEO, [Ed: The merchant Bank was Moktár] asked to see me in his office. He requested that I collect the keys to the secure locations of the Bank from Director Kalliwoda. Dr. Schmidt had to leave town at very short notice. During our discussion he said the trip was the consequence of the ultimatum issued to Serbia. His opinion was that the Serbian events would likely lead to war. He felt general mobilization was imminent and required that I return to Budapest next morning.

I went to Domonyvölgy. My brothers-in-law, Ottó and Jóska, were in total disbelief. Flórus, my wife, and I decided to move permanently to Pest. We arrived early Sunday morning. By the time we reached the town there were early notifications about forthcoming army service. My name did not appear among those affected by this order. Ottó, my brother-in-law, started marching along the boulevard within a day or two, carrying clothing and heavy boots. As a teacher in Budapest he was to join the army reserves.

I received my callup orders on 1914 August 21st. I was to join the 32nd revolutionary Battalion in Beszterce. This was not a surprise; in fact, I had already started assembling my army kit. After lunch I went to the Army Supply Store to purchase the rest of my needs. Included was a fine blanket and minor items I felt would be useful. My train was scheduled to depart to Nagyvárad at 7 p.m.

My assignment to my Battalion appeared ideal. My 3-year-old daughter, Icu, (Ed: Stolmár Ida, mother of Huba, Zsófi, Jenci) tried to think of what else I might find beneficial, running circles around me! My mother-in-law, Tóni, Aunt Guszti and my mother's sisters all came for a final farewell. I pretended that I had to deal with urgent tasks. During supper I removed my wedding ring taking care to avoid my wife noticing this. I was troubled with a dilemma: on the one hand, it seemed logical to leave it behind, in a safe place, while on the other hand if my wife were to find the ring accidentally, she would feel hurt. As it_happened, the hustle and bustle with my impending departure to my train obscured all else.

My dearest Flórus, my wife, (Ed: Flóra) assisted in the preparation for my departure without tears. When my carriage was departing, the tears flowed freely. "May God be with you" was the final message. I was fighting to avoid crying myself, especially when my 3-year-old daughter, little Icu, was happily chasing the departing carriage. This finally brought tears to my eyes. It took considerable effort to adjust to an image more like that of a hardened soldier. During the rush of my departure, I did not have time to think of the millions of vital problems that could be in my path. Being alone I was now able to organize my thoughts. The recognition that events could shape my future for ever was foremost in my thoughts. This included the feeling of mortality.

Gradually I was adapting to my future: to think and behave like an honorable soldier. I gathered my thoughts about my volunteer days in the Army. I had numerous memories which were forever stored in my brain's memory bank.

Let me recount some of these memories as a volunteer. The year I spent as a volunteer prepared me well to face the challenges of a "Real war". I felt secure in the conviction that I could and would serve with honor. I served my year in the Kaiser's and the King's 32nd infantry regiment. At the same time, my younger brother, Aladár, was a volunteer in the 23rd rifle regiment at Kolozsvár. Our mother had two sons in Army service, which caused her much stress. She died a premature death during that year.

Page 4 of the Napló.

The Mária Terézia barracks were located on Üllöi Út in Pest. This was the volunteers' domain. In charge was Captain Divéky. On the third day, we went to the training grounds at Rákos. In charge was 1st lieutenant Ákos Kárpáthy, who was my age (Ed: 36 years). During a break in the training exercises, he asked me to have a brief discussion. Apparently, he felt I would make a good "Klassenaltester". This resembled the high school class monitors. I told him that I was not a fluent German speaker. He cursed me and let me know that to any order the appropriate reply is "Jawohl, Herr Lieutenant!" So, I said "Jawohl, Herr Lieutenant!" The outcome of my interaction with Kárpáthy was that it became a matter of pride to learn German. I graduated at the top of the class and became 2nd Lieutenant. Out of 8O graduates only 4 of us reached this rank.

I enjoyed army life but did not get much joy in having to learn German! Although I did not advance much in the recitation of the Dienst Reglement, [Army Regulations], I did well in general infantry. I got particularly good grades for live fire exercises. This led to live fire exercises in Püspökhatvan, where I was placed as head of a battle-ready group. There I had the task of attacking the enemy's flank. I expected this to be a particularly effective maneuver in real battle.

There are several qualities of a good soldier. First of these is following orders. Another quality is the technical ability to understand and resolve tasks in an intelligent manner. I was occupied with these matters while on the train. The more I thought of flank attacks the more I considered these important because it took away a sizeable portion of the main attack. I tried to place myself in such a flank attack, aware of the risks and possible benefits of this move. My mind kept returning to the safety and loving environment of my family. These thoughts had to be pushed into the background.

At my request, when I left home, nobody accompanied me. At the railway station I met one of my colleagues from work, Jenő Faragó, whose orders sent him to Nagyvárad. All the 2nd class seats were taken. Jenő had a nice spot in 3rd class, and I joined him. At first, we discussed the politics, the possibility of a full-fledged war and the impact we could expect. He was also a family man, which was a topic we both valued, passing the time just chatting. I spent a day in Nagyvárad, bought a few more necessities in the stores and in a pharmacy. The wind of war caused a sudden onset of inflation, and I noted this phenomenon myself.

I left Nagyvárad in the afternoon of 1914 August 22nd. The Officers and troops received a warm welcome everywhere. Our train carried the newspapers, and thousands were thronging to get the news. This event recurred at every station. Our progress was further delayed by numerous troop transports everywhere, each attempting to gain advantage. The result was a lack of coordination, which in turn caused further delays. The troop transports were adorned with flags and green tree branches. Some of the soldiers were singing, others were just aimlessly gazing into the distance. I enjoyed watching the villages pass by between the hills. I did not make any friends; it was best to allow me to come to grips with my own thoughts.

I arrived in Beszterce late at night. After completing my registration at the Army Headquarters, I went to the Officers canteen. I surveyed my future colleagues. It did not take long to see that too much wine was consumed with supper. My Captain, Bertalan Fábry, appeared to be in a far better mood than seemed appropriate. He seemed to be a slow, quiet drinker who could hold his liquor. With the drinks his mood altered. He became more cheerful. Elsewhere many enjoyed playing cards.

After supper, our Captain requested a meeting with the Officers. His hangover was evident. He was trying to organize the Battalion's officers in the room the cardplayers just vacated. His approach left a lot to be desired. It was awkward, unpleasant, and left me questioning his leadership qualities. He asked if anyone would be interested becoming the Officer responsible for the economic aspects of the Battalion. He also asked if anyone was interested in becoming the Captain of a Company. Since I did not know much about economics, I hoped to get the post of a Company Captain or 1st Lieutenant. I was really hoping to receive such an assignment and I would have been most disappointed with not achieving it. The task of 2nd lieutenant was slated to Vilmos Fogarascher. However, his credentials did not pass muster and he was removed from the list of potential applicants. In his place a deputy sheriff, Dr. Loránt Vajda became an adjutant. As for me, I received command of the 2nd Company as 1st Lieutenant.

Out of the great blue yonder arrived 1st Lieutenant Dezső Vértes. The verification of this obese Jewish man's qualifications was rather superficial, Captain Fábry took the claim of rank and other pertinent matters as adequate, without checking his background and the veracity of his prior service. The long and the short of this event was that I was demoted and he received the leadership of the 2nd Company. Command of the 3rd Company went to Gyula Galamb, who arrived when I did. Dr. Árpád Pálffy, a 2nd Lieutenant, was unhappy. Having known me for just a brief time, yet forming a good bond, he did not feel it appropriate that my position went to this troublesome man. He did not mind expressing his opinion in public. The change in my situation, i.e., rank, made me somewhat depressed and my zeal for military life took a dive. To add insult to injury, many former 2nd Lieutenants were given the rank of 1st Lieutenants. Of course, the more cautious officers waited for the promotions to be confirmed in writing prior to broadcasting their promotions. Some less reliable officers succumbed to the allure of a higher rank obtained without foundation. They felt:" What's the harm in trying?" So, they promoted themselves. Mr. Vértes cheerfully added the stars to his uniform. When I attempted to ascertain his qualifications to this higher rank, he was evasive and getting answers to my questions was like pulling teeth. After a prolonged and unpleasant discussion, he admitted the lack of possessing the necessary qualifications of a 1st Lieutenant. This did not stop him from sewing on the extra stars, even after I said that he had two choices: remove the stars or I would notify my superiors of this unfortunate fact.

This did not faze him. He continued attaching his stars. However, Fábry acted, and upon further review Vértes was removed from the post I held previously. His fake stars were removed, and he lost the leadership of the 2nd Company. He was moved to the 3rd Company. I regained my former rank as Head of the 2nd Company. To clarify the officers in charge of the Companies, all 1st Lieutenants, Company 1, Fülöp. Company 2, Stolmár. Company 3, Galamb. In charge of the economy of my 2nd Company was 2nd Lieutenant Gyula Eperjessy, a former revenue officer. My adjutant was 2nd Lieutenant Zoltán Szántó. The officers of the 1st Company were Márkus Mayer, a former shopkeeper; Rákosi, a teacher and Dr. Gyula Vlayk, a Romanian lawyer whose qualifications as an Officer remained unclear to the rest of us! Also serving were Emil Tisca, a Romanian 2nd Lieutenant. The 2nd Company received Dr. Árpád Pálffy, a lawyer and János Heredek, who formerly was a mill employee. The 3rd Company received 2nd Lieutenants Lajos Surányi, Vilmos Fogarascher, Imre Lányi (who was a former Tax Office employee) and András Pópa.

Preparations reached a feverish pace. We all attempted to choose the most talented appearing men. We also selected our non-commissioned officers.

The remaining men were transferred to the Reserve Company. Our most difficult challenge was providing adequate clothing. We had virtually no funds allocated for this essential need. Unfortunately, we were not alone in seeking these items. The competition which inevitably ensued drove up the prices of the already tenuous supply of proper coats for the frigid winter. Since this never occurred to our respected superiors, the search was expected to be monumental. Since I could not foresee any action by the Army, however irresponsible such a lack of protecting the troops from the vagaries of the weather, particularly protection from severe cold and rain, I felt a personal obligation to my troops, and I was going to rectify this unacceptable mistake by using my personal funds and provide the proper coats for the entire Company. Heavy overcoats came in all styles and colors. Trousers, shirts, and underwear also came in all colors of the rainbow. Since beggars cannot be choosers, I bought what I could, going from one shop to the next. My efforts were physically and emotionally demanding. My supply of weaponry brought enormous surprises and even greater astonishment and sorrow. The rifles from the Werndl company were among the worst for many reasons. Just when I began to have a more optimistic hope for our future fights, along came these horrendous rifles ruining all my enjoyment of life as a soldier. These awkward rifles did not have a leather strap. The arrival of these naked and ugly pieces of heavy trash came with an equally ugly, impractical bayonet and heavy ammunition. Nobody cared about the protection of the rifles and the practicality of these rifles, or the troops. It must have been an imbecile parading as an engineer who was at the helm of designing this, not an ordinary, clear-thinking person. I wanted my Company to be equipped with leather straps, but the captain vetoed it. Against this order, I could not bear the thought of my poor Romanian soldiers handling these monstrosities without any handles or any protection of the rifles or the bayonets, to say nothing about the soldiers themselves. I ordered the protecting covers and handles. It was an awfully expensive strain on my personal funds, but the ingenious tailor did a superb job for our immediate needs. Seeing my Company so much better equipped by my tailor, made my spirits rise once again. I liked the practical, yet lightweight design of my tailor, who designed an excellent bayonet and rifle cover. My next task was to purchase cooking utensils and metal spoons, knives, and forks. The very large two or three pots, with matching and utilitarian large spoons and similarly utilitarian but smaller spoons, forks and knives completed the needs I could foresee. Not exactly my idea for elegant dining, but perfectly practical. I was pleased. My initial expectation of large, beautiful sets of copper pots and utensils carried on a Mannlicher Cooking Cart evaporated. But I achieved the desired purpose! No oxen were needed to pull the cart, a further advantage!

I had several problems relating to horsemanship. To tell the truth, I was a novice, and this caused me plenty of anxiety and worry. The Officers were mounted. I had no experience whatsoever in riding a horse! Then one day I got a surprise order to go to the riding school, where I was to choose a horse and learn how to ride it! You could have knocked me over with a feather! I was obviously in need of an expert, who could help me choose a well-mannered horse and advise me about the necessary paraphernalia that one needed to actually ride a horse. I found Mr. Bló, an ex-Hussar and thus a natural advisor about any aspect of horse riding. He was a kind man and ready to help me choose a horse. My requirements were that I get a fine looking and gentle horse, able to compensate for my lack of horsemanship! I had already bought my saddle and other essential riding gear. Mr. Bló selected Bella and did a trial ride, which he found satisfactory. Then it was my turn. After about a quarter hour ride, I began to feel the rhythm and the control of riding. I went to the riding school, where I displayed my horsemanship to Captain Fábry, who was satisfied. Thus, I surmounted my first test of horsemanship.

I was delighted with my great looking mount. However, this Hussar horse had her definite ideas about what she was willing to do. This stubbornness made my fellow officers concerned. The need for a very experienced horse trainer was painfully obvious. Finally, I struck gold. 2nd Lieutenant Zoltán Szántó, a former revenue officer, fancied himself as an outstanding equestrian. He was going to show me how simple horse-riding was and how, under a good rider, horses responded to tasks with ease. He had his Hussar Sword dangling and his boots equipped with spurs. Very impressive! So, he mounted the horse, at which point the horse reared up and bolted, whereupon the spurs went into my horse's side causing a wild waltz, which ended with an unfortunate, both sad and funny event: the horse expert was catapulted high into the air and the arc ended with the rider landing ungracefully, his sword dangling with no control, yet preserving the cigar which was still between his teeth! Perhaps it was unkind of me to enjoy the show. I was happy that I was not in the saddle.

Minor statistics of ages of our soldiers.

Age	32	33	34	35	36	37	38	39	40	41	42	43	Total
1st Company	1	--	3	8	13	29	37	26	22	32	23	11	205
	Subtotal: 54; 25%						151; 76%						
3rd Company	1	3	2	17	18	40	31	27	30	31	33	29	261
	Subtotal: 81; 31%						180; 69%						

Makeup of the 1st Company:

Soldiers, 3-year training	63
Soldiers, 2-year training	41
Reservists	101
Total:	208

Ethnicity:

Romanian	184
Transylvanian/German	10
Hungarian	11
Total:	208

On September 1st, we received orders to expect departure on the 5th. We commenced the preparations with feverish pace. The three 1st Lieutenants of the three Companies had their work cut out. We were rushing, mindful of the fact that whatever was not obtained prior to departure would not be acquired. We suspected our route might be towards the Eastern front. This would be towards the Carpathian Mountains. In that case we would have to change trains, since the first train was going to Kassa-Oderberg. Had the orders directed us to the latter, there would have been much less chance to see action on the Eastern front. The first alternative was more likely.

The orders received on 1914 September 2 stated that our departure date was the 4th of September. The first consequence of the order was a sudden increase of declared sickness. Two officers, Rákosi and Tisca, both 2nd Lieutenants, joined the sick list. I began to see the explanation for their lack of interest during our preparations for departure. They were plain lazy and never intended to follow orders. I was particularly offended by 2nd Lieutenant Emil Tisca, who let it be known to several people that he was expecting to be paid for his service and thereafter would be admitted to hospital for a "serious malady". I also began to feel that the stories about resenting Hungarian rule might have some truth. Vlayk claimed illness. He appeared eminently well; he had the appearance and physical ability of a Spanish matador! With two 2nd Lieutenants claiming illness, Vlayk did not follow through.

We asked the Romanians to swear allegiance to the cause. We also provided them with Orthodox crosses, which were well received. This also seemed appropriate, and I clearly recognized that we needed mutual trust to fight against a common enemy. All of us in charge needed mutual respect to each other. It needed to be a cohesive unit to fight effectively. I wanted to have their respect and wanted to earn it. My efforts were well received.

From my former office in Budapest, about Antal Vymetel, I received the unwelcome news that he sustained a severe injury to his ear on the Serbian front. He was moved to Budapest for medical care.
My Company was ready for departure. We had two sections of 60 each. We had 2 drummers, 2 buglers, 4 sappers (also called engineers). 5 medics, 5 aid-de-camps, 1 sergeant, 2 carriage drivers and 11 cooks. Part of our Company consisted of Wallachians, who preferred to wear their native garb, which was very distinctive and colorful from head to toe. The housing of their rifles and bayonets were similarly attired. While passing through Wallachia, the men from the area met with their wives and families and there was much joy and sorrow.

Pages 8 & 9

The Company's Wallachian troops were overcome with the hugging, kissing, crying, and laughing family members. I was deeply touched by this outpouring of love and sorrow. My memory drifted back to my family in Budapest. There was a kinship between me and these troops. As I surveyed the Company, it was clear we felt their pain of separation. The Romanians quietly accepted their burden the war caused. Finally, we departed. I led the Company, my horse walking in a dignified, slow manner, his head slightly raised while eating his oats from the feedbag with abandon. A strong bond formed between me and my horse. His appearance was pleasing. He had a lovely face. He was kind and entirely dependable. He disliked being petted and he let you know this!

After two day's march we arrived at the foothills of majestic mountains. The unexpectedly chilly weather surprised us. The first day we reached Borgo-Prund, the second day Tihusza and the third day Dorna Kendrély. Each community saw a relative amongst us and the repeated story of a difficult separation was disheartening.

In Borgo-Prund, Hugó Wachsman and I bought a few items at Albert's Pharmacy. We met a group of locals, who had thousands of questions. They were all happy to see us and we departed with a gift of a pair of great gloves. I came across refugees from Chernowitz. These were the first people I met under such circumstances, and I was abhorred at the cruelty the war caused. It was not just the material loss. In Prund we met with two wounded soldiers. They were hesitant to answer about the events at Rohatyn, where our forces were defeated. Their hesitancy to answer reasonable questions, combined with wounds at their back made me think of them as deserters. Later, we learned that the events occurred just as these two soldiers described. Not only was there a major battle at Rohatyn, but our forces were badly mauled. The loss was **not** the fault of the troops.

Our march was uneventful. Trekking through the Carpathian Mountains took us through majestic forests, gentle mountain streams, where peaceful valleys greeted us. We crossed the border at Tihusza. The Romanians removed their hats in reverence to leaving their homeland. I felt their pain. I was also getting further away from my home. The Company continued the march, thinking about what the future holds. I remember this location with perfect clarity. The border was along a mountain ridge. The road then took a steep decline. Old forests on the right and bald fields on the left. Our progress was also hindered by one precipice after another. The road then took a sharp left turn, now going uphill. We spent the night in Dorna Kendrény. Next day we passed through Dorna Watra, a beautiful village and popular spa. We spent the next night in Jakobény, where we set up camp on 14th September 1914. The village was located near Bukovina. An attractive village, populated by German speaking folk. We found them kind and likeable people. The Officers' dining room was at the center of the village, in a two story hotel. I was given lodgings with a sweet, old lady. My room was wonderfully comfortable. The furniture was well appointed, and I felt (almost) at home. East of us lay large forests, to the West steep hills rising to the sky, with a sharp ridge at the top. In the valley floor the flat arable land was providing the fields where crops thrived. The highway to the ridge was steep and one curve led to another all the way to the ridge. It took us over an hour to reach the ridge at Mestekanest. This divided the watersheds in Moldova.

We remained unaware of the purpose of the march. For several days we simulated maneuvers with our Companies. The Battalion Commander was not particularly interested in our activities, rather they preferred that the decisions be made by the Company commanders. Although we had orders to stay at the Hotel, except at night, we were not given further details. For a while we were anxiously awaiting orders, staying at the Hotel until midnight, the orders never materialized. This developed into an increasingly unpleasant atmosphere, having to stay at the Hotel until midnight for no good reason. Waiting anxiously for the so-called orders seemed pointless. Occasionally we heard news about the war when we received mail.

We were working on the reinforcement of the pass at Mestekanest on the 8th of September. The weather was cold. Flóra ordered a pair of felt lined boots for me. The cost was 24 crowns (korona) and it was to be taken out of my Army pay. By the 27th of September, plenty of snow covered the mountain peaks.

We began our march on 1st October 1914, toward Kirlibaba. We followed the lovely Bisztrics River, more like a stream here, where woods formed a crown in an idyllic manner. Our enjoyment of the view was hampered by the cold, rain mixed with snow, thus the mud further complicated our march. The mud was getting worse as time passed. We arrived at Lajosfalva where the Battalion was to rest. This was a small Hungarian village located just inside the border. It was on the opposite side of Bisztrics and Kirlibaba. Whereas Kirlibaba was an attractive town in the vicinity of Bukovina, Lajosfalva was dirt poor. It was in desperate need for improvement. The roads, which were just avenues of deep mud, were depressing. I stayed with the vicar, Mr. Kapca, a fine Hungarian, who graciously shared his simple, one room abode with me for a few nights.

Our Battalion was aided by field officers, who provided help with the task of digging ditches by the edge of the highway. We had no inkling that, later, this would be the location of serious, blood shedding fight. It was here that the Russian offensive was halted and reversed. The Russian forces threatened Bukovina. For the first time I witnessed Russian prisoners of war, six scouts dressed in heavy, fur covered boots, enormous furry headgear. There were 6 infantry soldiers. They were a good-looking bunch. They had fine, sheepskin lined winter coats, and, in comparison, we looked ill equipped for cold weather. I felt a pang of envy!

We returned to Jakobény on October 8th. However, my Company was ordered to defend the Mestekanesti Pass. I could foresee this and the need for protection from the elements. Since there were only 2 small houses at the Pass, these were quite inadequate for 250 people plus the carts. My construction of the shelters ahead of the need was fortunate.

One day we received an unexpected visit by Lieutenant Colonel Fischer, Commanding Officer at Bukovina. He arrived by car. By that time, he was well known on account of his defeat of the Russians in the defense of Bukovina, with his force consisting of volunteers, ex-policemen, revenue officers and the like. He brought Lieutenant General Schultheisz. They went directly to our defense preparation location. I hurried to join them and introduce myself. Serious discussions followed about where a future attack could be defended. The Pass was a likely place for the Russians to take Czernovicz, the most likely place to surmount the obstacle of the mountains was thought to be through the Mestekanesti Pass. Efforts to reinforce this defensive area seemed essential. Still, this was just a guess. I was particularly impressed with Lieutenant Colonel Fischer.

So, we began digging the trenches. We needed to clear 100 to 120 acres of the finest, old forest. This was done with hesitation. It would have been preferable to save the old forest, but the need for establishing an effective defense trumped the destruction of the forest. The trees fell towards the valley, thus providing additional obstacles to the enemy climbing the hill. Later, here, as well as at Kirlibaba, our efforts resulted in successfully repelling the Russians.

My orders were to remain at Mestekanest Pass until 20th October. We were ordered to return to Jakobény, where Captain Fábry recommended me for leading the first battalion of the 32nd regiment. General Schuller gave me the order. Their former 1st Lieutenant was a former gendarme Captain, Balascher. When the Russians attacked at Felsővisse, his Battalion was ordered to proceed to 0-Radna and to attack the Russian wing. This wing attack was considered key component of the battle. I heard he never made it. I heard later more details about this eccentric man, who often failed to follow orders and did not keep General Schuller in high regard. One memorable day, 2nd Lieutenant Dénes Sántha bought 18 large barrels of wine. I sampled it. The taste was unpleasant, somewhat sour and not fit for human consumption. It was obviously getting closer to becoming vinegar. The acceptance of the "wine" was cancelled by the General. My Battalion was not without shortcomings. 2nd Lieutenant Szánthó oversaw supplies that we needed. It became known that in Jakobény he held expensive and frequent gatherings, freely spending our funds on champagne. I had previous minor encounters with him in the past. Following this event, my trust in him took a dive. You bet I watched his every move with eagle eyes. He was transferred to another Company, he continued making poor decisions and his rank was reduced.

At lunch, when the leadership of the Company was transferred to me, I met my officers. Naturally, Balascher was absent. I met with unexpected warmth and they greeted me, shaking hands and introducing themselves. They were presented as follows: Gábor Kovrig, 2nd Lieutenant, a former sheriff's deputy; Dr. József Molnár, 2nd Lieutenant, formerly a teacher; 2nd Lieutenant Roth: 2nd Lieutenant Béla Groh; 2nd Lieutenant Domokos Pap, history teacher; 2nd Lieutenant Dénes Sántha (of the wine fame), former sheriff's deputy; 2nd Lieutenant Dezső Kölber, well-known painter. The Officers requested that a Lance Sergeant, Russ, a former General Staff Officer and former Hussar be allowed to join us in the Officers' Mess Hall. I welcomed the request and naturally approved it.

The superior division commanding officer sent us an order via a telegram on 22nd October at 1:40 a.m. Our marching order was as follows:

"The 32/111 logistics battalion advance toward Moldova with two Companies and one Company toward Izwor. The 32/1 and 32/11 battalions will move from Jakobény to Kirlibaba where they will sleep. 5 or 6 mounted scouts (Hussars) will reconnoiter the Seletin area. Tomorrow, 23rd October, one Company will proceed to Sipot and one Company to Seletin. The 32/1 and 32/11 Battalions were sent to Izwor. The train is to carry combat equipment and general supplies only over the high ridge. However, in the event of obstacles on the road, a train section will proceed through Jakobény towards Pozsoritta-Moldowa.

Captain Fábry will give 3 packages of maps to Lieutenant Colonel Fischer with further orders that Fischer deliver these packages to Colonel Fuchs, who will be marching tomorrow, 23rd October, through Jakobény to Pozsorita. The 22/1 Battalion will remain in Kirlibaba, where they will prepare accommodation for 5 Battalions. Res, 550th General. Schuller."

We now became part of a larger unit, part of the 55th Division, Field-marshal Schultheisz in charge, with his Staff Officer Tamás Pap, lieutenant Colonel. Our Brigade was under General Schuller. On 22nd October we marched to Kirlibaba, on the 23rd we marched over the mountains through Luczyan to Izwor.

Pages 11 & 12

Only infantry could reach lzwor, as the road was so awful. The muddy mountain roads and the steep gradients were too much of an obstacle and all the carts became stuck. All the Officers of the battalion slept in one room. This proved to be our first introduction to the conditions we could expect during the war. We reached Seletin on 24th October and we continued through Ploska to Storozinetz-Putilla. We were delighted with the upcoming rest and wonderful comfort! We arranged the furniture to our liking. Our joyful mood was premature: we received new orders. We were to depart without delay. It was a bitter pill to swallow. The road to Krzyworowna was a 45 km. march in one day, at the end of which we felt like death warmed up!

Along this march Lieutenant Colonel Bruckner met us and introduced himself. He was going to take charge of my Battalion. The formality took place in Krzyworowna. I rejoined the 32/II Battalion. On 27th October we had another long day's march, once again arriving in Kossow at night. There was much talk about the strong likelihood of the Russians imminent arrival. Therefore, we were ordered to stay in full uniform, standing, in the open in courtyards. We were not allowed to enter houses. Pretty miserable, especially with the cold wind adding to our discomfort. My Company attempted to get some rest leaning against whatever support they could find. The yard of the Salinen-Hof, a hotel, was quite large. I used whatever warm clothing I could find but to no avail!

After the exhausting march, the potential danger and the concern about likelihood of fighting in the very near future, added to my anxiety. I was so cold my teeth were chattering. Suddenly I remembered the flask of plum brandy I had in my pocket. I tried some and finished the whole flask. The improvement was almost magical. I went around the carts to find the bread cart. I found it and decided that the bread would be given to the troops without delay.

This was a lucky decision. The order to march immediately was given even before the bread was fully consumed. The other Companies were envious. They received nothing.

Our first task was to reinforce Kossow. We posted lookouts at several high locations surrounding Kossow. By this time another evening beckoned. My superior officer has already left to sleep. I was thinking to do likewise when loud rifle fire from a neighboring Battalion caused concern. My heart rate increased. "The enemy is attacking us!" Corporal Hartner, a giant of a man, volunteered to scout our situation. We got our answer rather quickly. One of our fellow soldiers from another Company came across one of my scouts. Mistakenly he opened fire and others joined in. My scout ran away, causing the loud, Hungarian exclamations: ' They are running away!" I was unhappy. Firing on a soldier of the same side is called "friendly fire". Of course, nothing is "friendly" about it. The second issue was that had it been the enemy, the Hungarian shouts could have made a true enemy take advantage of the information.

Our Division gathered in Kossow on 29th October 1914. My Battalion came to life and, according to my orders, I was the head of the Battalion. The orders were somewhat vague. The land was flat. We realized that another group followed similar orders. We were aiming toward Lysa Gora, a solitary hill. We arrived at the peak in darkness, in moderate rain and fog.

The Northern slope of the hill was quite steep, and it dropped down to the river Prut. We made our formation at the edge of the steep hill. I sent Lance Sergeant Vareci to reconnoiter the area. In the fog he got lost! He had a few infantrymen with him. I tried to rest for a short while, lying on a bed of corn cobs under my blanket, when I was awakened. The soldiers reported the ascent of the enemy. In the pitch darkness there wasn't anything visible. We heard the unmistakable sound of infantry gear. I ordered that the rifles should be loaded but strict silence was essential until I ordered otherwise. Approaching us was Lance Sergeant Vareci and his men. He was fortunate, that he was lighting his pipe and talking loudly, we all recognized his voice.

This fortunate event avoided his and his group's early departure to happier hunting grounds. I have no doubt he remained unaware of how close he got to meeting his maker!

After midnight 2nd Lieutenant Miksa Mayer was ordered to take his platoon to Zablatow and assist the sappers. Their task was to prepare to blow up the railway track. While all this was taking place, the Russians had long departed to the upper reaches of Galicia, and for reasons beyond anyone's understanding, never crossed the river Prut. Next day we crossed Prut. Before sunrise we heard gunfire and we expected our baptism by fire. The 8 preceding days' march took its toll. (This comment appeared quite important at the time, however, considering my later experiences it might have been better described as a minor skirmish. The fatigue I thought was beyond endurance would later be classified as a laughing matter.) One Battalion forded the shallow Prut, surprising the Russians at a cigar factory in Zablatow, who were guarding and ransacking the cigar factory. There were Cuban and Puerto Rican cigars stashed to the ceiling. We took two higher ranking Russian Officers as prisoners of war. The lower ranking Russians escaped. General Schuller gave his permission for the troops to help themselves to cigars. As for the troops under my command, I did not agree to a free-for-all, instead a few men loaded up a large tarpaulin with thousands of cigars and my troops could fill their pockets with cigars. I was not overjoyed with the generous order of looting the tobacco warehouse. My interpretation of the order was that our situation was weak, we obviously did not intend to return and make use of this large, well-built warehouse.

During our march we were under rifle attack, at times from the left and at other times from the right, from a long distance and thus inaccurate and ineffectual. We also noted Cossacks walking to and fro a fair distance away. In front of us the Battalion from Des provided security and also, we were at the front. Behind us were the four, heavy, old canons. Fine but persistent rain fell and eventually soaked us to the skin before we reached the outskirts of Snyatin by nightfall.

We had no idea about the upcoming events, which would befall us! Approaching Snyatin we got into repeated volleys of rifle fire, with the bullets audibly tapping on the road's basalt surface. The men leading the horses (which were dismounted on account of the severe cold, it was known that temperatures below -5°C would cause serious respiratory damage to the horses' lungs) and some of the regulars were taken by surprise and started to retreat. This resulted in an uncontrolled chaos which rapidly became dangerous. I ordered: "Feuer einstellen, tüzet szüntess!",(Ed: German and Hungarian for "Cease fire!".) My intention was to stop the disorderly retreat and regain control. I ordered "One Company follow me in the ditch by the road and march forward!". The disordered retreat slowly improved. The Russkies' repeated rifle volleys hampered my efforts to restore order. Suddenly, not far from me, a Romanian soldier shouted: "Feuer einstellen" and started firing in the air, which made me very angry and I was about to shoot him, but my gun was still on safety. I also felt sorry for the poor soul. Perhaps I benefited also: had my revolver functioned well during the very first need, I would have been left without a bullet in the chamber. Meeting the Russkies with a revolver with no bullet would have left me drawing the short straw! It took me about 10 minutes to stop the retreat and continue toward Snyatin in the ditches by the highway. The unfortunate result of the retreat was overcrowding in the rear, causing a bulge, then causing retreat of the artillery. Unfortunately, you can't put the horses pulling the guns in reverse, one gun ended up in the ditch, thus narrowly missing the General's carriage. Meanwhile there was rifle firing in all directions. We thought the attack was aimed at our flank.

Later, it came to light, that the entire Division was firing in the air!

Meanwhile we stopped at the town's walls. General Schuller soon materialized with his cart. I summarized the day's events. He issued new orders: we were ordered to search the houses along the way to the town center. This was accomplished without incident. The level of anxiety and confusion was gradually decreasing. Then a Hussar, carrying orders to the rear, was shot several times. In the poor visibility of the fading light, it turned out to be a case of "friendly fire". General Schuller arrived at the town center, very much to the town's joy and relief. We were given accommodation. My soldiers were given a school.

2nd Lieutenant Hilop's Company was sent ahead to assure safety. I was billeted, after taking care of my Company in the school, with a Jewish man. I had tea, but I was worn out by the day's events and could not eat. So, I went to bed and enjoyed this comfort. Earlier in the day I bought for myself a map of the town, for which I paid 20 crowns. My old shoes were not only worn but were taking their last breath! I thoroughly studied the map of Snyatin. By this time our letters were carried by Military Mail #350.

At daybreak on 31st October 1914, I received new orders. The task was 3 km away, where we were to dig trenches East of the Prut bridge. I received these orders with considerable doubt. First of all, our intelligence suggested attack from the East and I had a strong suspicion of the attack was from the North, where I was convinced that a strong presence of Russian forces was located. Next day at daybreak I heard the bugle followed by the sound of a volley of rifle fire from the direction of 2ndLieutenant Fülöp's Company.

Almost immediately 2nd Lieutenant Fogarascher arrived with new orders, now directing me to assist Fülöp, who was under Russian attack. Although I liked the new orders, I had mixed feelings, because the location would have placed us at a disadvantage.

Snyatin was built by the river Prut. The river was wide; on one side with relatively flat ground and steep barren hills on the other side. The enemy set up camp at the top. We were in a shallow depression. Anxiety reigned. Bugles rang in the air. This signified a serious situation. We were running double time towards the threatened Fülöp's Company. At this point Lieutenant Colonel Pap reached me in his car. He asked what my orders were, he immediately issued new orders that I reach the left flank of the enemy and relieve Fülöp's forces. Just for some effect, he threatened me with a Court Marshal. His order and the threats were just too much. I wondered whether I should laugh or cry. I suspected under fire conditions orders such as these were common.

I immediately turned left, the uphill march and the anxiety made all of us short of breath. I doubt that I took a hundred steps when I was called by Lieutenant Colonel Pap. He issued new orders, which directed us to the opposite hill. We were ordered to descend to the highway and the river, blocking the Russian advance. As before, he added that we would be Court Martialed if the orders were not obeyed. I decided to evaluate the tactical reality since my orders came from officers, who lost their heads in the chaos. So, I decided to get the men out of the ditches and try and locate Fülöp. I located him in short order. He was walking back and forth on the road without any anxiety. The men were sitting around nearby in relative comfort. I asked him: "Are you not under attack?"

He said we should complete the relief action soon, because he was very sleepy and added that we should not be lulled into a false sense of security because the Russians were getting close on the North and East front. He pointed out the barren hilltop about 4 or 5 km away where patrolling Cossacks were clearly visible. I asked about the rifle volleys. He said: "Ah, the volleys! I sent that hare- brained 2nd Lieutenant Somogyi with a few men to reconnoiter the area to our right, because we were at a disadvantage being in a low-lying ground. I gave strict orders that they were **not** to use rifles. This is always the case with reconnoitering and the rules are clearly laid out in our manual.

He got around some houses and saw some Russians. He initiated shooting at them, not only revealing his position but negating the whole plan of gaining information for our advantage. Needless to say, the Russians returned fire. As I said, he did not follow the rules and the volleys were not only unnecessary but put us all at risk.

I shared with Füiöp the events I had during that day and had a good laugh. We sent Captain Fábry a reassuring message about the status quo. I began walking along the road to see for myself the risks and benefits of the location between the river and the highway. A young Jewish guy came with me. He was on sick leave because of an injury to his fingers during an enemy encounter earlier. I suspected that his unit fell apart in that skirmish. While we were on our own, he told me that numerous Russian forces were in our immediate vicinity and recommended the utmost caution. At first, we walked on a ground which was covered by shrubs and canes. I sent scouts with bayonets ahead. Suddenly the brush and reeds cleared, and we faced an open field all the way to the arches of the bridge. To the left we saw houses, obviously the outskirts of Snyatin. I set up temporary headquarters in the reed and shrub area. It was thus less conspicuous (I hoped!). I sent a platoon toward the highway, a platoon toward the houses and fields while retaining a platoon amongst the reeds.

In the meantime, I felt quite hungry. I asked the young Jewish guy to get me some food. He said he would gladly oblige. He also said that he might be able to find out in the village the presence and strength of the Russian forces. About 30 minutes later he returned with some plums, an egg and bread. He said that there were many troops in the village, mostly drinking in a pub. The Cossacks were grand masters at this. For about 11 hours peace and quiet reigned. There was no shooting, and we began to enjoy our luck. Then Juon, Captain Fábry's bugler appeared. He informed us to retreat, because the Division has already retreated. Fábry was very angry. It was now not just a retreat, but a matter of escape. Fábry was livid. As soon as he saw my Company, he was on the go and we could hardly keep up with him. While crossing the bridge, riding towards us at breakneck speed, there was a Hussar heading back towards Snyatin. We thought we were the last but in fact there was a forgotten artillery group that was left behind! Hence the galloping Hussar. Soon Captain Weisz came with the artillery group, cursing away as he hurriedly passed us. We, on the other hand, were amused about this faux pas. It appeared that neither the artillery group, nor my Company received orders to retreat. Fábry, on the other hand, always knew our exact whereabouts, because I continually advised him of our position. This is why he sent his bugler to deliver the urgent message to retreat.

We marched through the village of Zalilicze, where we saw obvious signs of previous battles. There were graves here and there, houses burnt to the ground, broken windowpanes. Although retreating without gunfire raised our spirits, our hope remained that our division would see action. Perhaps as soon as tomorrow?

Though the retreat was by permission from the higher-ranking Officers, it was viewed by many as indicating we weren't brave enough to face the enemy. This was depressing to all Officers. Our task was to harass the enemy, which we did with courage.

We faced a long march. None of the men complained, none gave up and there were no stragglers. It may have occurred to the men that the further we were from the front, the safer we were. I heard next day that no sooner we left, the Russians occupied Zablatow. 2nd Lieutenant Mayer, whom I mentioned earlier in connection of the sappers preparing to blow up the rails, felt very comfortable after our departure. He and his men were billeted in comfort. He gave the order that a master chef be found and employed. Such cooks were found and big-time cooking commenced. Bakers were also found and were put to work. Soon soldiers realized what was going on and did not mind the inconvenience of fording the river for a great meal. Suddenly major rifle volleys dispersed the happy crowd, disrupting the culinary pleasures. The men were running aimlessly, most fording the river. There were quite a few Russkies but they stopped short of the river and did not cross the bridge either.

We marched from Snyatin to Rozsnow, where I had a local peasant serve us an outstanding chicken soup. We spent the night in Rozsnow and the next day we returned to Kossow. On the 2nd November, 1914, I received orders: Lieutenant Colonel Csics, commanding the 32/111 Battalion, got sick and I was to take his place. He was really **sick!** His Battalion just received Mauser firearms that saw better days. These were to replace the Battalion's also useless Werndl firearms. The firearms for one Company have not yet arrived. Just to add insult to injury, I left my Frommer pistol in the restaurant and I never saw it again.

Alarm sounded at dawn. The missing (undelivered) weapons turned up during the night. These were distributed and we rushed to catch up with the army. We marched toward Pystin. We knew advance

Russian scouts had been there. While in Kossow, the inhabitants had no complaints about the Russian scouts. We marched quite strenuously when we heard in Luczki our forward guards were sighting Russian forward scouts. So, the Generals got together to discuss this conundrum. The outcome was an order to stay closer together. We loaded our rifles. We hardly started moving when thick fog descended on us, with visibility about 20 steps. The gathering of different parts of the army under these adverse conditions was almost impossible to achieve. Slowly, improvements allowed some of the fortunate ones to reach Luczki but most had to endure a tough night, shivering in the cold fog. On 3rd November we received orders to proceed. My Battalion was placed on the right flank, another on the left flank and the rest, including the artillery, in the middle.

By morning, the Hussars captured a few Cossacks. We had to assume that the bulk of the enemy was not far. My General advised me that he expected serious problems during the following days. The Army commenced marching at 6 AM. It resembled my hunting days at home as lines of soldiers proceeded through brush, etc., especially as we drove some rabbits out of their domain. There was no rifle fire.

We were subdued and the concern about the possibility of the enemy firing bullets. In the end we reached Oslaw without incident. This small village had a small stream running through it. We marched along this stream and suddenly it made a sharp turn right across our ordered path. To my utter disbelief, the wide front marching in a straight line, did not ford the stream, instead opting to move as in peacetime without any recognition of danger, they strolled across the bridge, and this was approved by someone higher in the ranks! The bridge was overcrowded and became a bottleneck, thus an obstacle to rapid crossing of the stream. My Companies eventually crossed the bridge. I met the head of the Advance Guard, who received orders to supervise the crossing. He was only allowed to move forward after a large segment of the entire force crossed. Even most of us got through before the Advance Guard! Since there was no sign of the enemy, the General and Hussar Lieutenant Hencz got into a cart and went uphill toward the ridge separating two watersheds. We were ordered to march to Destyn. I was on horseback behind the General and received an order to move the 3rd Company forward. At this point the General just reached the ridge and was met with serious fusillade. This came from a hillside covered by shrubs and trees. The General and the Hussar immediately abandoned their cart. The Advance Guard started firing. I had no idea what they were shooting at, because the terrain and vegetation hid the enemy well.

I stopped for a second to survey the situation. I pulled out my sword from its scabbard and gave my order: "Follow me, in a row behind me, two men each side of the road, forming a line!". We reached the ridge where the Advance Guard was firing somewhat lacking vigor. The enemy responded with equal lack of conviction. However, when my men reached the ridge on the left wing, we opened fire in earnest. The right wing acted likewise, just as we were instructed in the training ground. Russ was the General Staff Officer, now Lance Sergeant, gave orders in a loud voice, he commenced further advance. Naturally, the Russians replied in a similar manner, volleys after volleys followed. I was running around encouraging my Officers to engage. A brave "Staffelweise" with a small group advanced in a spectacular manner. The two wings became a problem. The left wing went too far left, especially two sections of Companies went so far to avoid the danger, I was forced to gather them back to the flock. The same issue arose on the right wing. I suspected that many of these hesitant men might go AWOL. So, gathering them together was really the best option. I had to shoot in the air with my pistol and hitting some with the flat of my sword in order to persuade them to follow orders. By this time the Russkies realized that people running to and fro made perfect targets and their aim improved. The best alternative for me was to just lie on the ground and listen to the bullets hissing as they passed over my head.

I found my bugler hiding behind a small shrub. I joined him. At least the bullets passed **over** our heads. A very large and unhappy Corporal passed us, one little finger barely attached, dangling in the air. He was on his way to the rear to seek medical attention. This was my first sight of an injured soldier. How I hoped it would also be the last!

Whenever I remember and mull over that day's events, our baptism by fire, I believe we did our duty honorably. It took around 10 minutes for the return of discipline and obedience to materialize. Considering the bullets whistling overhead, I still think it was exemplary. I felt my men had faith in me with the task of making the **right** decisions and I was thankful for their trust in me. It was more a feeling of gratitude rather than simple thankfulness.

As soon as the left wing resumed their volleys, the right wing advanced. The enemy always aimed at the advancing troops. After leaving our temporary shelter by the bush, we advanced. To my surprise, there was a copse of trees. This provided another shelter, where I could think about the next course of action. My men found shelter also. The view of the valley was picturesque. In the valley, we could clearly see all the way to and including Delatyn.

From the direction and force of the enemy fire, we could deduce that we were facing their Advance Guard. Now they started to retreat. We saw the khaki uniforms of their Advance Guard retreating in a single file. All firing stopped. I was concerned about the left wing, where I could anticipate a sudden unpleasant surprise attack. This did not happen, and we made our way slowly and quietly toward the valley. As we advanced, our anxiety mounted. We expected to face the main force. The river opened and ahead of us was a large, about 2 km wide floodplain. Through it went the river Prut, with Zarzecse on our side and Delatyn on the other side.

We arrived at a narrowing of the river. The left side was level, but the ground was higher on the right by 10 to 15 meters. We found the trenches built by the Russians. These trenches faced Delatyn. Many of my men jumped in and felt secure. Others followed. Understandably, they were hesitant to leave, and it took some effort to move on. We hardly moved a few steps, when we heard the distant sound of guns, followed by the whistling of the bomb that landed in the vicinity of our front line and exploded. One of the Companies had a dog, who ran forward, barking, objecting to the intrusion into our peace and objecting to the unfriendly intent toward us by this missile. The men laughed. Their mood turned sour when the sound of a second gunfire was heard. Then, shrapnel passed near me and went toward my men. Someone was crying. The desire to advance not only declined but men were running back to the trenches they just left.

I joined them but moved to the left wing. The troops were near the woods, and I did not want to lose any who might be inclined to use the safety of the woods. I placed my reserve troops on the left, instructing them to reinforce that wing.

The Russkies were on the far side of River Prut and using their guns well. Shrapnel travelled from one side of us to the other. Meantime our artillery arrived. They set up their units in a hollow behind us. They started firing and our hope was that the Russkies would feel the stress. It turned out to be the opposite; the Russkies doubled their efforts. Since we were in the proximity of the artillery, an unexpected risk was that the Russian artillery firing on our artillery meant that we received some of the presents aimed at our artillery! The artillery quickly recognized that their presence put us in danger. They moved near to our right wing, much to our relief. However, the issue quickly resolved: thick fog descended on us and peace and quiet reigned once again.

A night without worry was not to be. We all worried about the events of tomorrow, hoping for the best and expecting the worst. During dusk, we resumed good order of the different components of our force, supplying them with food, ammunition and other necessities. We sent a dispatch rider to the Brigade Commanders. During the day I happened to notice a barn. After a very tiring day, filled with dangerous artillery fire, it was most reasonable to provide shelter. The barn was a gift. The cold, assisted by sharp wind still managed to get into the barn, but it would have been much worse without it.

As I laid down on some hay, the thoughts in my head were chasing each other like the swirling wind of a tornado. The silence was occasionally interrupted by loud shouting by the drivers of the carts and the neighing of the horses. The wind was still quite wild and a restful night was unlikely.

After midnight, 1st Lieutenant Hencz visited our quarters. He was very tired and extremely cold. He laid down next to me and his teeth were chattering because of the cold.

He told me that General Schuller's aide, a General Staff Captain, was near the explosion of a bombshell and suffered shellshock. We had no orders. We could expect difficulties next day. We took care of feeding the troops early, just in case of an unexpected development. The carts also made good progress and we were happy about the early light and the fog, which managed to hide our progress.

Around 8 a.m. the fog cleared and the panorama of the countryside was pleasant. To our left there was a deep valley, followed by high and heavily forested hills. I sent my reserve troops there and kept constant communication. This was the most likely way in which to avoid unexpected clashes. The River Prut opened to a large flood plain, which looked rather muddy. Farther on was the village of Delatyn, built mostly on elevated hillocks, on the far side of the Prut. Zarzese, a much smaller village, was on our side. In the forest we could hear the enemy. Fairly soon the Russkies decided that our viewing of their movements was not to their liking. They resumed the symphony of vigorous volleys which were well directed to the center and both wings of our positions; this was a threat. The soldiers had some protection in the trenches. The artillery did not engage as they considered the action too risky, much to the anger of General Schuller. Ahead of us, to our West, the Attems-Schreiter Division was engaged in vigorous fighting. The same was true to our right. Adding to the melee were machine guns. A narrow fog arose reaching the river. This was caused by the smoke of guns firing.

Around 10 a.m., orders arrived. We had to advance to occupy Delatyn. At the forefront of the attack would be the Stolmár Battalion. I gave the orders and quickly reviewed my troops. We marched slightly to our left and thereafter aimed directly toward Delatyn. I had no reserve troops. Neither did the others. General Schuller arrived to see me at 10 a.m. on the dot. We hardly took a few steps and shrapnel was directed at us. We had a few trees, hardly enough to provide any cover. We were about 1 ½ to 2 km. from the village. But the terrain was wide open. The presence of a General also made a difference. The orders were followed. I don't quite know how, but our orders to advance were perfectly followed. The Battalion advanced with confidence and even I found their advance impressive. With half of our route completed we were doing well. The General became somewhat short winded. The Russians were consistently aiming 20 steps behind us, which was quite fortunate. We were about half-way to Delatyn when I realized that our General, now 60 years old, simply could not keep up with us. I asked him to seek the safety of a haystack as the ground became unsteady and our boots sank into the mud. He was simply unable to keep up with us and he became a liability for us all. He complained that his Adjutants deserted him during his hour of need. We agreed to meet in Delatyn.

The General was a true and honorable man. He was not only very highly regarded but people under him had a warmth toward him. They had respect for him as a fighter who would do just about anything and viewed him as a friend. I left him at the haystack and I was concerned but it still appeared to be the most reasonable alternative. The shrapnel seemed closer and I saw the left wing getting loose again. So, I ran there to reestablish order and aim toward the village. My orders were followed and I was satisfied.

While approaching the village I had many dark, pessimistic thoughts. I tried to keep these thoughts at arm's length but my mind brought up images of volleys fired in museum pictures and soldiers advancing against that village. For a moment I could see my men collapsing under the volley. As we approached the village, I ordered the bayonets to be fitted just as we were told on the training grounds. So far there was not a single gunshot. With each second, I just knew that the volley would get us. We were 20 to 30 steps from the town walls, when the lads broke into a run all the way to the wall. The stress was just too much for them. There was the joy of not being struck by bullets.

We were very cautious searching through the houses, paying special care to attics. We reached the North boundary by midday. The Prut appeared two to three meters deep and the width of the riverbed was 200 to 300 meters. We saw few inhabitants in the streets. A few women appeared afraid and curious. Men and the Russkies were absent.

The sound of artillery ceased. As some of my men appeared at the last couple of houses, they received fire from the far side of Prut, from the thickly wooded area. We replied with cautious fire, which resulted in the enemy's slow retreat. 2nd Lieutenant Mészáros was at the right wing of the Battalion with his Company. He was to advance in small groups; instead, he advanced with the Company. They had hardly commenced the downhill move towards the Prut when they were met with severe enemy fire and were forced to retreat behind the houses. There were casualties. Following this experience the decision to halt the advance was obviously the correct one. My General arrived and I informed him about the *status quo*. I had no choice: we could not advance. After evaluation, the General said that we could advance only if both the left and right wings could advance together. At that moment both wings were under serious attack.

Upon the ceasing of gunfire, a few carts braved the downhill road with the ammunition, past the narrowing of the river, toward the village. This turned out to be the wrong decision. Some of the horses died. There was no chance of us receiving food or assistance. Our situation remained critical from the afternoon of the first day.

We just received news that our fellow brigade suffered a devastating loss on our right wing. They were armed with Werndl armaments. My former Battalion and Captain Fábry did not get involved with this loss.

As evening beckoned, 1st Lieutenant Orosz arrived with his Company. He was on the left wing. Around 4 p.m. he met a Romanian General Staff Captain, who ordered him to cross the bridge and post guard on the other side. Orosz said that since the Russians occupied the far side of the bridge, the occupation of the bridge should be the first step. He was told to just do his job as per the order instead of trying to outsmart a Superior Officer. Orosz was fortunate. He waited until daylight faded. Then he approached the bridge. There he found two foreign Companies who had similar orders. They attempted to cross the bridge in broad daylight and returned with casualties.

We spent much of the afternoon studying the maps. My General tried to convince the Artillery to open fire several times, to no avail. He was full of rage over the unwillingness to open fire. In the meantime, he also attempted to contact the left wing, who were still under heavy fire. We were in one of the first line of houses, when one of the men jumped up and cried. He was shot in the thigh by a projectile which came through the wall. Other injured men started arriving. We moved to the next row of houses for safety. My lair was shared along a row of houses with Lieutenant Adjutant Aladár Kölber, a noted painter, and Alajos Stróbl, a sculptor. When they met, they were overjoyed and hugged each other. The meeting could have taken place at a better location. They met at a point which was between two houses and the gap presented the Russians with the opportunity of a volley aimed at their location. Kölber started to run, but in the rush, he tripped on his own sword and fell. Stróbl got terribly afraid assuming that a bullet caused his friend's fall. In the end, all turned out well and they had a good laugh. They recalled a previous pleasant time they spent at the Kossuth Mausoleum.

Time passed waiting for orders. Not only were we without orders, but we had no intelligence about the general situation in our vicinity. As we waited there was sporadic rifle fire but there was heavy gunfire from the East and the West. That sound somewhat tempered our otherwise pleasant atmosphere. The General was relaxing on a bench when he received a communication from Artillery. As the General took the message from the Artillery ensign, a piece of shrapnel whistled by and exploded in their vicinity. The General remained on the bench, but the Artillery ensign was gone in the blink of an eye. The General's comment was: "Now I know why my Artillery is so hesitant to fire!".

The note said our Artillery was assigned to another unit and they had already left. The General's mood was not happy. The afternoon produced no surprises. There was some action during the night, but apart from disturbing our sleep our situation had not changed. The 5th of the month also passed without incident.

However, our situation remained increasingly risky. It was quiet behind us. We heard no news about spare troops. There was no word of us receiving reinforcements, just the opposite. We could foresee having to escape somehow, not retreat. We spent the afternoon studying maps with the idea of considering alternative routes of retreat. The news was that the road to Bukovina was compromised and Fábry's Battalion was retreating. I saw no other route but one over the mountains.

We received orders that we were to be moved from the General Staff of Schultheisz in Bukovina to the Attems-Schreider Division. This cheered us all, especially the General. My bugler was immediately sent to the Division involved in fighting West of Delatyn for further orders. The second night came and went. By daybreak of the 7th, movement on both our left and right side was now a matter of grave concern. I was forced to withdraw a Battalion to the village. The Russians were preparing to cross the Prut to our side. My General, with whom I had frequent discussions, was particularly unsettled. As for me, I feared that we might face an escape with heavy casualties or the possibility of an escape becoming impossible. I suggested to the General that even without orders we should retreat using the fading light as cover. My proposal surprised him. Obviously, he had similar thoughts. However, he would have preferred a movement through the Russian forces. Although a heroic act may have sounded noble, the reality was that we would benefit more by attempting to avoid enemy contact and save our men. My bugler just returned. The order was to remain and defend our position. The bugler told us that they already commenced retreating and that any effort of attempting to dislodge the Russians from their trenches failed. Facing Russian reinforcements and lacking any hope of our side receiving reinforcements, the order was given to retreat to Kőrösmező. Of course, this applied to the other troops, not to us. With the information from the bugler, I repeated my former advice to the General. I explained the numerous, and to me logical reasons for my opinion. Simply put: our presence here would make little, if any, difference. I felt retreating to Luczki would make more sense and, if achieved, it would prevent the possibility of us getting encircled by the enemy. In short, we should avoid a mousetrap.

The action of the other Officers was interesting. After I met with the General, they wanted to know what was happening. Some had ideas that they thought I could talk to the General for consideration. Like the proverbial Sword of Damocles, the matter of retreating or remaining under the threat of encirclement hung over our heads. Going against orders was a very difficult matter for the General. At dusk, the General wanted to have a meeting with all the Officers. It was easy to round them up, as they were nearby anyway. We gathered on the highway on the South side of the town.

The General discussed the orders and the proposed time sequence of our departure and projected route. He had hardly finished with his orders when he received another order from General Headquarters. It was as follows: "The Schuller brigade will retreat, with utmost silence, during dusk, without delay, through Magura to Mikuliczin. I will ensure the safety of the Brigade in the event of an enemy action in the Valley by providing support until the arrival of the Brigade. Pfanzler s.k.".

Since the likelihood of a retreat had been fully discussed several times, we took hardly ten minutes to gather the Battalions. It was pitch dark. It was so dark that one Battalion nearly collided with another! It was all as quiet as a grave. The increased level of danger was palpable. The General arrived. The hard freeze added to the tension. In the darkness the General was unaware of the presence of a Battalion ahead of him, as were the troops. When they collided, one of the men shouted: "Here come the Cossacks!". This resulted in a temporary disruption but it took the Officers a short time to resume order. I suppose this kind of event should not be surprising under such stress.

On our way we did not meet any military personnel. Bialy Oslaw had no military personnel. The civilians told us that all military left some time ago. We arrived in Luczki very late at night. There were large groups from assorted places huge concentrations of carts and animals, people from apparently all sides, even from the South and our rear guard congregated here. Some were remnants of former units. The enemy was well entrenched in Bukovina. When I studied the maps, my conclusion was that we had but one option: the route would have to be via Magura and Rokiela. It would involve a difficult climb to 1114 meters. After that feat, there is the downhill road to Körösmező and its beautiful valleys.

After a short discussion with the Officers, with our General presiding, the decision was to go with the escape route through Magura. It was impossible to restore order in the darkness. There were too many widely different groups. For example, some of the cart drivers simply cut the leather straps and rode away as fast as the horse could go. The General also set off in his carriage. Two local big wigs preceded him. Off they went, jockeying for advantage on the narrow mountain pass. Behind them all semblance of order evaporated.

The moon also attempted to hide yet cast a ghostly light on the giant firs and deep canyons and on the tired, hungry troops. The overall mood stabilized and improved with the feeling of better security. At about 2 a.m. the line of men, hiking two abreast, halted. Then came the shout: "Officers to the front!". I, with my Officers, went ahead. We found a group of lower ranking Officers debating which route to take. There was no sign of the General's route. In theory, there was a guide for avoiding such complications. It was a quandary: exactly where were we? At this point I realized how useful my maps were.

With my maps and compass I was able to decide the direction we needed to take. Of course, being in the middle of the forest with huge old growth trees was a real challenge. It was obvious that we had to reach the summit. Therefore, I accepted the role of leading the crowd to Mikuliczin. I had absolute confidence that I could do this, even though I never travelled these parts before. It was a matter of going uphill to the ridge and downhill to Mikuliczin. Our progress was exactly as I predicted. We went uphill, facing shrubs and other obstacles, eventually reaching the ridge. Vegetation was sparse at the ridge. We saw soldiers at the top but we didn't know whether they were ours or Russians. We approached with stealth, in silence and revolvers ready if needed. They turned out to be our troops. It was a Border Battalion.

In the meantime, we had a brief rest while studying the maps to locate the road downhill. We found that we left with two to three thousand people, but now had 150. I guessed the missing 2000 odd were wandering around in the forest but generally in the right direction. A different spirit seemed to dominate us, more positive and looking forward to our journey. The short rest was refreshing but the hard freeze motivated us to move on. Shortly after our rest we found the road. We soon found the Company, sleeping. The Commanding Officer was awakened. We explained what supplies and services we required. He said they would not leave before daylight.

A few men came with me. I did the advance to Bukovina with them before and it brought back pleasant memories. The daylight gradually improved our progress,; we could see the awesome vista! It was our thought that the Wild West must have looked somewhat similar. The beauty of this place was incredible! By 10 a.m. we reached the highway to Kőrösmező. I ordered a brief rest, while I went to scout the highway. I met groups of disheartened soldiers with their Officers. They told me they were going to Kőrösmező, on their way to Hungary.

The valley by the river Prut widened. The hillsides were heavily wooded, the fields bright green and there were several attractive and well-designed holiday homes where the well to do of Galicia could spend their holidays breathing pristine Alpine air. There was a railway station nearby. The locomotive appeared ready to go. Soldiers were everywhere, some resting, some marching. It was quite disorderly. The overall appearance around the station resembled a crowd going to a county fair.

After an hour's rest, while I tried to contact Headquarters without success, I gathered my flock and resumed our pilgrimage to Kőrösmező. Our troops, quite fatigued, still marched in perfect order, an Officer at the front and me at the rear.

Page 24.

I unexpectedly heard someone inquiring:" Wer ist der Kommandant?", Where is your Commander? with a harsh, unpleasant manner. He was referred to me. So here comes a man on horseback, patent boots, polished beautifully, complete with a whip. A cocky General Staff Officer approached me. "Wohin laufen sie?", "Where are you going?". I introduced myself and told him that the details would be released only at the Headquarters. He went into a fit of anger, understandably, and behaved as if he were high and mighty! He said, menacingly, that he would deal with me at the Headquarters. We arrived at a small house, not a bit like my expectations.

 I met a General Staff Sergeant with shiny boots, just like his predecessor wearing a shirt with a very high collar. He had a whip in his hand, but no horse. The Captain said: "Auch ein Herr, der weglaufen wollte". Which means, "Also a gentleman who wanted to run away".

I said perhaps I might be allowed to defend myself against these insinuations. When they saw that I was not about to roll over and do whatever they said, they allowed me to speak. Once again, I introduced myself as the head of 32/III logistics division. I stated that we were in Delatyn, under attack for three days and we left as ordered by the Attems-Schreiter Division Orders. It was to be their responsibility to support us and to help us prevent Russian threats to our forces. Their whole demeanor changed; they were offering me cigarettes. I specifically mentioned the apparent disorder and lack of leadership which could, and perhaps would play into the enemy's hand. I further stated that there was no effort to rectify this situation. I asked what their role was in dealing with this dangerous risk. They had nothing to say. The Captain said: "Das geht sie nicht.". I pointed out that my troops had no decent food for four or five days. At this point they said that we could take our troops to the train, where they could be fed. I was expecting orders. I was sure our 60-year-old General would turn up sooner or later.

We were looking forward to a warm meal and transportation by train to Kőrösmező. The Almighty, however, had other plans for us. As we approached the train it started to move. There went our expectation of a hot meal and transportation as well as resupply of our ammunition. It also seemed that several train cars carrying ammunition, meant for several companies from Mikuliczyn departed with the train. I saw danger ahead. I returned to my men to prevent them being sent to the front lines while protecting these officers who were at the rear. Fortunately, I met General Schuller. I felt like hugging the old gentleman! He left Luczki on a cart, wandering around in the forest. He soon realized that the cart would not be able to get through Rokiel. During the night he unhitched the horses and hiked the long distance on foot. In the meantime, I gave an account of our experiences, especially mentioning the officers from the General Staff and their unkind reception. I knew he was not particularly keen on them, especially since his General Staff officers were nowhere to be seen. Just as I finished my report, we arrived at the small house.

I am not sure exactly what transpired in the small house but, through the closed windows, I clearly heard loud shouting. The fact that the train had gone upset him tremendously. In the meantime, I occupied a larger house and gathered my men and officers in that place.

Page 25.

We opened tins of food and whatever other edibles I could find for a makeshift dinner, inviting our General to join us and ease his anger about the unreasonable state of affairs.

This was a particularly beautiful area marred by ravages of war during the past year. The Cossacks attacked Hungary last fall through this valley. They also left their mark when they retreated. The beautiful vacation homes were robbed of most items and the houses themselves were damaged. At another house, they used the middle of a flower bed as a gun emplacement, destroying the garden features.

In the meantime, around us about 8,000 soldiers gathered. Daylight faded. The officers got together and discussed our progress with the General who shared his experiences. Gradually our soldiers who were lost in the forest reunited. I was amazed at the soldiers' ability to find their unit in the cold and pitch-dark forest. They went to sleep immediately because of the extreme fatigue. It is amazing that our dispersed troops could reorganize without major incident.

The Russians remained in their trenches while we were able to have a comfortable night here. We received our orders late evening. This directive was for us to go to Tatarowka, where food was awaiting us. The morning brought beautiful weather and our hope for the future improved because we did not feel that the lost battle was catastrophic. Intelligence suggested that the Russians will attack again. In part, our orders were to rejoin our forces in Bukovina and to continue to harass the enemy. This meant an independent march for two days.

General Schuler announced that he did not plan to stay there for a long time. Surprisingly, our forces, which became completely disorganized in the forest, got together. The soldiers knew what the future of a POW would be in Russian hands. It was no surprise that, despite the thick forest, the darkness and all the difficulties with orientation, the soldiers found their way.

In Tatarowka we received the food. We left the small village, got off the highway to Kőrösmező and marched toward Bukovina. The civilian armed forces and the youth armed forces did well in assisting us.

It should be noted that when the Logistics Battalions were combined in preparation for a major military move, the colonels, lieutenant colonels and majors, normally recruited from the retired military, were **not** chosen to lead the Divisions.

Page 26.

After the first battle you could hardly find Officers in the entire Division. Their role was taken over by Commanders of the civilian armed forces, revenue officers, bank employees, Sheriff's Deputies and artists. A notable exception was our good old General Schuller, who stuck with us through thick and thin.

We left Tatarowka on November 10, 1914. Our first stop was Worochta, the first place we found a peaceful place, untouched by war. It was a picturesque village, now covered with snow. No soldiers had passed through before us. The shops were full of items we had not seen for a while. There was cheese, salami, ham and wine. The Officers went on a buying binge. The Officers had a great time demolishing the edibles and wines. When the combination of fatigue and the empty carafes, it was time to sleep.

Next day we marched through the most beautiful scenery. We had a relaxed march to Zabie. During the day it was cool but not unpleasant. With sunset, and through the night, it was freezing. The soldiers tore up fences, burning them to get some warmth. This angered the General since these fences were built by innocent civilians. He demanded payment to replace these fences, which was only right. I paid my share but wanted to be certain the scheme was not abused. I found a Polish bearded Jew, who collected payments both from my Battalion and another one but it was evening and I was unable to find him. Next morning as we were about to depart, I noticed him. Since we had no time for holding court, I sent a well-built soldier to try and persuade him to return our funds. After a brief physical encounter, the money was refunded.

We continued our way on November 12, 1914. Although the march was tiring, it was on a newly constructed highway. My Battalion had a particularly long route to conquer to Spetki. I made a mistake: instead of crossing the river at Ustericky on a bridge, and electing to cross at Ceremócz, assumed that we'll find another bridge there as well.. There was no bridge. We had to hike to Uscie-Putilla then to

Spetki. There were only a couple of houses but our severe fatigue and the bitter cold at night necessitated that we rest like sardines, overcrowded but not freezing to death. Next day we were directed to Berwinkow, where we spent two days. The food trucks also reached us. They had managed to make their escape from Delatyn through Kozmácz.

During these days the remnants of the Schultheisz Division gradually assembled in the small villages and using both banks of the river went from Czeremócz to Kuty and Wiznitz, where I got the order for my Battalion and myself to clear Kuty of any Cossacks. I was very happy to receive this assignment, since it indicated the trust placed in me by my superiors. I moved to Kuty without meeting opposition and I discovered that Captain Fábry and the 32/II Battalion, which was my former Battalion, got there an hour earlier and cleaned out the Cossacks. We remained in the town until November 20th. The weather was rainy, with wet ground and mud. Apart from reinforcing our trenches, we also provided general safety measures in town. In particular, we dug defensive trenches North of town to the river. These were, up to this point, our largest projects. Later, we had plenty more trenches to dig! We saw the enemy only at long distances from us. They were mostly Cossack patrols.

Page 27 & 28.

We heard occasional rifle shots. Otherwise, we were living a grand life. We even had the occasional redcurrant wine and other delicacies. Captain Fábry was my neighbor.

During a windy and bitter evening, we received orders to advance to Koszow. Departure: November 19, 4 a.m. We gathered in pitch darkness. Our soldiers were housed in different locations, in houses located nearby on account of the cold and snow. It was quite difficult to assemble them. We departed slowly, thus allowing the rest of our battalion to catch up with us. The departure was chaotic. Despite all the adversities, all the stragglers caught up to us as we approached Koszow. We received new orders to dislodge all the Cossacks from Koszow. I had no prior knowledge of Russian presence in Koszow. When we got to the town, we searched all the houses as we progressed. The inhabitants told us that when the Cossacks discovered that we were on our way, they vacated the town. I met Colonel Somogyi, an art teacher and painter. He had a kind, pleasant personality. He came across the Cossacks first but they rode away and disappeared. One of them became a POW. Somogyi had admired his sword and confiscated it. There was lively rifle fire on our right. It did not last and we thought it was another interaction with the Cossack scouts and we formed a defensive perimeter along the North side of town.

The night was spent fighting the snowstorm and the very cold wind. Even the idea of sleeping was an impossible dream. I was staying in an attractive house with furniture, clothing and other items strewn about. The Cossacks obviously looked for items of value. Judging by the appearance of the house, the Cossacks' forte was not good housekeeping! I went out several times because the wellbeing of my troops was a grave concern. I ordered much shorter outdoor duty periods to avoid frostbite and other health problems. In the morning another battalion took our place. On the highway another battalion built a mound of snow as an obstacle. They were proud of the work, but I thought even if they were just props in an opera, their structural

68

integrity would not pass muster. From the East our position was compromised. There was a chance of encirclement. It was not surprising to receive an order for us to retreat. We arrived at Kutyn at 2 a.m. and proceeded to Wiznitz. We searched for the Headquarters for over an hour and found them enjoying themselves with a large party. General Schuller was very angry. He read the assembled crowd the riot act. He bitterly complained that no accommodation was made to house our freezing soldiers. A school was suddenly converted for the troops. The Officers and I were lodging in the school caretaker's house. It was nice and warm.

I was unable to find my orderly. After a prolonged search I found him in a dark corridor, fast asleep and drunk as a skunk. To add insult to injury, he drank my liter of plum brandy, which was in a beautifully designed flask, which I Just bought in Kutyn. I dismissed him and appointed Michael Lőw, a very decent Transylvanian German, who remained with me until the end of the war.

Next day, 23rd November, Lieutenant General Schultheisz, who somehow turned up in a car, inquired after the general health and welfare of my Company. This inquiry was suspicious to me because it is usually followed by sending us on an unpleasant mission. So, I replied that I have lots of old, tired soldiers, not career soldiers, equipped with old, worn-out Mausers and even worse Werndl rifles with useless bayonets. He promised that he would "look into" my complaints. After telling me how proud he was of our achievements, the true issue surfaced.

Lieutenant Colonel Fischer's forces were involved in a very difficult fight in Waskoucz, where large Russian forces were on their heels, trying to prevent passage at Csermócz. Were they to succeed, Bukovina would be lost, since the forests, rivers and other obstacles would not be available as natural obstacles to the Russians. There was no possibility of resupplying, let alone providing reinforcements to even the odds. Bukovina was a constant source of headaches for the Russians. It also interfered with Russian military operations in Galicia and Poland. So, they decided to take Bukovina. This would prove to be advantageous for the Russians, since it would expand the front, and it would be definitely a bad blow for our side. Little did the Russians know that Fischer's somewhat depleted forces had only us, with our old timers, to prevent the Russian advance. The poorly supplied elderly soldiers were no match for the enemy. Fortunately, the Russians were unaware of the sorry state of our weakness and they numbered 60,000 troops complete with Artillery and Mounted Personnel.

We continued to hear gunfire all day long. This confirmed their need for help. Three other Battalions also joined us. From the General Staff, Major Pap (previously mentioned when he threatened me with a Court Marshal twice in one day) joined us. We were to get as much ammunition and food as we could carry, because the railway line was cut past Wiznitz. A locomotive and a couple of railway cars got stuck here. The plan was for us to travel under Waszkoucz by train. The importance of this move was stressed repeatedly. Pap, true to form, threatened us with a Court Marshal. After a friendly departure we followed the orders.

Next morning was unbelievably cold. Our advance guard noted the Cossack and Infantry advance guards on the far side of the river. As daylight faded, the first train left. Smoking was forbidden. We knew that Russian artillery was at one location, trained to hit the rail line. I was to take the second train. The temperature was -18C and I opted to hike instead. Schultheisz agreed and provided us with machine guns.

Around midnight we arrived at Banilla Ruszka, where, in a tiny waiting room I found my General. His orders were for the lads to stay together, and we would not try to sleep in houses around us, because the enemy was very near us. The Officers were cramped in the small waiting room. The men were advised to seek some shelter. When I got back to the station, I heard that Lieutenant Klein, in charge of the advance guard, had been fatally wounded and had died.

By the time we reached our assigned location the Russians had successfully crossed the river and defeated Fischer's forces where the river narrowed. I still had telephone connection with Máramaros Sziget and could receive orders from Beltin Pflancer, Commander-in-chief, and awaited further orders. The constantly changing situation resulted in constantly changing orders in response to the Russian attack. The future of Bukovina hinged on the outcome of our defense. We were keenly aware of this heavy burden.

Around 4 a.m. Lieutenant-General Schultheisz called my name and ordered me to advance, under Major Pap (you guessed it: the Court Marshal General). He gave no idea of where, or for how long our march would be or the location of our destination. Behind us were the heavy guns and the machine guns under Captain Weisz.

When I left the railway station, there was no Battalion. I informed Major Pap that a short delay was needed for assembling my Battalion. I located the entire Battalion from the houses nearby and we were on our way to Waskoucz. We were troubled with our thoughts of the unknown, we wondered what danger awaited us. Since the Russians crossed the river, it was obvious that they should be stopped. The reality was that our troops were, likely, inadequate. Even our resupply of ammunition evaporated.

We hiked East for a while when we met refugees at a farm. They confirmed the battle we lost. They escaped from Waskoucz. We could feel their sorrow. Their carts, overloaded with people and some of their most precious belongings saddened us. From this farm we turned South, with our backs to the enemy. This decreased our anxiety. We were moving faster than earlier but the cannons were too heavy on the thin ice of the tiny rivers and could not support the artillery. We soon traveled uphill. The paths were far too narrow for the cannons, and we had to widen the route. With the mud now frozen, hard as marble, digging the route was no joke. By daybreak we were near the village of Karapceu. While the main force rested, the Officers went West of the village to reconnoiter the area. We found a place with a good view of the highway to Waskoucz and Cseremócz. We had no inkling what Major Pap's intentions were. There was no knowledge about the forces around us. Were there enemy reinforcements? An immediate task was moving the heavy artillery over the hill toward better roads. We had civilian help. They used horses and a makeshift leather harness to get the guns over the peak. The task was completed without incident. We were not visible to the enemy.

The area around us appeared peaceful. We could see occasional civilian movement around the houses. To the East we noted troops. Even with our binoculars we could not tell whether they were friend or foe. I sent a patrol to clarify the situation. The patrol had hardly left when rifle shots were fired. The above-mentioned soldiers were firing at the Cossacks, who were approaching them from Cseremécz. They were too far away to be effective. The soldiers very quickly packed up their tents and disappeared in the woods. They made no effort to engage us. From the village farmers we heard that they were the rear guard of the forces defeated at Waskoucz.

About 15-20 Cossacks, approaching from the river, soon reached the Northern edge of the village.

They disappeared amongst the houses, which were spread around the hillside. It would take them no time at all to take up positions on the roofs of the houses and on top of haystacks. This would tell them our location and strength. Our patrols reported the Cossack presence in the village. We had no orders regarding a response. In the afternoon we reached the Southern border of the town. In several houses we were somewhat shielded against the bitter cold. Evening beckoned when our Lieutenant-General gave me the following order: "Lieutenant, you will take two Companies, along with a machine gun squad, and eliminate the Cossacks from the village".

After a short overview of the recent events, I set off with my crew and examined the houses in the area. A young man told me, in German, that 17 Cossacks had been in the village but had departed. He also told me that a force of 400 infantry and some mounted riders were at a large farm, planning attacks against us. I inquired about the best access to this location. First of all, this large farm is separated from the village by a large drop off on one side and a small river on the other side. He strongly discouraged me from attacking the area, because it was saturated with Russian scouts, and it would only take a single rifle shot to alert the entire force. He thought the Russians would encircle us in no time. He also warned me that there was a possibility of some Russians still hiding in the village, possibly in cellars. By the time we reached the North of the village, it was dark. I was facing several challenges. I was unfamiliar with the terrain, my men spoke several different languages and both the issuing and understanding of orders was difficult. Attacking without machine guns was impossible. We were walking in knee high snow in cold that was unbearable. Against orders, I turned around and walked through the village. My men found several curious characters in the village. They claimed they were transporting materials. They had valid Hungarian papers, but none could speak Hungarian. Under guard they were transported to Headquarters.

By the time I got back to Headquarters, I was very tired. While I was going through the village as well as assessing our advantages and liabilities, the Headquarters were moved to a new location. They listened with interest. They received news from other sources which were the same as my report. My orderly took me to a room with straw on the floor, where many officers were asleep. I rapidly also fell asleep. I thought about the previous night's events next day. Some Officers were awake after I went to sleep, and they heard that we would attack the Russkies today. I heard some noise above me. Apparently, the displaced civilians were in the attic sleeping.

We got up early in the morning at 7 a.m. I received an order to see the Artillery Colonel Suchomel. He advised me that he would be taking control and gave me the following orders:

"On the left wing, Colonel Stolmár Battalion along with a pioneer detachment, behind which the Artillery will take a defensive position; on the left and right sides of the highway Colonel Biró's Battalion; on the right wing the Fogarasi Battalion will take a defensive position. Aim: occupy defensive position and prevent Russian advance".

For the Fogarasi Battalion, this will be their baptism by fire. I knew the previous day that this would be the likely scenario. I could guess that our efforts to resist the Russians were likely to fail. The reasons for this were quite simple: our old and inexperienced troops, equipped with third rate, practically useless weapons along with us being isolated from other friendly forces added up to an exercise in futility.

I informed the troops about the orders at 7:30 a.m. I added orders in the event we were forced to retreat, should an order be issued to retreat, it would be on my order, and the route would **definitely not** be on the highway, but in the woods, preferably aiming for higher ground, preferably a ridge, toward Majda. At this time, we received a message that Fábry's Battalion would be joining us.

Our messengers to Headquarters had hardly left, when a Hussar, riding at top speed appeared. He said that large numbers of Russians, in battle formation, were approaching. From that moment on I was unable to contact Headquarters. They did not even send a messenger to me. I immediately ordered our carts to move toward Majda. Lieutenant Domokos Pap was ready and his forces started to retreat. Lieutenant Biró also wanted to be certain that I ordered the withdrawal. He was satisfied that the order was genuine. The other battalions received the order and withdrawal commenced.

There was a nervous silence for a short period. This quiet withdrawal was unsettling. Our scouts all confirmed the approaching enemy. We were in a valley on the edge of the village. The choice for slowing down the attack was not done with much thought, and we were at a distinct disadvantage.

I concluded that our orders were given without thought and were to our detriment. The better choice would have been to occupy the Northern rather than the Southern edge of the village on the previous day. Our location would have been better, as the Russians would have been obliged to climb a steep hill to attack us. They would have lost a far larger number of their troops.

Events rapidly followed. As soon as rifle shots erupted on the left wing of my Battalion, the Russians replied with gunfire and shrapnel. I was able to see the area well. Even though the shrapnel exploded far above our heads, it was enough to disrupt the Fogarasi Battalion and it took a lot of effort for the officers to restore order. But, because of this, my right wing and Biro's Battalion were left without support. From the woods a mounted Officer materialized. He said something to Colonel Biro and rode back to me. Biro contacted me and informed me about an order from Headquarters.

Page 32.

Our assignment was to resist the Russian offensive. Retreating would be an option if so ordered by Headquarters. Otherwise, it would be on the basis of personal responsibility.

Another mounted Officer from an unknown Battalion rode up and down the highway, looking here and there. From one of the houses a rifle shot was aimed at him. He sustained a neck injury but remained in the saddle and returned to us at high speed. From our left we received heavy rifle fire. From our right a line of soldiers, in their greatcoats, followed by another line and yet another line of well-organized soldiers also approached us, firing their rifles. We had no way of guessing how many lines were approaching us.

Our artillery fired one or two shots in my immediate vicinity. As a result, a civilian ran out of a house and frantically waved his arms. Then he rushed back to the same house. The Russian artillery aimed at our artillery with remarkable accuracy. We received some shrapnel also. Our line had the shortest rifle range on account of the topography; I expected an attack from our left. Sure enough, a line of Russians appeared on my left. I ordered my men to open fire.

To my right the Sergeant of an adjoining Battalion, standing a few steps from me, was hit and fell. We were also receiving fire from straight ahead. Wherever I moved, shot whistled past me from all directions. I realized the shots came from the houses and I ordered the men to shoot at every window of those houses. The same applied for every door or roof opening. This put an end to shots.

In front of me there was only moderate shooting but the left wing was under intense fire. I saw one of the machine gun operators leave his place in the line and move to a more secure location behind a house. The artillery was rapidly retreating. A runner arrived: the request was for us to hold our position, because reinforcements were on their way. If they arrived soon, the outcome may be favorable. This message made me proud and full of courage. So, I went around encouraging the men to take as accurate aim as they could, making every shot count. Meanwhile the situation with my right wing became rather dangerous. After the first round of shrapnel the line retreated about 100 steps. The Russians were virtually upon us. Our lines were lying down in a ditch in the valley. During the entire attack I was the only person standing. The troops were in a line. The Fogarasi Battalion was ineffective. They either forgot how to fight or disappeared into the forest. The Russkies had a good idea: they placed themselves so that they aimed **along our lines.** I noticed that the machine gun detachment was silent. I sent a runner to report to me about our machine guns. He reported that one machine gun crew had absconded, taking the gun; the second crew disappeared but the machine gun was there. He also reported that, while visiting the left wing, there was intense rifle fire. Although Russians were 50 steps away, they were shouting in Romanian. The troops were Bessarabian. I realized that it was time for us to move, especially to avoid us getting shot to smithereens from the left, while encircling the two Battalions on the right. I warned the troops to avoid running in the deep snow. They were to follow me. I told if I found a soldier attempting to overtake me, I would shoot him. The clear order was for the troops to follow me.

Retreating was the most significant and most difficult task. While facing the enemy and the danger I remained calm, keenly aware that my thought process absolutely demanded an inner peace allowing me to recognize and properly deal with the demands of retreating. The risk of a disorderly retreat was great. To hear rifle fire aimed at your back meant that during retreat you could not return the fire. It was hard to accept that we lost a battle. I also felt my responsibility to return my men intact. Being on the losing side is depressing enough. Losing control of the men during a retreat would be disastrous. The situation was bad enough to make me stumble and almost fall on an obstacle the height of a threshold.

I regained my self-confidence. The men followed me in an orderly manner. Then we reached the top of a small hill, where our tempo suddenly increased as we came under enemy fire. By the time we reached the first small hill, the retreat became universal. On my right wing we experienced strong machine gun fire directed at the highway. I shouted: "Avoid the highway!". Because I could see the danger with the road. We ran to a small depression. The Russians were hunting us down as if we were rabbits. It was disheartening to see some troops not listen but go headlong into danger, then get picked off by the Russians. I shouted: "Bear right! If you value your life, follow me!". Above a small hillock the rifle shots were thinning out the brush, but we were out of immediate danger. With Lieutenant Kölber and his 80 men we were heading to a slight slope and woods. The slight downhill direction was leading to a valley. There we met some members of my left wing and a Pioneer Captain. I noticed that several men did not have their knapsacks. I stopped and ordered them to go back and retrieve their knapsacks. To instill confidence in the troops, I sat down and started eating my cheese sandwich. The worried Captain settled down. The troops retrieved the knapsacks. We continued on our way, this time uphill, undisturbed snow underfoot. The captain asked me where we were going. I said don't worry, I know this area like the back of my hand. The truth was a little different. I had maps which I had studied thoroughly in the days before. I could foresee the potential retreat and did not need surprises. I said at the top of the hill there is a road we could use. The captain added: "Unless we are chased by Cossacks!". This did not enter my mind. But avoiding the road made sense. The Captain, whose rank was higher than mine, did not attempt to take over control, much to my relief. Sensing the trust of the troops I was happy to devise my plans for withdrawal.

Page 34.

Arriving at the peak, we reassessed our options. Rifle shots were still present but muted. The sound came mostly from the direction of the highway. Intermittent machine gun fire was not of much concern. We found the path I originally aimed for with no difficulty. A sleigh carrying a badly injured soldier approached us. When informed that they were heading to the front, rather than away from it, they turned around but much to the anger of the Romanian sleigh driver. Next came a horse drawn carriage. They claimed they were going to turn left later. To this day I am at a loss why I allowed them to pass. Their faces displayed fear. Looking back, I suspect they were spies, returning from a well prosecuted task; we were the last thing they expected, on a logging road, in the middle of nowhere.

We still had daylight when we reached the edge of the forest. The vista was that of fields and in the distance the community of Majda. There was a large farm on the right. We were tired. I requested that the men stay hiding in the woods while Kölber, the captain and I looked around. The men inside were artillery soldiers.

We decided to continue toward another large farmhouse. As we reached the highway, a Hussar came with orders. At this time our artillery fired two shots. The reason for these shots was a mystery. To me it sounded like the final movement of a serious musical score, probably the 1812 Overture!

The order was to support the artillery under Colonel Suchomel. We occupied the large house of a wealthy farmer which was very well organized and, in a way, resembled a medieval castle. It seemed the ideal location for a brief holiday. I decided to review the artillery situation while the lads rested. I asked Kölber to take charge in my absence. I reminded him that an attack from the nearby forest could take place.

When I arrived at the artillery location, they vanished. Much to my joy I found a large section of my Battalion and many of my officers there. They joined us at the large house. I sent a note to the Spare Headquarters in the village. The term "spare headquarters" was my term. I coined it to signify the absence of our Lieutenant General Schultheisz, who departed without explanation, leaving Karapceu and transferring the role to Artillery Colonel Suchomel. It was not as if he had been assigned elsewhere.

The train carrying the wounded had 100 cars and was, of course, full of wounded. In the village lads from the defeated and disorganized units were wandering around. We were wondering what could or should be done. Without orders we were in a mess. Very frustrating! The Colonel finally ordered retreat at 4 a.m. Just as we were about to disperse, a mounted soldier told us that Cossacks were present in a large farmhouse at the edge of the village. The order stated that the Stolmár Battalion will attack and dislodge the Cossacks and keep it safe for our troops' withdrawal. I requested that I be allowed to start the occupation of the "Cossack house" at 2 a.m. My reasoning was that on ground which went downhill, darkness would benefit us. Furthermore, if the departure of the train carrying the wounded could be delayed somewhat; our wounded – after the attack on the Cossacks – could be loaded onto the train. I also discussed my dilemma with the physicians. I advised them that in my opinion they should wait to depart until they knew that the Cossack risk was eliminated. At that point the train could depart, stop near the "Cossack farm" and, after loading the new casualties, proceed.

The order, issued in German, read as follows:

Marschbereitscha:rt für die Truppen 2h 30. Train 1h30 der Queu bei der vYegkreuzung auf der Strasse nach Luka.wetz abzumarschiren. Weiter1narsch über Mihodra. BrUcke Luka.wiec "K" und Berhomet. Truppen Co lonne : Baon Stolmár, Batterie, Sa.peure, Baon Birg Nac11hut Baon Biró. Téte der Colonne Ba.on Stolmár hat um 2 53 von der Wegkreuzung Cote 488 den Marsch anzutreten. Train-Bedekkung Sapeur 1 Zug. Genera.lko1ra11ando mit der Batterie die um 2h50 an der vVegkreuzug nac11 Lukawiec iN die Colonne sioh einzurangieren hat, hinter Baon Stolmé.r. Ab "K" Lukawec scheidet

Baon Stolmár 1 2ug der auf den HÜhen Truskowa 499-513 na.ch Berhomet nördliche Abhang beobachtet. "

ENGLISH: (Ed: Using Google translate.)
Ready to march for the troops 2h30. Train 1h30 the Queu to march off at the vYeg junction on the road to Lukawietz. Continue1narsch about Mihodra. Bridge Luka.wiec "K" and Berhomet. Troops Co lonne : Baon Stolmár, Batterie, Sa.peure, Baon Birg Nac11hut Baon Biró. Téte der Colonne Ba.on Stolmár has to start the march at 2 53 from the crossroads Cote 488. Train-Bedekkung Sapeur 1 train. Genera.lko1ra11ando with the battery that at 2h50 at the vVegkreuzug nac11 Lukawiec iN the column sioh, behind Baon Stolmár. From "K" Lukawec separates Baon Stolmár 1 2ug, which observes the northern slope on the heights of Truskowa 499-513 na.ch Berhomet."

The plans for withdrawal suggested by me were accepted and left me to decide the mode of attack on the "Cossack house". I had a runner who took my orders to Lieutenant Kovrig, who was to attack from below and I would support him from the higher ground. The security of the Colonel and the area surrounding his place troubled me yet I really saw no immediate danger.

As I left the Headquarters, I found a sizable crowd outside. There were Officers and all other ranks. They were all looking for orders. The Officers were happy to oblige me as were the men. I talked with the doctors, who were happy that action was taken. I asked them to go to the edge of the village and wait for further orders. It appeared that the entire village was going to the designated meeting place.

Our troops marched in good order towards the large house. This was surrounded by a substantial stone fence. As we approached, we were challenged: "Stop! Who are you?!". It was in Hungarian, and we knew they were friends. During the evening the Cossacks quietly departed and Lieutenant Kovrig's people did move in about 15 minutes later.

I immediately notified the doctors that they could come. Under Fischer, they were in far better hands than Schultheisz.

The train with the wounded soon arrived. I pointed out the highway to Berhomet.

The owners of the large farm were fine people and they invited us for supper. We had butter, sour cream, and ham, there was no shortage! After such a fine meal and the comfort of a bed we lay down and were soon sound asleep. I woke up at 1 a.m. and in preparation for a safe withdrawal I studied my maps thoroughly. At about 2 a.m. I got up and decided to reconnoiter my intended route for the morning.
With snow on the ground the light was sufficient to see my surroundings well. I reached the forest, where we had to turn left, off the highway, at the right location. I had the most unusual thoughts while hiking the highway. The events of the previous day were of great concern. How many died, how many were wounded and how many became POWs? My soul was reexamining my role. I was trying to assess how many died or suffered on account of my decisions. Then the question arose: why was all this necessary? Then came the thought that this was all to do with the security of my homeland. I remained uncertain as to what I could or should have done to arrive at a better outcome. Did I learn anything that would help me to make better decisions in the future? In the end I concluded that such decisions were the primary responsibility of the upper military echelons. I had to trust that they had more experience and possessed much wider overall knowledge than a mere Lieutenant. They received regular updates from different units, and I had no choice but to obey my orders.

My men approached me in the distance. I stood behind a stone cross, lest one of my men failed to see me and used his rifle. In the cold weather the men needed no encouragement to step up the tempo. We reached Berhomet around noon. There was a train, much to our joy as we could have done with less walking. Our joy did not last. The track was cut off by the enemy and we had to face the task of continuing our retreat through the steep hills. We were also told that we could not hope for reinforcements or other assistance. As we hiked along the highway, who should we meet but Lieutenant Colonel Schultheisz. I went to greet him, which was accepted. He immediately gave me orders in the most serious manner: "Colonel, you and your Battalion will defend the road to Wiznitz and protect our forces from attack from either side". It took a lot of self-restraint for me not to laugh. He talked as if we had just left our barracks in Budapest. I did not even know my Battalion's strength. After a short while I spoke up: "Your Excellency, the men are not capable of further marching." At that moment the Artillery Colonel arrived, but without waiting for his report he was given the order to defend the highway at the same location as specified by my order. The answer was: "Your Excellency, the Artillery is quite incapable of hiking, let alone fighting". He added that it was a miracle that the heavy guns were pulled this far.

After the two disheartening reports, he said that we would retreat through the valley on the far side of Berhomet. I knew this was coming even before His Excellency did. My question was exactly how were we to pull the very heavy guns over the Magura?

The fact was that His Excellency did not have the faintest clue that we would all have preferred to go straight home, especially under His Excellency's command, who not only didn't lead but was totally unaware of the suffering the men endured, but he also didn't know what these troops achieved, where they were or whence they came. My 3rd Battalion, under Lieutenant Dr. Molnár would take the rear and were to find accommodation to the rear. The rest were to find accommodation in the town. We all desperately needed rest and a chance to get warm.

My location was in the house of the Postmaster, on a hillside. His wife met me, crying, because her husband was called up and she did not hear any news since his departure. Her two- or three-year-old son was smiling and contented sitting in my lap. There was an older sister also, but she was shy. I was a foreigner, yet they met me with kindness and warmth. The lady was complaining, sensing our retreat. She was afraid of the Russians, who were known to treat women without compassion. I felt that her fears were not only justified, but very likely real. To add to her woes, should her husband not return, how could she make ends meet? I felt that her situation was worse than ours.

Towards evening we left Berhomet toward Seletin in massive cold with me leading the Battalion. Behind us were the artillery and the rear guard. We got to Sipot and took a short recess. Our bread in our rucksacks became as hard as large bones. There was no chance of riding my horse in such intense cold. After Sipot we became the rear guard. We occupied the last few houses, the fortunate ones enjoying some heat and the rest trying to get through a very cold night as best we could. The rooms were full of refugees. I asked the owner for just enough space to lie down. The owner was a Jewish shopkeeper, who said there was no space left. I examined his own room upon which he offered me his bed which I took. I doubt it took me more than a few seconds to go to sleep!

My men shook me to wake me up. Our forces had already left. On the road tins of food and slices of toast were in a large pile. We took as much as we could carry, leaving the rest to the civilians or the Russians who were not far behind us. We soon caught up with the artillery, who faced impossible odds trying to haul the heavy guns up the increasingly steep serpentine road leading through the Magura to Seletin. As early as the first hairpin turn on the road the horses were no longer capable of hauling the heavy guns. About a hundred civilians were brought from the village to assist the guns' progress which was incredibly slow.

Being the rear guard, the two Battalions were obliged to match their (lack of) speed. To some extent the high trees and the slow progress allowed for the men to start a fire and warm up. Once the hairpin turn was completed, the men established another fire at the next hairpin turn. We reached the top at 4 p.m. by which time the daylight was fast fading. The artillery disappeared without saying a word. Then came the wild snowstorm. The area was foreign to us, but we thought the downhill progress would lead to the highway.

Page 38.

At first, we followed the hairpin turns, but later we figured it would be faster to slide down the steep hillside. Some men were able to do this and others were not. I gave the order that those who could reach Seletin should do so and the others could stop at the nearest houses and catch up in Seletin later. Gradually even the Officers started to get left behind. When we reached the highway my horse, Bella, and her minder were already there. She was very weak due to the combination of the severe cold and the slippery path. It got into my head that we had to reach Seletin before resting. After the exhausting night we stopped at the first better looking house. Maximillian Glinsky was the very kind owner. The furniture, in fact the entire house, was beautifully designed and furnished. He was in the employment of the bishop and his job was to take care of the bishop's properties. He extended kindness and we had instant mutual respect. The room was lovely, the furniture was attractive and most of all the room was warm. The bed was so comfortable I think I was asleep before my head touched the pillow!

Next morning my first task was to place guards on the highway. I had to gather my men who arrived in groups of two or three. While this was unfolding, I rushed to give my report to His Excellency, thinking that he would want to know our progress. On my way I met Artillery Colonel Schumel, who had the same requests in mind as I did. His Excellency was involved with two officers. When our turn came, he was not in the least interested in our reports but wanted to inform me that I would have to face a Court Marshal on account of my actions in Karapceu. I informed him with the utmost tranquility that such action would not concern me, exactly the opposite: I would be delighted to discuss the action in Court. His Excellency was taken aback by my answer and by my lack of fear. So he offered me a seat and cigarettes, the latter of which I declined, and he inquired about my actions. He was surprised with my total lack of fear. From this point on the change in his demeanor was abrupt. Noting this change, I was emboldened to say that instead of a Court Marshal my men deserved medals for exemplary courage. After all, my men were elderly by military standards, yet they fought well allowing the

Russians to advance within 50 steps from our front line, thus enabling them to aim their shots more accurately. As for using bayonets, I complained **in writing** several times that the bayonets did not fit the rifles. An additional factor was the promise of support by Captain Fábry's Battalion to our vulnerable right wing. What we received was a strong Russian offensive, not friendly support. My third complaint was the lack of orders and inability to contact the leadership. My fourth complaint was the lack of machine guns and artillery. The overall lack of leadership was inexcusable. After my quiet tirade, His Excellency underwent a complete change in attitude and became kind and considerate. He informed me that I would be leaving that afternoon to march to Rostoki, where they expected a Russian offensive. I stated that my battalion would not be able to comply. The main reason was that the previous day and night, the troops faced tremendous challenges first going uphill on a steep grade then descending a steep grade. The temperature of -8° Celsius (Ed: 18° Fahrenheit) as well as the wicked wind made it a huge achievement, but the effort took such toll that rest was an absolute necessity. The artillery was still somewhere in the hills. We received a three-day rest.

We received news from Máramaros Sziget. An independent Major was the judge and he took statements from many officers and 800 men. From what I heard the investigation did not originate from His Excellency, but the origin was external. I suspect we will never hear the full story, except that the order came from Baltin Pflanzer. We heard very little about His Excellency for a short while but nothing later on.

Amongst my notes I found an interesting item. It relates to military meals, a subject which seldom pops up in Military Diaries. Yet it has significance and provides an insight into the glamorous aspect of a soldier's life. This covers a few days:

Time	Nov. 24	Nov. 25	Nov. 26	Nov. 27	Nov. 28	Nov. 29
AM	Coffee	Battle	Coffee	Tea	Coffee	Tea
NOON	Soup with meat	3 cans	---------	Hominy	2 cans	Soup
PM	2 slices of bread	At camp	---------	Hominy + curd	2 cans + toast	Meat + 2 slices of bread

Time	Nov. 30	Dec. 1	Dec. 2
AM	Coffee	Tea	Coffee
Noon	Soup with meat	Soup 2 slices of bread	Bacon
PM	Bacon	Bacon	Rice soup & onions with lard

Dr. Molnár's Battalion vanished. We waited for three days but he was gone. As rear guard they had a difficult task. When they eventually turned up, they were assigned to another unit. We had a wonderful three-day rest and felt rejuvenated. The two Battalions were now organized. We received the results of the Karapceu battle. We lost 140 men and 3 Officers. Of these, two became prisoners of war. The third one was Dr. Molnár. He suffered a leg wound and somehow missed the train that carried the wounded. The leg wound was not healing well. After missing the train, he either died of the infection or froze to death. He was a pleasant fellow. I miss him.

On the 4th day we began our journey to Rostoki. Our much-appreciated General Schuller was in charge in Rostoki. During our march we had no additional orders, and the march did not pose a threat to us. I was able to ride my horse and I was not tired. We reached our destination at noon. After our departure from Wiznitz the

General kept three companies in Rostoki. He greeted me warmly but said that he was expecting serious developments next morning and he would be unavailable to hear my report until 6 p.m.

The General's attitude to forthcoming problems was exemplary. He prioritized his actions carefully and spent his time to consider different enemy plans and ways to best resist. The Officers were fully advised about the tasks they were facing. His orders and the explanation for the reasoning supporting the plans were to the point. Not verbose but accurate and complete. The situation was such that we had no time or appetite for any merrymaking. I doubt there were many Officers who felt like having fun.

After the general meeting I met with him and described the history of the last few days. I was particularly critical of the lack of leadership, to which I largely attributed the unacceptable losses we suffered. He was very upset about my story. He asked if a different outcome might have resulted had I been in charge. Uncharacteristically he was critical of Schultheisz's habit of disappearing during the battle and attempting to hold others liable for his shortcomings. He was not enamored by Pap's actions either. He discussed his plan for the morning briefly and placed both of my Battalions on reserve. He was convinced that a Russian attack would take place next day.

Captain Fábry's Battalion received orders to commence marching toward Lopus. The Russians attempted the route over Magura, as we did, but they were not successful. They were easily beaten during the really challenging Magura attempt. In the surrounding area we knew the Russians had considerable presence. The plan was that we attack them on their side. This was an excellent idea and reminded me of my army training and my strong belief that a lateral attack is a very good tactical maneuver. I was independent, trusted in a well-planned course of action and I was happy. I had a concern about the aging warriors in my units, who did not have the physical abilities of the younger men. Bearing in mind the reluctance to fighting with my former Battalion, it would not have surprised me to experience the same with this group.

I awoke at 3 a.m. on 3rd December 1914. I warned my officers to expect an early departure and asked them to be punctual. Absolute silence followed, signifying that they all understood the crucial importance of our attack and were clearly aware of the potential risks and benefits of our plan. The advance guard came and went to keep us informed of the situation. The Russian guns started firing at 10 a.m. - their usual method of announcing their intention to attack. Like an alarm clock, but a lot louder. I went out and met General Schuller on the street. He noted the Russian attack and asked me to have my troops at the edge of the village to our left where he expected to join me later. He gave the artillery an order to place their guns about 100 feet from the edge of the village. Rifle shots came from our right. As I was ordered, we marched to the last two houses and established the men in the large barns. Later we took up a position where the river met a very steep and solid rock formation necessitating that the river take a very sharp turn. This was an ideal location for my men. To our left was a steep hill. To our right was another wooded hillside. I was unable to witness the encounter because a stream was next to us and the rock formation obstructed my view. On my left wing the new Fogarasi Battalion was placed. This was their baptism by fire, and they ran away, allowing the Russians to reach the edge of the woods. Although too far from us, the Russians opened fire on us. The shots pinged off the rock and the General was swearing at the slow and rare shots the artillery managed to fire off. They started bringing the wounded from the front lines.

From the rock formation we received a request for assistance. I sent Lieutenant Groh with 80 men. They emerged from the barn in disorder. They soon disappeared amongst the shrubs. The General commented: "They will not reach their allotted positions today". I told him: "They will start shooting in 10 minutes." My pride was wounded. Sure enough, we could see our men ascending the steep rock face, and the sound of our rifle fire increased. The General looked at me and nodded his head with approval.

I did not receive communications from my right wing. The General sent Lieutenant Dezső Kölber to get an update. There was risk with this assignment. Kölber knew that part of his route was within Russian rifle range. Nevertheless, he took off on his horse without hesitation. As he rode along the delicate part of his route, the Russian firing intensified. I felt for him.

From the steep hills across from us the Russkies had the nerve to fire at us! The General gave the order that some of my men return fire at the transgressors. My men found a location to respond in relative safety. In the depression of a small stream, in part of a garden, between houses I found a location ideal for defending the men from enemy fire yet allowing us to fire at them. After a few volleys directed at the forest's edge, not only did the enemy fire get silenced, but the previously dispersed and hiding Fogarasi men regained their confidence and started firing. Some even advanced and with the Officers' encouragement reached the edge of the forest. With my men in a safe location, I returned to General Schuller. Kölber arrived at the same time as I did, out of breath and with his horse wheezing. He completed his assignment and was so proud of his achievement his face was positively glowing! With a modest smile he gave his report. The enemy stopped their attack and appeared to prepare for retreat. The General ordered us to follow the Russians.

No sooner did our runner depart with the new orders, another runner arrived from our rear. The brigade was to retreat immediately. The artillery control was to be transferred to the Polish division, as they were under Russian attack. The Russian forces were particularly threatening North of us near Pystin-Kossow. We contacted the artillery immediately. The sudden rush caused an unintended consequence. One gun overturned. Captain Weisz demanded the artillery. General Schuller refused and stated that the gun would have to be dug out of the ditch, because without the gun the artillery would be useless.

The order for retreat was given. The General was unhappy. To win a battle and retreat made no sense. My evaluation was different. I did not think we **won** the battle, but felt that although we did do well, causing heavy losses to the Russians, the fact remained that the Russians advanced on both our left and right sides. Thus, they knew that we would have to retreat, otherwise the risk of encirclement of our troops could follow. The action would avoid heavy Russian losses. Later we learned that Russian losses in Rostoki resulted in many bodies collected and left by the church there. We were certainly the last forces to retire. We reached Uscie-Putilla and proceeded to Dolhopol. During this march, Lieutenant Kölber was happy about his previous achievement and, most uncharacteristically, drank a fair amount of rum.

Page 42.

Then he recalled some of his amusing stories and jokes.

My first responsibility was to plan the retreat. I was particularly concerned about transportation. The passage through the Carpathian Mountain range was most challenging, especially for the carts carrying our gear. Yet we **had** to cross the mountains since no other option existed from Dolhopol. I reviewed my maps. I found paths suitable for infantry. Even those were questionable: I wondered whether the footpaths would be passable in winter, with possible flooded areas. I went to see several merchants in town, as well as the Head Forester to get a reliable route.

I met the General at 6 a.m., 4th December to report that I researched a route over the mountains to Hungary and would be pleased to guide the men. He said he would prefer a direct route, rather than lose men due to hunger. My personal view was such a heroic plan was unwise. The Officers all supported my view, but the General was hard to convince. During our deliberations we received an order: "March to Rostoki and attack". We alone could clearly see how absurd this order was, a prime example of the Schultheisz/Pap manner of placing orders not supported by reality. According to the orders we proceeded to Uscie-Putilla. The General refused to go any farther. He said he was unwilling to walk into a mousetrap. The General, in his small cart, reached me and began asking me about the route I had researched previously. I laid out my reasoning for the route I considered most likely to succeed. When we reached Uscie-Putilla we met Captain Fábry, who was very surprised to see us.

The Captain said that by the time they reached Lopus, the enemy had long departed thus drawing up a plan to attack was unnecessary. We travelled back to Uscie-Putilla in severe cold and over terrible roads, arriving at 3 a.m. Another order awaited to immediately march to Lopus. The General had had enough. "These men are issuing orders from their comfortable beds!". He approved of Fábry refusing to return. My personal observation was that Fábry was never in a battle and probably never would be. People like him were full of excuses. My Officers had much the same sentiment about Fábry, but in the military, everything was different. Many Officers suffered under bad or downright lazy leadership or cowards.

Towards evening we heard fire from the advance guard directed at some Russians. It was not serious but caused a lot of anxiety in the village. My carts were ready for departure. I went to see the General. He was hesitant but agreed to allow the carts containing food items and ammunition to go as far as the edge of the village. I rushed to see Lieutenant Pap and assigned the leadership to him. I asked him to leave right away and not to stop until reaching Seletin, where I would advise him the reasons for the orders.

As it turned out, my decision not to follow orders to the letter saved all our food and ammunition by the early departure of the convoy of carts.

As per orders, all the soldiers went on the highway to Seletin and stopped at the edge of Uscie-Putilla to resist possible opposition. We waited for 1 ½ hours but met no Russians. The men and I stayed in houses at the edge of the village. My bed was incredibly dirty, and I slept fully dressed until 6 a.m. There was absolute silence. We had no orders. Several Officers stood around outside the General's house. Soon the General joined us. He sent me to his quarters where I got hot coffee. He suggested that I might wish to add a tip. While I had my breakfast, the light fog cleared further and we were able to see the peaks, which were full of Cossacks. If the Russians could reach the peak during the night (no mean feat) they could occupy the road South of us. The General asked if any of us were sharpshooters. The distance was estimated as 1,200 yards. Somogyi was the first volunteer. I was next. A third officer also volunteered. We all missed, but caught the attention of the Cossacks. On the stroke of seven o'clock the Russian guns indicated the beginning of their action. A few minutes passed and a sergeant arrived on horseback. His demeanor indicated that he and his horse experienced something awful. He read the handwritten note to himself and he asked me to return to the house.

He summarized the note to me. It said our routes were cut in all directions except through the Carpathian Mountains. At first the General thought of just fighting his way through the Russians towards Seletin. Then he remembered my conversation with him on the day before, when I offered myself as the guide to get us through the mountains. In any case, the idea of being in the valley while attempting to break through an unknown enemy strength appeared dangerous if not foolhardy. He reviewed the maps and had enough confidence in me to take my two Companies with me to Sybéni and prepare lodgings for the entire troop.

He assembled all the Officers-in-charge and gave out his orders. We were to defend ourselves until the first gunshot and return through the Carpathian Mountains to Hungary. As for my orders, I left immediately accompanied by Lieutenant Fülöp to Usceriki; he would be my guard on my left. On the opposite edge of the river Cseremócz we saw several men with questionable motives. We suspected they were Russian spies dressed as peasants. Fülöp and I parted company. I was pleased to have escaped the trap awaiting us on our former route! My two Companies and I continued our way to Stebne. We reached Jablonica that day. Meanwhile I also ordered that the town leaders bake some bread for the troops.

I also went to see a priest who lived in a small room. I asked him to help providing bread for about 2000 troops, who were on their way and explained that our supply routes were cut by the Russians. He replied with a bitter smile. Unfortunately, they had a very poor harvest that year in the entire valley and the military already took some of their food. The utmost simplicity of the room, the bare walls, the sad and tired priest spoke volumes. As it was, this area was on the verge of catastrophic hunger. This simple and sad meeting with this priest deeply affected me. As I was leaving, I met with the advance guard of a different military group. I left with my companies immediately, hoping not to meet the advance guard's main force. I hoped this would give us a day's advantage from their main force.

I could not understood how the main force was able to reach us so fast. I got some information later. The Russians attacked the advance guard shortly after our departure. Our troops were on the steep hillside as obvious targets on a target practice range according to 1st Lieutenant Galamb. The Russians thought the situation was so funny, they could not help laughing uncontrollably. Not many shots were fired. Of course, the only way to escape was uphill and therefore in the general direction of our escape route. This was the encouragement our troops needed, and it was the reason for their rapid pace thus catching up with us. My two companies marched without worry.

The main force stayed in Jablonica but we marched to Hryniawa where we found a school where we slept on straw. We awoke before sunrise and continued our march. By this time, we were in thick woods where visitors were rarely seen. The people were interested in us but were not fearful. Not far from the village we met Alfred Miltsovits, the head of forestry management. He offered milk for the troops and invited the Officers inside for a light meal. He had two fine daughters, Valéria and Aloizia, both blessed with good looks. They had a table with plenty of food. My heart really felt for them because they had no idea what was in store for them only a few hours later.

Initially the conversation was lighthearted but turned serious when we told them the horrendous reality. Our advice was for them to flee now. They realized the terrible risk that, so far, they had been unaware of. The lovely house in wonderful surroundings was obviously hard to leave. The rest of the way we all felt depressed about their future while marching toward Sybéni.

The road was incredibly beautiful, with high mountains and old forests.

We arrived in Sybéni, surrounded by the magnificent Carpathian Mountains and old growth forests, near Hungary. On the hillside was the forester's house. The view from there was spectacular! The area consisted of four houses. Maybe there could be enough room to house the Officers, but the men would not be under a roof. We had a wonderful meal. During supper the man of the house was called out. When he returned, he asked me to resolve a problem. My men had caught a forester but, not being able to speak Romanian, were unable to communicate with him. Our host vouched for him as his employee. When I heard that the main force was approaching, I placed my sword on my belt and rushed to meet them. I reached them just as they were arriving. I advised them on our exact position. I went into the woods where I found the General in his light, horse drawn cart. In front he had two soldiers, each with a candle, guiding him. It was raining and the General was in foul mood. I was not sure whether it was the weather or our strategy that angered him.

He asked if I had made adequate sleeping arrangements for the troops. I told him the troops would have to sleep in the open. His anger was now even worse than earlier. Did I provide enough firewood for the troops? There was enough wood for the fire, but I had no chance of having it transported to the desired locations. He got yet angrier. He well knew there was plenty of wood, after all, we were in the middle of a forest! He said it was fine for me to have a nice supper while forgetting the rain-soaked troops and that I obviously had no thoughts of the suffering troops while enjoying a fine meal in a warm room and I went ahead not giving any thought to my men, who had to fight. That I did not care a damn about my men! I was thinking of the fine venison and smiled. In the darkness he could not see my face. After a while he had vented his discontent and was ready for my report. When he heard that all the men had assigned places, the leaders of each group were already appointed and dry wood was already stacked, he was in a better mood. When he got a fine room, he was almost happy. I went out to be sure that everybody was taken care of. When I returned, soaked to the skin, I found the Officers in a very good mood. The hot tea certainly helped. There was a relaxed and friendly atmosphere among the Officers. I then went to see the General. He was obviously less stressed and said a few kind words which I took as an apology for his earlier outburst. I took him to the window where the view was simply wonderful. In the large clearing one could see the soldiers in neat rows and hundreds of campfires were a pleasant sight. The distant soldiers moving around reminded me of the French revolution, which was taught in school, and I remembered the illustrations in the books. In the end, the General was genuinely touched by what was achieved.

We went to rest. I found a very tight place in an unused building. The men unfortunately could not sleep, having no cover and steady but light rain did not let the men lie down.

Some were able to rest by the fire. At 7 a.m. we started marching to Kopila, on the Hungarian border at 1,699 meters (5,500 feet). Returning to Hungary was pleasant, although the circumstance with having lost a major battle was disheartening. With our experience crossing the Carpathian Mountains we knew the enemy would also meet an unkind experience. We felt that defending our country was the most important task. Somehow the retreat did not feel so bad.

For several days we did not receive newspapers, so we were unaware of the war's progress. We started ascending the steep hillside. We were unhappy as we talked about the past experiences and wondered what future awaited us. Two Polish men approached us on horseback riding smaller horses which were better suited for this hilly area. They were looking for the General. I had a bad feeling about what this might mean. I discussed my fears with the Officers, and we decided to stop. We soon received an order to retreat. I looked at the deep valley and my concern was where could we get bread?

We just stood still and waited for our gray haired General to reach us. He said his orders were to return to Dolhopol. He said he was not moving until we received our food carts. He was feeling the pressure especially because he knew that with no food, we could not fight an enemy. The food arrived around noon and was hardly adequate for that day. The Russian advance to our north was successfully prevented by the Poles. Ahead of us the Russians advanced and our food supply was compromised. In the morning, we climbed the snowy peaks again. We then proceeded along snowy meadows. There were barracks at the peak, but we opted to carry on to Havasmező. (Ed: An appropriate name, translated, means Snowy Meadow.)

On 8th December we arrived in Havasmező, dead tired at 10 p.m. I had travelled this route in the past as Head of 32-II Company. In Sybeni 3 active Officers were present. From my two Battalions I was obliged to transfer 80 men to 1st Lieutenant Spalt. This was the Zilahi

Battalion, and I finally had to bid them farewell, about which I will make a note later. This Battalion met a sorry end later. The bloody Carpathian and Bukovina battles were also connected to the Dés Battalion and all these units suffered nearly total losses.

I had a disagreement with Gyula Vlaik, a Romanian. I strongly disagreed with him and Headquarters decided in my favor. I was headquartered in the comfortable house of Herman Fliegelmann, a businessman, who looked so young and reached such fine achievements. After all the shortages of food it was so wonderful to enjoy thick slices of ham, huge wheels of cheese, appetizers, wine and other fine food.

In the evening, we gathered in a large hall adjacent to a restaurant. The gramophone played Hungarian songs. I had some roasted goose thigh. As I got these a messenger arrived with a telegram. We were anxiously awaiting the General's comment. He continued eating. I had bad vibes about this telegram. Amongst all of us present only Captain Fábry and his Battalion had their original number of soldiers. Why? Because they did not take part in any battles. Possibly because they were Romanians. Somehow, I felt I would be the one most likely to face an obstacle yet to be defined. I no longer enjoyed my goose when the General finally spoke. He said a Battalion was needed. Fábry's Battalion was chosen. The Battalion was to depart at 4 p.m. from Leordina in two trains to the Carpathian Mountains. I was very sorry to lose my General.

We were very fortunate to get our carts going early, against orders but smart, as they were directed from Uscie-Putilla to Seletin. They arrived this morning. Lieutenant Eperjessy had to avoid the enemy and chose to go via Dorna-Watra and Felső Vissó.

We rapidly finished lunch and had to check our lists of items and orders. The Battalion stood at attention when our General departed. He said to me: "I would have loved to take you with me, but I have so little time to make decisions." We got going and I felt sad when I should have been happy. We thought our stay in Havasmező would be longer. We liked the sight of these majestic mountains. The Russians had other ideas. They harassed our troops along the border. During a counteroffensive the Hungarians lost badly. The losses were so profound that few were left alive out of two battalions. But I will return to discuss this saga later.

In Leordina half of my Battalion got on the train and left for Máramaros-Sziget. (Ed: This area is about 130km east of present-day Hungary, 2024, on the Romania/Ukraine border.) At 10 p.m. we arrived at Vissóvölgy, awaiting the arrival of our second detachment.

The second part of my war experiences is titled: "In the Carpathian Mountains". It covers my experiences from 11th December, 1914 to 28th June, 1915.

Part 2

IN THE CARPATHIAN MOUNTAINS

1914 December 11 to 1915 June 28

The two sections of the train were joined and we resumed our journey. Attacks by Cossacks left visible marks on the landscape. Portions of the stations were burned, others had parts demolished. We arrived at Máramaros-Sziget at about noon. The place was so busy, well-dressed men and women rushing around; since we left Beszterce we have not seen such pleasant sights. The atmosphere did not seem to be affected by the war. It was a real joy to sit at a table covered by a white tablecloth.

The civilians viewed us with interest. They appeared to appreciate the efforts the armed forces displayed and were noting our worn clothing. I was somewhat troubled by our poor display in our worn clothes. Many people looked down on us, judging us by the clothes, or in our case uniforms, that we wore. Many people looked down on us, judging us by clothes, or in our case uniforms, that we wore. I was sure most of them took cold beer on tap for granted. Many of my friends will not be enjoying cold beer on tap in Máramaros-Sziget, or for that matter, anywhere else.

Huszt was busy preparing for our arrival. It was cold and hot tea was brewing, food was arranged in appropriate portions, and it was made clear that we were not to waste any time. These were placed on the carts. The rush did not please us. Someone was obviously hurrying the loading. Eventually it was my turn to get into a cart with plenty of hay, and we were soon asleep. I was awakened by much shouting. I wondered what the cause was. Apparently, we were ascending a steep hill on partial ice slabs and the drivers were encouraging their horses to pull harder.

We arrived in Dolha at 7 a.m. on 12th December; the destination and the reason for our deployment remained unknown. We then received orders to march to Bereznek. The civilians along the route were pleasant and relaxed. To us this signified there was no immediate danger. Some of the Officers accepted an invitation for dinner from the Director of Animal Husbandry. I and a few colleagues had lunch at a restaurant. As a result of our rush at departure and with no clear knowledge of our whereabouts we got off the carts before reaching Bereznek, where we arrived at 2 p.m. We never saw nor heard any enemy action. It was only later that we heard of battles. Northwest from us at the gap at Verecke there were battles and Northeast of us the Russians made significant advances at Ökörmező.

Bereznek is surrounded by steep, crescent shaped, snow peaked mountains to the North, with thick, ancient forests in the valley. The valleys are deep, with plenty of sheer cliffs. In my opinion, this would be an ideal hunting area. The owner of the land is Baron Schonberg, whose woods are well guarded by gamekeepers. The summit was to be defended by us. The inhabitants of the village did not pose any concern to us. The Catholic priest was Cyril Rakovski, a pleasant, pro-Hungarian gentleman. My captain, along with two officers, 2nd lieutenant Fogarascher and myself, were billeted at the manse. In charge of housekeeping was Anna Szabó whose older sister, Kornéiia Szabó moved there from Ungvár. She was a teacher who became unemployed with the onset of the war closing schools. Thus, there were women in the house.

The first day was spent with trying to organize billeting for my Company. We left with our Captain on 14th December, aiming toward the snow-covered mountain to relieve 2nd lieutenant Fülöp and his Company. At first the road followed the valley floor to a hunting lodge. This "Hunting Lodge" was more of a small castle. Unfortunately, it was unfinished and uninhabitable. The gamekeeper's abode, "Rika ", was barely adequate for him, let alone several others! There were other outbuildings. The rest of the Company had to endure the miserable shortcomings of these buildings and just grin and bear it.

We left Rika on 14th December. We had a guide from the village and left the road and began a steep climb through the thick forest, in pouring rain. Ascending the mountain took us four hours. At higher altitudes the rain first changed to freezing rain and then snow. We reached the edge of the forest with slush underfoot and freezing rain alternating with wet snow. Brisk wind added to our misery. We identified 2nd lieutenant Fülöp's group's location; it took another hour and a half to reach them.

When we encountered the half frozen, miserable soldiers, it was obvious that moving the entire Company to the ridge would have been ill advised. Fülöp's Company built an improvised tent and a fire which was difficult to maintain with the competing wind of the storm. Heavy rain further hampered their location and maintenance of the fire. I set out with a small group to relieve the guard at the ridge. At first, the ground was clear as the harsh wind of the storm blew away the snow. At the ridge, however, the snow was knee deep and the storm's intensity was increasing. We had a real challenge locating the guard! North of the ridge there was a steep drop off. The snowstorm was now in whiteout condition.

Thus, it was abundantly clear that bringing the Company to this location would be ill advised if not impossible. With my Company soaked to the skin and freezing, without a roof giving protection I had no hesitation: I could disobey my orders and save the lives of my group. We desperately needed a dry place with a roof over our heads. Without orders, I took the responsibility for returning to the hunting lodge. The Company was well motivated for the downhill move with the hope of dry clothes and a roof over our heads. To me, this was a no brainer!

Next morning I sent a scout to ensure that the Russians had not occupied the ridge during our retreat. On the third day I received orders to move to Bereznek. Since only half of the Battalion was actually serving at any time, we felt at ease in Bereznek. Our billets were comfortable. I had my meals in the Officers' Mess Hall. Life appeared normal. I was able to do shopping in Bereznek. The food was outstanding. Baron Schonberg's wine cellar provided excellent wine, which, at times, was consumed to excess.

Two mounted officers brought new orders at 2 a.m., December 19th. We were to be under Polish command. Until now we were unaware under which command we served. We had no telephone connection with the main division. Later, we attempted to resume communications to the left of Unszolasom but maintaining the lines of communication over long, snow-covered terrain did not seem practical. The difficulty of the physical maintenance thus outweighed the advantages of the communication lines. Our orders were to depart in the morning of December 21, marching over snow, to attack the Russians' right wing.

Since Bukovina, this was our first real challenge. To our advantage was our ability to act totally independently, to do what appeared most reasonable, based on our intelligence and after a thorough discussion of the different avenues of action we could take. Our superiors felt that we would make the best decision under rapidly changing situations. Thus, no specific orders were given. During the night we discussed the proposed excursion to Bükköskő.

We sent scouts to every road and footpath to prevent unexpected problems. One scout went to Bükköskő, then continued to Kispatak. Another scout was sent to lszka. The third scout was sent in the direction of Rókamező. The battalion left at 7 a.m. to the Eastern, snow-covered footpath to Hrab and then Bükköskő. Ammunition and food were carried by pack animals. These poor beasts of burden also found it difficult to advance on these frozen and slippery footpaths. The infantrymen, marching single file, resembled a row of geese. The gentle slopes presented further problems on account of the lack of friction on the ice. In the early afternoon, as we were descending on this slope, we were without the protection of woods and were vulnerable to detection by the Russian forces. To our relief, in the reduced visibility of the early afternoon light the Russians did not see us. Really lucky, considering that we were so exposed without any other alternative to marching over such barren terrain. We surmised that the Russians thought that such open, treacherous space provided good protection from us. The right arm of the Russian Southern army was located East of Tyuska on an elevation. The Northern arm of the Russian army had their left-wing North of lszka. Our descent from Bükköskő landed us right in the middle of the two armies and the land was not fully occupied. What a fortunate turn of events! We proceeded to Bükköskő unmolested.

Bükköskő had Hungarian families. (Ed: Bükk means beech (tree), Bükkös means beechy and kő means stone. So together it means beech forest over rocks.) They provided information about the most recent events, especially the location, size and direction of movement of the Russian forces. This was helpful in planning the orders for the next day. Our task was to attack the right Russian wing in the morning. During the night my Company had to ensure safety occupying an area South of Bükköskő. In the pitch dark night, it was nerve wrecking to try and find the scouts and put their findings in perspective. The scouts were awake and alert. They obtained further updated information about the location of the enemy. We could clearly see the Very lights our main force used at Ökörmező.

We awoke to a foggy morning, unsettled about the expected guns blazing, which preempted the onset of our attack. Our task was to support the main attack by our forces on the right wing of the enemy, thus reducing their ability to counterattack. The expected gunfire was delayed. The Battalion slowly progressed from Kispatak, a small village, to the East, over undulating ground, marching South toward Tyuska. Our scouts warned about the presence of Cossacks. Sure enough, we saw some of them on horseback, appearing totally relaxed. We suspected that they either assumed that we were part of their units or simply did not see us. Fábry was dead set against initiating an attack. Only the Officers, especially I, wished to keep to the plan we devised during the night. We planned to occupy the "Djill" mountain's ridge. We had no idea who, or if anybody, might be there.

2nd Lieutenant Fülöp took half of the 2nd Battalion and went first. I followed with the 1st Battalion. We kept the 3rd Battalion in reserve. We faced a bold hillside with small bushes at the ridge. The overall appearance of the hill and the surrounding smaller hillocks resembled the shape of the back of a giant fish. When Fülöp and I reached the ridge, we noticed a large herd of horses on the next mountain top, guarded by Russian soldiers. We estimated the distance and direction of this group and we started a fusillade of gunfire on the unsuspecting troops. We saw some limping horses and running scattering about. I think we caused an unexpected and unwelcome surprise without causing much harm. After much delay, they halfheartedly returned fire in our general direction. I am sure they had no infantry at that location. They had a few heavy guns directed at Rókamező.

114

The return fire gradually intensified, from ahead of us, behind us and from the side. The situation was definitely becoming more interesting. More and more Cossacks appeared, often in pairs. Only our right, only the snow-covered flank was free from enemies. In the meantime, our Battalion made it to the ridge. We organized a well thought out attack, using the shrubs for concealment.

Unfortunately, the reserve contingent was caught in the unprotected area. Captain Fábry and his adjutant organized some protection for the troops behind a large haystack. Around 3 p.m. the Russian infantry increased in size and the shooting became more intense. I would estimate the distance between us and them to be 800 yards. 2nd Lieutenant Batta and his platoon attempted to descend on the hillside to attack the enemy, but they were driven back by fierce rifle fire. He was forced to abandon his attack. Soon small caliber shrapnel shells arrived. These were not suitable for their purpose, as they were unable to ascend the steep hill and exploded hitting the hillside. Our troops watched the events without concern, until a well-aimed shrapnel shell flew above our heads and exploded right on top of the haystack serving as protection for Fábry and his troops. At the exact moment of the explosion our Valiant Captain Fábry was about to take a sip of brandy, with his lips just touching the flask. Both the Captain and his adjutant ran to the higher elevation at breakneck speed. It was a sight watching our fearless commander run for cover, one hand on the hilt of his sword, the other hand on the flask of cognac, in a leather coat reaching his ankles! The rest of his group followed his example with no hesitation. It was difficult to stop them and resume appropriate formation.

As daylight faded, the rifle firing lessened and eventually stopped. Around 5 p.m. Fábry ordered a retreat to Bükköskő. We did not want to abandon our position, but one did not argue with a Captain. In the darkness of the fading light and the forest I had scouts to lead us and not get lost. Our erstwhile Captain, in the meantime, got into a heated discussion or argument with a patrol and did not keep up with the rest of us. The patrol spent all day attempting to make contact with our forces south of us. Eventually he succeeded. The patrol's superior, a smart non-commissioned officer, felt that it would have been better had we stayed at our former location. His opinion was that we would then have been in place to defend the left wing of our forces and avoid serious damage by our adversaries. Some retreat would have been an acceptable alternative. The advantage of holding the higher ground would have been preferable to moving down to Bükköskő. Fábry's argument was that food was not deliverable over the snow-capped trails. So, we went to Bükköskő and spent the night there. We were told that 2nd Lieutenant Eperjessy got through with the pack animals and the supplies. 2nd Lieutenant Vertes, in charge of delivering our ammunition did not reach us. A restless night was spent by all of us. From the South we heard heavy guns firing. It seemed our attack was to be delayed by a day. Captain Fábry ordered a retreat to Bereznek.

I found an unexpected ally in 2nd Lieutenant Palffy, as well as other officers. However, Captain Fábry's mind remained rigidly opposed, even though we now had ample food.

The ammunition did not reach us because 2nd Lieutenant Vertes was, in my opinion, afraid of the Russkies to do the trip to Bükköskő.

We rested for a day. This provided beneficial relief for all of us. We received new orders late at night of 21st December, to be implemented on the 22nd. We were further advised that the date of the larger, coordinated attack would be postponed until December 23rd. Upon hearing this, Fábry declared that he was sick and I was to take his place. So, I was suddenly in charge of the Battalion. Three of us officers, the 2nd Lieutenant and his partner shared our billets. I immediately sent 2nd Lieutenant Titieni before daybreak as Officer in charge of patrol. He was off to ascend the snowcapped hillside. Meantime, several others claimed sickness. As a result, only half of the Battalion was available. I was anxious to retain the good name of my Company, especially bearing in mind our most recent events which cast a shadow on our pride. Without further delay we left with only a half of the original contingent.

The unexpected attack on the Russians came as an unpleasant surprise. They made tactical alterations to avoid a repeat outcome. They reinforced all their forces, thereby making our tasks more demanding and dangerous. By the time we arrived at Bükköskő, it was pitch black. We met Titiani, who told us that he was sustaining rifle fire in the vicinity of the village. Residents confirmed the presence of Russian infantry in Kispatak, a neighbouring village. They estimated their numbers as being two to three companies. They possessed one cannon. Infantry was also seen elsewhere. At one time, infantry was located at Kispatak, but they moved elsewhere. I decided that we would be safer by moving out of Bükköskő and relocate to a safer camp on the hillside. That location appeared more defendable. Furthermore, I would have been able to withstand an attack by the left wing of the main, large Russian forces. We crisscrossed rather steep hillsides searching for an ideal location. The most promising place was above Kispatak. It had a truly amazing view of the village and the vista of the sprawling valley.

Initially the vista was not obvious with the dark night. The firepits of the Russian guards were clearly visible. To the South, we saw numerous *Very* lights (flares) and heard exploding shrapnel.

We spent the night under the protection of an enormous pine tree, in the comfort of being rolled up in our blankets. Whenever I was in charge, without precise orders to follow, I felt confident that I would make the most appropriate decisions and felt at peace with my conclusions. My fellow officers and Dr. Csendes, our Regimental Physician, concurred with my evaluation and accepted my orders with perfect equanimity. This allowed me to relax and fully enjoy the rather cold, but otherwise wonderful night. We moved at first light to an even better location. I posted sentries around us with orders to shoot enemy troops and hightail it back to us with their reports. To our right there was active fighting with cannons and rifles. There was no abatement in the fighting, as the sound of firearms continued all through the day.

As night fell, the cold intensified and we needed a source of heat. To avoid detection by the Russkies, we needed to move to higher ground so that we could build a fire without alerting the Russians. At one point they became aware of our presence and sent shrapnel in our direction. Their guns from Kispatak were hopelessly underpowered and we were never threatened. As the light faded, it started to snow with a vengeance. This was accompanied by the arrival of fog, which seriously impacted our orientation. The badly fatigued troops made it necessary to move out, especially as our situation having worsened by the snowstorm. We ascended snow covered hillsides with the aim of reaching Bereznek.

Returning to Bereznek was easier said than done. We did not use our usual route because it would have been longer. Instead, we slowly descended to the valley. In a way I could describe the route as an impossible undertaking between huge trees. Perhaps it might have been a romantic stroll through the wilderness on Christmas night. Instead, we faced babbling streams, giant trees fallen over and huge rock formations impeding our progress. The snow still falling just added to our troubles. Dr. Csendes was on horseback and extremely concerned about his mount and continuously appealed to all the Saints to get us out of our dangerous circumstance. The saints may have helped, as we reached Bereznek late at night. I went to the Officers' mess, which was deserted except for Mathe, our beloved cook. While others went to Christmas Mass, he remained to provide a feast as well as wine. They departed at 1 a.m., just in time for Mathe to attend to us. He was regaling us with the events of the Christmas Eve and the stories he overheard while preparing our meal. He made outstanding hot tea, which took care of our fatigue and we finally stopped shivering.

In the meantime, General Headquarters received the report of our first retreat. They must have been wild with anger, which I deduced when I was walking from the dining hall to my quarters, where two officers and new orders awaited me. The Colonel, who did not always make the best decisions, and his adjutant seemed frightened to see me. Apparently, they were aghast while reading the scathing letter. They did not expect me and were shocked when I walked in. They were not sure how to deal with this major dilemma. The Colonel started with an anemic claim, blaming me for a premature retreat and said that he sent reinforcements and food to Hrab. Without doubt he was afraid that next time I would claim sickness and will not join any action. I immediately replied that I was ready to return to the snowcapped ridge. I read the orders again; my task was to reoccupy the same snowcapped ridge we occupied before. Compared to previous orders I thought it would be child's play. The day after

Christmas I gathered as many willing souls as I could and set out to the ridge for the third time.

I was mulling over the different aspects of this task. The main aim was to defend the ridge. It was wide open, subject to severe wind and the snowbound, naked ridge had no shelter worth considering. A better choice was still in snow, being in a somewhat sheltered location by the edge of the woods. It would provide access to firewood, which in turn provided much desired warmth in the bitter cold, snow and wind. Upon arriving at the edge of the forest I found 80 men, who were sent there to provide reinforcement. The snowstorm prevented them from leaving. I organized the scouts to prevent surprise attacks. I organized substantial fires to deal with the frigid cold.

My task was to protect the ridge. Easier said than done! One side of the ridge was steep and rocky. The other side was less steep and there was a forest not too far away. On the ridge, wicked wind and snow made the idea of establishing a post impossible. However, if a post were established near the forest, we could build fires protecting us from the cold, and not being on the ridge meant that the fires would not be visible to the enemy.

When I reached the location, I found 80 men who were sent as reinforcements. I arranged patrols to prevent a surprise attack. I used my hut, but after 2-3 days the smoke got the better of me and I moved to a hunting lodge about 20 minutes away. Although the smoke now went through the chimney, the bitter wind still managed to blow through the walls. By January 1st, 1915, the patrols functioned well, and I was relieved from that post.

The Russians didn't move. Our patrols established that the Russians were still stationed in Kispatak. (Ed: This is a Hungarian word. Kis means small and patak means stream, so together it means Small Stream.) While I was in the mountains, other officers enjoyed themselves in warm rooms in Bereznek and kindly supplied me with all sorts of goodies on a daily basis: roasted meat, wine, and pastries.

Their kindness and gratitude felt good not only to my stomach but to my heart and soul as well.

Page 55.

I returned to Bereznek from the mountain ridge and my colleagues welcomed me with celebration, since I had successfully saved the reputation of the battalion.

After this friendly welcome, time went by rather monotonously. In the Officers' Mess, drinking and card games were ongoing activities, neither of which was my cup of tea.

Activities at the mountain post were running smoothly, as were the barracks inspections; patrols regularly relieved one another from their posts. I was kept on as a battalion commander, probably to save Fábry from again having to report in sick upon receiving an order. At least, I didn't have to be up in the top of mountains. The postal service was working well; letters and newspapers arrived daily. The only reminder of the war was the sound of distant cannon fire coming from the canyon of Vereck.

More letters were arriving from home and from the comfort of a temporarily peaceful life, homesickness was getting hold of my mind and soul. My dear wife was also hinting at visiting me in her telegrams and letters. I tried to convince Fábry to allow my wife to visit, but he wasn't interested in the idea, so my suggestion fell on deaf ears. He treasured the temporary peace and comfort of our post and was afraid that by allowing such a favour, he would endanger our pleasant circumstances. He was against upsetting the status quo. For example, I had suggested putting up a roof over the troops kitchen and building log cabins on the snowy slopes for the patrol services. However, it looked as if he didn't even want to consider buying lumber for these projects since he didn't want to draw attention to himself, which might have resulted in his possible reposting. The soldiers at the Bereznek base had also made themselves at home in the village, lonely women were happy to find companions for themselves and overall, life was peaceful.

On 1915 January 13th Captain Fábry again took command of the battalion. On this day, two commissioners appeared at the parish priest's residence with an order to arrest the priest, Ciril Rakovsky, and transport him to the city of Pécs. Fábry and Fogarascher accompanied him as far as Dohler. We couldn't imagine the reason for Ciril Rakovsky's arrest and we decided to investigate.

Lieutenant Dr. Walye issued a request for an investigation into Cyril Rakovsky, starting with his arrest. He strongly recommended that Rakovsky be taken to Beszterce immediately. Dr. Walye was a Romanian lawyer and he often expressed his hatred toward Hungarians. We were very happy when left a few days later. We could imagine what this wicked "oláh" (Ed: Romanian from Wallachia) would have done to the displaced Transylvanian Hungarians.

On 1915 January 17th I went up to the snowy slopes again and stayed in the hunting lodge on the side of the mountain. The snow here was neck high and the mountain ridge was covered with beautiful bluish white snow, giving a majestic vista to onlookers. After three days of service came three days of rest. Since we had enough personnel, we established another patrol in the mountains. The two patrols used the same reserves stationed in Rika. It looked as if something was afoot with the neighboring troops because Germans were arriving and we had to guide them to the Western side of the mountain toward Stog. On the 21st, there was already some movement among the Russians, and they moved up to Hrab. They ended up a little to the North of our patrol station and observed people in the horse corral. Anytime they saw the slightest movement within 2000 to 3000 steps, they would shoot in that direction resulting in one of our men receiving a bullet in the heart and dying of his injuries. There was no officer on location at the time, so our soldiers bolted believing that the Russians had gotten too close. We were sitting at the priest's residence having afternoon tea when a Romanian militiaman arrived, completely beside himself and delivered a report from Fülöp. According to the report, an overwhelming number of Russian troops was occupying one of our patrol stations and Fülöp was requesting help.

Page 56.

This led to great confusion, especially for Fábry since he didn't have the foggiest idea where the attacked patrol station was located and how and where the Russian troops had entered our territory and he even authorized me to take necessary steps immediately. I sent Lieutenant Galamb with half of his Company to Rika. The other half of the Company was sent to strengthen Fülöp's position. I moved my Company to higher ground east of the village in the valley. The village and the valley were the locations most threatened by Russian advances. Based on what I had seen on my walks, I knew that from that position the whole area was clearly visible and was, strategically, a perfect choice for a defense.

We had a fantastic view of the snowcapped mountain peaks and we could easily observe both of our patrol stations. We spent the night in haystacks. One might think that to sleep in haystacks during the night in January would be very harsh but that would be a mistake, because we prepared our beds very well. We leaned wooden rods against the haystacks. Between the rods we put branches, spread hay on top of them and created a shack, where it was relatively pleasant to stay. The next day, we observed the mountain with our binoculars and there was no sign of either the Russians or our own people anywhere. The following day, I sent a firm order to Fülöp that he and his company should immediately move from the forest to the location of the previous patrol station at the edge of the forest.

Such a message would take two hours to reach its destination. Finally, Fülöp decided to send a patrol up to the mountain. As soon as his three men started off from the edge of the forest we noticed that the Russians had already reached the top from the other side of the mountain. It was a breathtaking sight to observe the two opposing troops approaching each other. It looked as if the Russians had noticed the Hungarians first, because they shot at the three Hungarians climbing up the path. Thereupon, the Hungarians started running down the mountainside as fast as they could through the deep snow towards the valley. While 16 of the Russian troops continued

124

walking down toward the edge of the forest, 34 of them remained on the mountaintop and we could clearly see them standing in the snow. A footpath started off from the edge of the forest and about forty feet away it took a slight turn. That meant that it wasn't possible to see into the forest from above, nor was it possible to see the trampled down snow path from below. When the Russians arrived at this part of the path, Fülöp's men shot at them. The Russians ran back towards the top carrying their two injured men with them and leaving behind two guns. From our lookout we watched the whole thing as if on a movie screen.

Before I continue telling the story of this incident, I must note that I was very upset by it. My fellow officers also stated that with the previous Company this would never have happened because the patrol station would never have been left without an officer. Furthermore, even our junior officers wouldn't have run away from a few gunshots without first investigating their origin. We never left the mountaintop unpatrolled. Changing of the guard took place on location. The only way the Russians could have reached the top is if the patrols were absent.

The retreating Russian patrol reached the top of the mountain and disappeared out of sight on the other side. We sent a note to Fülöp to move to the top immediately. Of course, that message would arrive at its destination with a delay of two to three hours but timing was still on our side and we watched them move to the top without incident.

The real surprise hit when I found out that Fábry, in response to Fülöp's first report, had packed up and left for Kereck. That wouldn't have been a tragedy in itself; we could have borne the embarrassment ourselves. However, Fábry had sent a report to general headquarters without concrete knowledge of what had just taken place on the mountain. Straight from Linsinger came an order that we must stop the Russians from entering our territory at any cost before the arrival of the German support troops.

The Germans were there the following day. Our poorly attired freedom fighters looked so forlorn alongside the well-dressed, healthy, young Germans.

1914 January 27th. The Germans organized a great celebration on a boat on Baroness Schonberg's property for the German Emperor's birthday and I attended with my Company. After the choir sang, a Calvinist clergyman gave a speech, which was accompanied by the distant sound of cannon fire. The soldiers listened in solemn silence as the clergyman expressed his blind faith in our victory in this war. The pleasant milieu made a great impression on all who were present at this celebration.

Soon after the Germans appeared, the battle got stronger both from left and right and the Russians soon retreated to the borderline. The Germans left on the 28th. They left without saying as much as a goodbye. Many battalions came through Bereznek and we led them to the mountains. We never saw them again and we received an order that our troops should secure and back up the mountain troops. Our main troops passed us by and we stayed put in our location. From this time on, we didn't receive any orders and it looked to me as if the mountain service had lost its importance, since, according to our newswire, the troops ahead of us had already joined forces. On January 30th, the Parson's son, Rakovszky János, who was the town clerk in Iszák, was already ordered to his office. The Parson came back on February 1st. He told us that Baroness Schönberg had reported him out of revenge. Somehow, she found out that he had sent civilians to reconnoiter the Russians and reported this to police, essentially accusing him of spying. But she didn't reveal the fact that we had requested him to do so! We tried to convince the police that his actions were patriotic but to no avail. So, we sent a letter to the Mayor that the Parson acted patriotically and we requested the action the police is taking be stopped. He was no spy at all. It appears our intercession action was successful. The Parson kept saying that the baroness would regret her underhanded behaviour.

In my report to the Captain, I will make mention of this and the financial mismanagement of Lieutenant Vértes of the Officers' Mess account. Auditing that account, I found out that Vértes, who oversaw purchasing wine, was lining his own pockets in the process. As a gentle punishment I sent him back to his Company.

In a peaceful and quiet interval, the question of letting our wives visit us was on the agenda. Fábry finally let go of his resistance and reluctantly gave my wife permission to visit me. On February 8th the telegram was sent. Flórus reached Munkács by civilian train and she spent a night there. The next day she found a military train in the train station and she found out that it was heading toward Szolyva. She inquired around whether she could get a seat on it but the answer was no.

A railway employee noticed her efforts and quietly told her that he had just recently hauled an officer's wife's luggage onto that train. If that lady could travel on the military train, then Flórus could do the same. He suggested that she go to the commanding officer of the railway station and ask him directly. That encouragement was enough for my Flórus and she went to the office and requested a seat on the military train heading to Szolyva. The Lieutenant flatly refused because of strict regulations. Then she mentioned the lady who had gotten permission. The officer smiled and she won a seat on the train. However, he asked her not to attract attention and stay in her seat until the train left the station. The officers on the train received her with kindness and offered her tea and the time went by pleasantly until the train arrived at Szolyva. By then it was dark. I sent a sergeant with a horse drawn sleigh to the train station to receive her but since no civilian trains were announced, he went to sleep thinking that she would be at the train station the following morning. Flórus naturally couldn't find him at the train station when she arrived and it was too late to get any kind of accommodation. She spent the night in a train cabin. In the morning Sergeant Steiner found her, put her on the sleigh, covered her up with blankets, placed a warm hat on her head, and her own hat came on top. That is how they started to their destination in the frigid cold weather. They arrived in Bereznek in a very cold temperature but in beautiful sunshine. I went to greet her on horseback at Kerecke since I was concerned about her late arrival.

We spent very happy days together. We had a sleighride to Rika and enjoyed the lovely countryside. And most of all, we enjoyed being together after the long absence from each other. We didn't go to the Officers Mess, since I didn't want my colleagues to get envious of me having my wife with me. I decided to put up a fight that the other wives also should gain permission to visit their husbands but I was already too late doing that since my colleagues had got wind of my wife's arrival. Their wives soon arrived too: Mrs. Lányi, Mrs. Pálffy, Mrs. Somogyi, and the mother of Lieutenant Batta.

We kept quiet about the wives' arrival. Flórus enjoyed great popularity. The captain was happy to come with us to visit the priest where we spent many pleasant and cheerful evenings. Flórus' departure was drawing nearer. However, the Captain himself suggested that she should stay longer since she had a cold and was coughing. He didn't think that traveling in this condition was a good idea and suggested that she stay a few more days.

My Flórus left on February 21st in nasty weather. She boarded the train in pouring rain. The farewell was very difficult. We didn't know how much time would go by before we could see each other again. The captain naturally was very angry when he found out about the other wives' presence. He had no reason to feel that way. Nevertheless, he gave them permission to stay a few more days.

The Russians were pushed back to the border and our services became unnecessary. I often talked to my colleagues about getting new orders for the battalion. However, Fábry had definite orders and chose to do nothing. As we lived our lives in barracks style, he was always very strict and rude, and in tough situations he always lost his power of reasoning. To be precise, he drank his mind away a long time ago. He was always drunk; none of the other officers had an aversion to drinking and they always reported to their posts when they were needed. To make our time more useful, we decided to inspect our weapons and we organized target shootings.

We benefited from our diligence later on because we established the fact that most of our weapons were faulty and it wasn't possible to calibrate the gun sights.

We were not willing to carry the liability much longer. I demanded that Lieutenant Eperjessy, our supply officer, go to Beregszász, request money from the army headquarters, and request further orders for our post. We received immediate marching orders on February 8th at 2 p.m.
]
March 1st, the following officers were at the battalion: Fábry, Fogarascher, Galamb, Stolmár, Vértes, Eperjessy, Somogyi, Pálffy, Titieni, Csegey, Fülöp, Mayer, Mészáros, Lányi, Dr. Csendes.

March 1st, we departed on a dark winter morning in heavy snow. The same day, we marched through Dolha to Lipcse. The following day, we reached Vucskómezõ and on the third day we marched into Majdánka. We had difficulty getting accommodation in Majdánka. Strong icy winds made matters worse. Some of the officers went to a wooden church and I went with them. However, I couldn't bear the cold and moved to a store, which had been hit by a shell creating a hole in the wall. We filled this hole but the cold wind was still whistling in the store. Only Máthe, the cook's, hot tea could warm up our frozen limbs. From Majdánka (Ed: About 75km east of present-day Hungary and 60km north of Romania.) we marched to Felső-Sebes where we stayed in a nice apartment for two days. Lieutenant Eperjessy left our battalion and went to Beszterce. Lieutenant Lányi became our new supply officer.

We could see the signs of destruction left by the war in Ökörmező. Destroyed cars, dead horses and damaged carriages were scattered all over the road. Villages were riddled with bullets. Only a lucky person could find a heated accommodation in this place. 1915 March 6th, we got a new order and continued our march to Titokvölgy (Ed: Hungarian for Secret Valley.) We were again in the middle of the vast Carpathian Forest. The road from Huszt was hardly adequate for the military transportation of food and weapons to the front. Trucks, ambulances with the injured, horse drawn carriages, and cars stood bumper to bumper on the road. These highways had a great strategic importance during the war; they were the lifeline of the army. If the highway from Huszt hadn't been built, we wouldn't have been able to chase the Russians from our country.

Titokvölgy was a beautiful place, with few houses scattered across mountain pastures. We were assigned with the Germans. Fábry sent me up to the post with Lieutenant Fogarascher. The Russians were stationed far up in the mountains and had taken a defensive position. This is where a long line of trenches was developed from the North toward Romania on which the Hungarian-Austrian-German army faced the Russian army.

As we approached the trenches, the Germans warned us about the exposed and dangerous locations. We passed by our reserve troops. They were spread out in the valley under the trees on the mountain slopes. Our posts were very smartly camouflaged. They had built structures like palaces in the ground. We were assigned to a German Commander who was an officer of the Dresdner Bank. We looked around the posts. The trenches were very well dug out with a few machine gun stands. The enemy had dug in about 800 feet from us where their posts were clearly visible.

They noticed us at a curve and they were shooting at us with machine guns.

However, by then, we were safely in the trenches. Personally, I found the whistling bullets around us very unpleasant after the peaceful life we just had in the last while.

In these posts, with our freedom fighters, I wouldn't dare relieve the Germans. They had only two Companies posted here but they worked wonders establishing the posts even though the Russians were relentlessly firing cannons at their positions. Their Commander wouldn't accept our presence yet ordered us back the next day with the request that we report to Colonel Steinbeck and to General Putkammer the following day. That day, we climbed back up to their position and reported to the general. He was a short man and he climbed up to the location with his walking stick. He received us with a pleasant, calm, and engaging manner. He acknowledged that our freedom fighters couldn't be used in these posts because their weapons were bad. However, before noon the following day, the first thing he did was to arrange an examination of all our weapons. We discussed with Lieutenant Ripple how we could secure the valley. Since we knew about the local people's intolerance to working with the Germans, the idea that they might collaborate with them was out of the question.

The weapons were examined, the fighters looked over, and were thanked for their service. The firearms examiner stated that the quality of the weapons would not be efficient in an experienced army. The next day, we marched back to the Austro-Hungarian troops.

We headed towards the summit of Mount Cote, 1,210m, where underground shelters were available for us. After a difficult march, we reached our destination. The dugout huts were covered with spruce branches from which meter long icicles were hanging and that's **inside** the hut! Nevertheless, we were happy to have them since the brutal winter night made it impossible to camp outdoors. The men broke off the icicles and took them outside and we settled in, more or less. We officers, the ten of us, slept together in this "palace" the first night and we heated the space with a Schwarm stove. This primitive heating gadget with its tin chimney cut through the spruce branches worried me. Since my spot was far from the entrance, I taught my men what to do in case of a fire. We placed our bags to the left and right of our beds. In the case of fire, we would simply pick up our bags from either side and run outside. We drilled this procedure and the rest of the men laughed and made fun of us. Sergeant Steiner was on fire watch. He fell asleep and at 2 a.m. we were woken up by his shouting "Feuer!". My men and I picked up our bags as we had practiced earlier on and ran out the exit. The roof, which was made from branches, was already in flames and heavy smoke filled the hut. Lieutenant Batta was sleeping even farther from the exit than we were. He had comfortably taken off his boots and his belongings were scattered all over the place. At the exit we were pulled outside by soldiers and we had our bags but nobody else did. We put out the fire by pulling out the roof beams. The rest of the roof with the heavy snow just collapsed and we threw more snow in the hole. It was tragic but at the same time a comical sight to see Lieutenant Batta in socks outside in the snow.

It wasn't easy on a cold winter's night to find another hut. It was already morning by the time we found one. We didn't have much luck with this hut either because two days later it also burned down and everything burned in it, including a wonderful parcel that I had just received. It contained a beautiful new rubber coat and many more great gifts from home. Commander Fábry didn't enjoy the hardship of the mountains and, using sickness as an excuse, moved down to Pereszlő. According to ranking rules, Lieutenant Galamb became the commander and took me as his assistant. We spent quite a few days on this mountaintop where the cold wind was constantly howling. On March 24th, we received 100 Mannlicher guns but without bayonets. The Russians were firing at our positions in the valley and we returned fire but they still managed to land their bombs close to us. On March 25th, we received news of the fall of Przemysl.

Galamb and I received an order one day to meet the red nosed Colonel of the Austrian-Hungarian troops. Colonel Burggasser drank all day and kept his fingers crossed in anxiety. He had reason to worry since the Russians were shooting cannonballs and they hit near his quarters. The Russians were also heavily shelling some part of our route and we were forced to a standstill. Since we needed to get to our meeting with the Colonel, we had to take advantage of the time between impacts. On a dangerous part of our route, we had to run fast in single line. The Colonel wanted to push the battalion to the firing line. We would have followed the order to our deaths. In the meantime, Fábry arrived and firmly stated that with weapons like ours, and men like ours, he would not be willing to go to our front line, which was only 100 feet from the Russians. It was not possible to attach our Werndl bayonets to either our Mausers or to our Manlichers. The management decided that the whole battalion would be equipped with Manlichers but, unfortunately, there weren't more than 100 available. As a result, we didn't get to the front line and we marched to our next post.

In Rozanka Nizna we met up with Lieutenant Fülöp's Company whose men were carrying ammunition and food up to the front line. That job was appropriate for our men. The village was being heavily bombarded by the Russian cannons. We, one by one, quietly moved through the village and reached the last house where we stopped for a short time. A frightened German soldier ran out of the house and demanded our immediate withdrawal from the house. Since we were dragging our feet in obeying him, he eventually decided to leave. He picked up his coat and left in a hurry. He was right because shortly after he left, about 100 feet from the house, we heard a terrible crash. A large caliber cannon ball hit the ground and that made a huge spruce tree fly in the air with its roots and branches.

On the edge of the village, in a little forest, our artillery was set up and the Russians aimed to silence them. After a second cannonball impact and because the highway went by the edge of this forest, we decided to continue our way to Rozanka Vizna, through the mountain in the adjacent side valleys. From the house, we sneaked through to another valley and climbed from there to the high mountain peak. There was hardly any snow on the South slope but we got the surprise of our life when we reached the other side where the snow was a meter high. Because our horses couldn't handle the deep snow, descending the mountain slope was fraught with difficulties.

In Rozanka Vizna, we spent two nights outdoors in makeshift twig-tents. We were the reserve of the 131st Brigade run by Commander Kneifel and we were proud of that. Our fellow soldiers were lying in makeshift trenches when the snow began to melt. In the beginning of April, they suffered immensely from frost at night. We also heard that the Russians were weakening and there was news in the air that we were going to the front soon. Then we got an order to exchange our good Mannlichers for the old Mausers of the younger battalion which was posted at the front. This was carried out and we returned to Rozanka Vizna where we spent two days of the Easter Holidays in spectacular weather. This is where we got the order to march to Slawsko. Fülöp also joined us and the whole group set out again.

The Russians were stationed at Tuchlán, aiming their guns on Slawsco. Under these circumstances we could only march in a spread-out manner and luckily we didn't suffer any casualties or damage. Because of snow melting, the roads became literally impassable and life threatening. While the battalion kept marching, the food delivery trains from Pereszlő, moved through Tornya, Repenye, Bezskidok, and arrived at Lavoczné.

On 1915 February 18th, I was informed that my valiant behaviour during the battles at Bukovina had earned me the Signum Laudis as an acknowledgement of distinction. Order Bulletin 1st Issue, 1915 February 13. This was the first decoration presented to an officer in our battalion.

1915 March 29th, I was promoted to lieutenant and this was communicated in the Bulletin 29th Issue. Besides being an honour, it also meant more money because it was made payable retroactively from 1914 November 1st.

I mentioned that the battalion's cash balance on 1915 March 6th was 51,501 crowns and 86 fillér. The reason I took note of this fact was because I wanted to supply data that shows the huge cost of war.

On March 28th the battalion horses, pack animals:

Pack animals	27
Saddle-horses	9
Harness horses	32
Dr. Csendes' own horse	1
Total	**69**

Full number of the battalion:

I Company	265
II Company	264
III Company	261
Total	**790**

At Slawosk we were assigned to Commander Hoffman's division. They were headquartered in Oprzec, so Galamb and I walked over to receive orders and let the rest of the officers take care of accommodations for the battalion. We arrived at the headquarters in the dark. The offices were in large barracks built with planks, full of desks and officers working away under electric lights. It was an unusual sight for us. While fighting at Bucovina, we never had the chance to see a huge military operation such as that. We were always stationed in the Carpathian Mountains; we didn't have telephones and never got anywhere close to such a military center. We had to wait until a few engaging young officers acknowledged us. Mostly our shabby uniforms and Galamb's white hair induced them to show us respect. The Captain of the chief of staff, Sípos, inquired about our activities up to that point.

Page 63.

He indicated that he would most likely form a working battalion from ours. Lieutenant Galamb wasn't resourceful and he couldn't speak German. I was worried he might waste an opportunity for our battalion so I never left his side, not even when we were presented to Count Lamezán, a colonel of the chief of staff. As we walked into the room, the Count eyed the two of us skeptically and in a dry tone (and in German, naturally,) asked how many commanders our battalion had. I immediately got his drift and quickly explained that Lieutenant Galamb didn't speak German and I had come to translate for him.

The powerful man relaxed after my remark and then he asked us many questions after which he concluded that our battalion could be used as a service troop to the area. He let us go by telling us that at the train station of Lavoczna we should try to get good Mauser weapons. We went to Count Stillfried, the German commander of the train station to whom we passed on this suggestion. He didn't think that we would be able to use his weapons but he was willing to show us what he had. We went outside the train station where a few wagons stood. He opened one of them and inside we found the weapons lying on top of each other in disarray. We quickly realized that these weapons wouldn't serve our goals. Count Stillfried stated that he wouldn't allow these weapons to be used by our old freedom fighters. We also got an order from army headquarters that we should hand over our officers under 40 years of age to the I/21 battalion. This is how some of our young officers got transferred away: Titieni, Batta, Mészáros, Somogyi. We were sad to see them go and wished them good luck.

The following officers remained in our battalion: Commander Fábry, aide-de-camp Fogarascher, Lieutenant Galamb, Lieutenant Stolmár, Lieutenant Fülöp, Lieutenant Vértes, II Lieutenant Pálffy, and commissary Lieutenant Lányi. From then on Fábry was no longer with the battalion but was moved to the food transporter trains 30-40 km away. He took Lieutenant Fogarascher, now an active officer with him, who was very much missed from our midst.

The next day Count Lamezán decided that he would send us as a working battalion to the troops and he ordered the Captain of the Chief of Staff, Sípos, to supply our battalion with proper equipment. This pleasant gentleman, whom we had already met before and whom I met again several times later on, pampered us. I met him on 1915 April 4th at the train station, where I was trying to find out where and to whom I should hand over our weapons. He found the storage officer and ordered him to upgrade our current weapons and at the same time supply us an adequate number of tools, like spades, hoes, picks, and other miscellaneous equipment. We didn't waste our time and one and half hours later we were on our way toward Plawie, where we were made available to Colonel Guilleaume (19th defense of the infantry regiment Pécs.)

We had to leave behind the wagons because the roads were in terrible condition, and they were impossible to use. Even walking on foot presented difficulties in moving forward. Often, we were in mud halfway up to our knees. Lieutenant Fülöp's Company was retained and then assigned to repair the roads. Even though this didn't require bravery, it did require devotion, perseverance, and hard work. Our battalion in this regard, from the very start considered it our patriotic duty to fully apply ourselves to the task.

Page 64.

With our old freedom fighters - uneducated, unlearned, exhausted - we wouldn't have been much help to our country on the front line but I can state with all honesty that every one of these people, even the Romanians, did as much hard work as humanly possible.

We arrived in the evening through Kalnen to Plawie. This village stretched 10 km along a babbling brook with scattered houses standing in a row in a wide, open valley. Our troops were stationed parallel to Zwinin where we were holding a strong defense line which was also connected with the Uzsok Pass.

I was amused by the quiet, relaxed atmosphere in the village; people walking around despite the enemy being in close vicinity. We thought that providence had placed us on an insignificant part of the frontline, but we were mistaken. There was simply a ceasefire because of the Easter holidays.

We found Lieutenant-Colonel Guilleaume at the far end of the village, which was located at a higher elevation. He was the Commander of the division. He patrolled the mountain tops, Ostry, Pliszka, Makowka and our battalion. Galamb addressed the Colonel in German, and immediately realized he couldn't speak the language. In Hungarian, the Colonel rebuked Galamb for not speaking Hungarian. We were happy to be able to communicate in Hungarian since that made communications with the Colonel much smoother.

We couldn't understand why the headquarters was higher up on the mountainside in shabby little huts on the other side of the creek instead of the tidy, nice houses in the village. We wanted to be close to headquarters and picked a smart little house that stood on its own this side of the creek. It had a perfect view to the West in the direction of Zwinin, to the East, over the valley of Rikow, and to the South, towards the village of Plawie. The house we picked was abandoned which made it very tempting to occupy. The rest of the houses were all occupied. Over the next two nights we were very comfortable in the pleasant house but then Lieutenant Colonel Sipos appeared and requested that we give him our house. We were happy to accommodate him since we felt grateful to him for his past kindness. In the meantime, our work had started. At first, we had to repair the broken-up roads. After the Easter holidays, Captain Sipos experienced some very unpleasant activities around the nice house we passed on to him. If anybody approached the house, the Russians immediately started shooting in that area. Captain Sipos packed up, and moved to a house that was not nearly as comfortable. The situation also became impossible in the part of the valley we stayed in. The Russians were targeting the bridge and the road and we had to move farther back into the village. The repair of the roads was stopped and our men were used for trench repairs and digging new. The two companies were split into smaller groups. Lieutenant Vértes with one group went to Ostray and Sergeant Fortleff went to work in Rikowon. Commander Galamb of the battalion and the chief of staff stayed alone in the village.

As long as our troops didn't attack, our circumstances were OK. Later on, while we were preparing for a general attack against the Russians, I wasn't in the most comfortable position. The bridge and the road, which we constantly used to receive new orders from or provide reports to Lieutenant Colonel Galamb, were under constant fire. It happened right at the beginning of our stay in Plawie, when a group of workers were assigned to Major Wiblinger. To receive our first order, we started off according to our usual preparedness.

Page 65.

Battalion-Commander Galamb and I as his aide-de-camp, our battalion's trumpeter, and my messenger, all departed on horseback. We barely got over the bridge when we were fired upon. Our horses got spooked and danced around madly. We quickly turned down towards the valley and reached a place where we were under cover below the village of Rikow. Soldiers ran toward us with horrified faces from headquarters. They told us to get off our horses, before the Russians started shooting. Wiblinger found out that we had come to receive orders for 60 workers. He was amused by our keenness. We immediately realized our mistaken tactics and from then on we tried not to show up at headquarters.

Most of the positions were dug into the snow. When the snow melted these positions disappeared. Our poor soldiers had to do the hard work of digging new trenches in the rocky ground. Our men were very popular since they worked non-stop. Their boots got ruined in the deep mud and we asked that they receive new boots. We received the new boots whose bad reputation preceded them for their paper soles. These boots were the shame and the sin of the war suppliers. Some of them I took apart and I could see with my own eyes how thin the soles of these boots were. The soles of these boots had hardly any leather. Under the thin layer of leather there was pressed paper sewn in, which I could tear away with two fingers. We sent back the leftover boots accompanied with strong criticism. Before we could get proper boots, however, our men suffered a lot in the wet and slushy weather without proper footwear.

With the Spring weather upon us, war activity came to life. Troops arrived and the sound of gunshots mixed with cannon fire was ongoing. They were heard frequently. The Russians were destroying houses in the village day by day. They had a nasty habit of finding a house to target and launching 5 or 6 grenades until nothing was left of it. In the lowest part of the valley, roads were heavily damaged by Russian shrapnel, and it was impossible to use them in daylight. Life began during the night on the terribly damaged roads, which were full of potholes. Nevertheless, with superhuman effort, we started receiving food and ammunition. Deep in the mountains the transportation of the injured had begun with terrible suffering along the way. I will never forget the heart wrenching cries and the spine-chilling screams of the injured being transported away.

People talked about sad stories along the front. Amongst them was Major Drasser's tragic death which generally generated the most compassion. He was a man who was loved by everyone. His corporal was injured during an attack and couldn't get himself to safety. Dresser displayed several Red Cross flags and went out to help his corporal. The Russians obviously didn't honor the Geneva Convention and killed him.

During the fights Lieutenant Titieni, our colleague from the past who had been part of the attacks with the I/21 battalion visited us. The strains and the horrors of the war terribly effected his mental state. He would tell us one story after another and repeat them over and over until he got to a feverish condition. We all worried about his sanity. Somogyi also dropped in like a true bohemian. He told us stories about the killing field with his usual humor and he added that the only reason he was still alive was because each time there was an attack, he would climb up onto the steep slope on hands and knees and put his head between his hands.

His troops chased the Russians out three times from the same trench until they had hardly any men left. Unfortunately, they only succeeded in chasing them out of Ostry mountain's main ridge. The Russians were holding to the five-pronged mountain ridge and both of the battalion's cannons were able to get at them. Word went around that the Russians were going to counterattack. All through the night, we listened to the continuous gun and cannon fire which sounded like a bubbling hot porridge and we stood by all packed up ready to leave. On May 8th, German troops arrived. One of the groups stopped in front of our barracks. When we asked them where they were heading, they answered that they were going to Skole, which meant that they hadn't taken any notice of the enemy around us. Their discipline, self-consciousness and briskness was very impressive. After their long tiring walk, they washed themselves in the creek and after a very short rest they did exercises on the mountain slopes. When I talked to them about the difficult terrain and also informed some of their officers about it, I felt they were smiling at my presentation and they didn't hide their belittling views of our troops. However, the next day they got a taste of the terrible fights which were going on here amongst these mountains. Their splendid soldiers fell in large numbers. They finished their unnecessary exercises on the mountain side. We thought that when the Russians abandoned the neighboring mountain ridge at Zwinin, they would also withdraw from Ostry and Makowka. We didn't have to wait long. The Russians indeed disappeared without any further bloodshed by the morning of May 13th.

At the beginning of May, at the time we occupied the Ostry positions, a battle took place before our eyes. There were enormous artillery preparations and the half size cannons also participated in the battle. Our infantry walked toward the Russian positions and occupied them. By the time they got there, there wasn't a living soul left. Our large cannons caused terrible destruction everywhere. Later on I visited the site. There were corpses, torn arms and legs scattered around the ground. Bloody body parts were hanging on branches of the few trees which escaped destruction. We befriended Major Kraus Genie and in Rykow, Sapper Lieutenant Schindler whom we met again later on. The huge Russian army, with its injured bodies and souls, began its withdrawal from the high peaks of the Carpathians. We got an order to collect the remaining army supplies and bury the fallen heroes. Within a day everybody left and on the site of what had been fierce battles, a deadly, eerie silence reigned.

We moved to Rykow. Naturally, Captain Fábry also reappeared, since the danger had passed. During the four days we spent here, I took long walks in the mountains. I looked at those sites, where I walked during the night when the battles were raging. I could see how close we were to the enemy's trenches. Then I walked around Pliszka, which was foolishly attacked by a stupid Russian group. We were positioned on the side of the area and well covered and with one quick attack, our machine guns killed them all. They lay there in a line. We were shocked by the horrifying sight that lay in front of us. They looked as if they had been hit by lightning. The whole incident was over in a minute. The poor souls! Their pockets were turned out. Many of them had family pictures lying beside them, the smiling pictures of wives and children. Next to their bodies there was fresh green grass, and hundreds of thousands of violets.

Page 67.

The magnificent meadows, the fresh green trees, the vast valleys, renewable nature, all created a contrast to the unimaginable pain, suffering and destruction on this hallowed ground.

On the ridge of Ostry, in front of the wire hedge, German soldiers lay in a row with bullets in their heads. They were brave, healthy lads. Farther on, behind the wire hedge, in front of the second row, valiant Hungarian soldiers. From a young soldier's neck his identification card (Ed: dog tag) stood out. His name was Demeter. He received the fatal shot two steps from the Russian trenches. Next to him lay two of his comrades. They must have fallen in earlier battles judging by the condition of their bodies. In this area we buried 487 Russian, 102 German, and 181 valiant Austrian-Hungarian soldiers and gathered 493 German, 962 Austrian-Hungarian and 1980 Russian weapons. While we worked on this, I caught a man who was inciting our men to loot the corpses. Money was sown into every part of his caftan. We found 40.000 crowns, lots of rubles, marks, and even blood-soaked money on him. I called the police and they took him to the court of justice.

Rykow by then was completely shot to pieces; we couldn't make out where the houses used to stand, such was the extent of the destruction. We hadn't received orders and despite all my effort, I couldn't establish a telephone connection. Once we finished the clean-up job, we also packed up and left. When Fábry in Slawsko announced that he was sick, he received an unpleasant surprise on the train. The doctors wanted to take him by force to a hospital. He knew exactly what was wrong with him and he knew that in the hospital they would quickly heal him from his sickness and he would be released back to the front again. He resisted but to no avail and he ended up in the hospital. He escaped within three days and signed up again for service. He probably knew that the Russians were already gone.

After these eventful days came the endless marches. On May 17th, we started from Rikow, across Smorzanka's deep valleys, through

Holovieckó, and we marched into Koziowár. The Russians' reserves used to be stationed here in this deep valley among 100-year-old trees, in a well-protected place. There were thousands of little caves carved into the mountainside where the enormous army used to live. Despite their large numbers, the Russian army wasn't able to break through our thin lines. On the contrary, in the end they were forced to retreat. They left behind deer skins and stag skins, which were scattered around. They almost eradicated the game stock of this beautiful area. Our troops shot Koziowa to pieces. It had been the Russians' main strategic line and the line of their retreat. Along that way we found many cannon stations and the destroyed barracks used by the Russians. We marched on to Augustow, where we stayed in Groedel's forest ranger's home. Groedel was an ultrarich timber merchant. My men stayed in an abandoned factory building and found it a bearable place to rest for the night.

The Russians stopped again before Stryj. I went to Skoleb the next day to receive further orders but I couldn't find out any information or receive any further commands. The only order I got was that we should march toward Synewuck where we could expect to receive orders. We set forth and marched to Synewuck and then further to Scoleb. Good fortune brought us together with Major Krausz Genie. We were happy to see each other. When he heard my report, which only contained continuous marching, he decided to move the whole battalion under his command. (picture of a bombed bridge).

He had to make the troops build a Prügelweg (mountain path) through the mountain Peak of Sukiel since it had been agreed with the Russians that no passages should be built in the valleys of Scole and Bolechow for troops or cannons. He directed us to Kamionka. When I looked at the map, I immediately realized the importance and the urgency of this order. I thanked him, and with the arriving battalion, we were ready to start toward Kamionka. We were in a hurry to get started before anyone could change their mind.

Kamionka did not suffer much in the war. In their nice and tidy houses, we found comfortable accommodation. Since the Sukiel Mountain peak was a long distance from us, we left behind a battalion and moved to Brzoza where I got a very neat little room at the forest ranger's house. The last few days of difficulties had taken a toll on me and I stayed at home. The whole battalion, even Captain Fábry, was walking out to build the planned road. Around noon the chief of staff officer appeared and asked me to give my accommodation to him. I didn't show any willingness to comply but during our conversation, it came to light that Commander Hoffmann would come here with his Joint Chief of Staff. I immediately gave up my reluctance and gave an order to load up everything, and within an hour we were on our way to Sukiel. On the way to Sukiel, we met Captain Fábry as they were returning from work with the battalion. He got raving mad when I told him what happened, however when I mentioned Commander Hoffman's name, he quickly realized that I was in a delicate situation and had no choice but to obey. We could have found ourselves in close quarters with Commander Hoffman and the Joint Chief of Staff. He actually was grateful to me and thanked me for my immediate action. Commander Hoffman's habit was that he sent everybody whom he met on the road to the frontline. People said that in the Carpathian Battles, this was the way he collected his army corps.

Sukiel was a little mountain village with a few little houses. Nevertheless, they were able to accommodate the two battalions. I got a room in the teacher's house. There was an ancient piano in her home which could have been in a museum. As the battalion's aide-de-camp, my activities turned to making the battalion exactly the way the command described it. The road was rarely used by troops or carriages. It looked as if the road was built for withdrawal purposes. We stayed in this place for three weeks. We worked diligently on the road but often wandered around the mountains and in the meadows and visited the creek teeming with trout. Suddenly Spring had sprung, and the road building slowly came to an end. We had to orient ourselves to find new jobs. Major Krausz Genie occasionally visited us and was very pleased with our work. On May 24th, we first read about the Italian betrayal.

I set off and drove into Bolechow to learn about future prospects. However, I couldn't get that far because it was very warm, but I got to Salamonova Gorka, where I found the sappers in an excited mood. I also went through Brzaza which had gone from being a small village to a town. They built a large barrack hospital, pioneer and sapper depot, and a line of barrack palaces had sprung up. Many wounded were carried by trucks. I was informed that the Russians were planning a possible attack. South of Bolechow was especially critical. I had no chance to get further orders here and I returned to Sukiel, where we heard bad news from the front.

Page 69.

I got into the car again and left to find out more information. The Russians had indeed attacked during the night unexpectedly on some parts of the front. They captured many prisoners, which created huge confusion. On the road there were soldiers drifting from the crushed troops. There were make-shift kitchens established for them. Elsewhere, trains were waiting for battalions but they couldn't be found and only a few men reported that the rest of their troops were marching toward Moscow because they had been captured by the Russians. I found an exhausted officer friend of mine in a tent. He told me that he had been sleeping in a house near Bolechow when his man barged in his room saying that the Russians were coming. The terrain was intersected by the numerous branches of the mountain river Swica. Islands of sedges and reeds made it very difficult to get one's bearings during the night. He ran out of the house in pitch dark and tried to escape crossing a small river and finding himself in high weeds where he met a man in hiding. In the meantime, the troops had got over their surprise and started shooting frantically. The cannons started to ring out and they also used flare pistols. They were shooting randomly, not in an organized manner. In the light of the flares, he realized that the man in hiding was Russian and constantly beckoned him to walk with him in another direction. Eventually, it dawned upon him, judging by this man's behaviour, that he was trying to escape from his own troops, save my friend too from imprisonment. He then joined him and indeed the Russian got him out of a dicey situation.

After these events, I went to Bolechow for the third time. By then the Russians had bolted. On June 4th, our army headquarters also disappeared. The whole area became empty and only the doctors remained with the wounded. Our road was more or less complete but there was no longer any need for it. We packed up and started off after the troops.

I only found out after the war that my younger brother László was stationed in the same area at the same time but unfortunately, we didn't meet. He was injured and captured soon after in Lamberg. He returned with a 7cm shorter right leg. The way he got back home was through a prisoner exchange program.

Our first stop was in Boleshow where we did some necessary shopping. The second day, we slept in Dolina, the third day, in Krechowiecka, and the fourth, on 1915 June 10th, in Kalusz. It was obvious that the next line of Russian attack would be in Dnyeszter and we were prepared to reach their troops soon. They ordered us from Klausz to Bednarow. Most of the time I was ahead in the car in order to get the orders as soon as possible. I didn't like to hang around without orders. I went through Babin, Bryn, Antowka and Sapahow. The battalion stayed in Bednarow for a few days. Our men worked on the trenches. I stayed in the village with Captain Fábry who occupied himself with continuous drinking and card playing with the Commissary officer. I had to watch over my "gallant boss". I was looking after the battalion's affairs. Our troops were rarely in the trenches. For that reason, we wouldn't have been able to defend ourselves from even a small Russian attack. Around that time the Russians rarely used their cannons. We found out later that they were running out of ammunition.

On a nice day, our whole battalion was ordered to Pawelecz. We got some unpleasant news on June 15th. Our working battalion was going to be dissolved.

Page 70. The reorganization took three days. Fábry stayed with the army corps headquarters. They were created for him to command a working battalion and from the existing battalion they formed two battalions: Arbeiter Abteilung I/32 and II/32. Galamb was the Commander of one of them and I was the Commander of the other but I had to give up my position to Fülöp since he was out of service Ist Lieutenant, and he was a senior officer, although, up until now, occasionally I was a commander over him as the commander of the battalion. Amongst the officers, Fülöp and Lányi stayed with me, and Lieutenant Vértes stayed with Galamb. Pálffy, as the youngest officer, was made to join up. We were assigned to a Brigade Bolsánó and we set up camp at the side of Wiktorow in the forest behind the firing line. To the left of us, between Wiktorow-Krylos were 130 brigadiers. We developed the post beautifully since the Russians didn't disturb us for quite some time. On one occasion, Commander Hoffmann visited the post. Troops were arriving slowly. We met officers who were engaged in the war in Galicia in 1914 who told sad stories in detail about fights that took place in that war. If we had been properly prepared, we wouldn't have had to lose so many people. The city of Stanislau wasn't too far from us and since my great grandfather did stay there, I made a tour of that pretty city.

For a short time, the war activities revived but the Russians were retreating behind Dnyeszter. We stayed at our post, and then we marched to the suburb of Halicz. We were billeted here in a convent. The convent and the church were located at a higher elevation where one could see far into the countryside. The Russians also stayed here, so they could watch over their enemy. They developed great posts, most likely when their troops were far ahead. However, without cannons, they couldn't defend these posts. They had to give them up once our artillery shot at them, and they didn't have the power to silence them. The church was built out of carved stones and over centuries, it served its people. Now it collapsed under our artillery fire. The surrounding hundred-year-old trees were torn to pieces. The convent also received two shots. One of them made a huge hole in the building's side, the other shot hit a beam which had been sticking out from the building. The school and the teacher's home couldn't escape the destruction either and here a Russian Commander and his aide-the-camp found their death. In response to our cannon fire, the Russians retreated from the houses and escaped into carved holes on the mountainside and into the ravines. The nuns prayed in the basement during the bombing. Now they had become our hostesses. They made very comfortable beds for us. Although our cannons had broken all their windows, we slept like babies in the convent. Lieutenant Fülöp arrived in pitch darkness in Halicz. He considered his comfort very important and didn't like to sleep outside. He wandered about in the village until he found an empty house. He made himself comfortable there and slept very well until breakfast time. However, he woke up to a very uncomfortable realization since he found himself in the mortuary of the cemetery. He complained to us for a long time that he smelled of the dead, so naturally we made fun of him.

Our troops crossed the Haliczi bridge and made camp there.

Page 71.

We also got an order to appear in Tusta. We could work only at night. The middle pillar of the bridge was blown up leaving the bridge broken in half. The pontoniers built a wooden plank at the site of the damage during the night, creating a footpath through the damaged area of the bridge. The Russians would shoot at that temporary footpath when they found the traffic too high there. When we crossed the temporary plank, they shot at us but nobody got hurt. We picked up our feet and ran as fast as we could.

A young lieutenant greeted us at the post, which contained improvised trenches one meter deep. We were walking on the ground farther away from the trenches when the bullets started whistling around us, and we quickly climbed into the trenches. Toward the evening the shooting increased and the captain informed us that we wouldn't have to work too hard since the Russians were about to leave. It was a pleasant warm evening. I didn't go back to my troops, but I did send a messenger to Fülöp that he should stay with my troops until I sent another message. Then I went to sleep under a beautiful large tree.

After midnight the villages behind the Russian posts were set on fire, which was the sure sign of the Russians' withdrawal. In the darkness of the night, I saw in the distance the burning villages with sky high flames, and in contrast, the warm and quiet summer night gave me an eerie feeling. The Russians were burying their huge losses by setting huge fires.

We left the Carpathians behind, if not with happiness, since the fight was still ongoing and we had lost so many of our people, but with hope in our heart. The huge Russian army was retreating, and we trusted our own strength.

Part 3

IN GALIZIA

1915 June 28 to 1918 February 25

We were deep in Galizia, as we crossed over the Dniester at Halicz. It was the start of the long fight, which ended in 1918 with the entire Russian army driven out, or perhaps more correctly, with the final withdrawal of the Russians.

I was stationed on this front till 1918 February 25. This long period can be divided into three periods:

1. Strypa and Studynka Valleys
2. Feldbahn and Brzezany
3. Road building

Strypa and Studynka Valleys
1915 June 28th – 1916 August 11th

On 1915 June 28th we started to march forward with our first stop in Meducha. On the first night I ended up at the house of a Polish man, who received us with warm hospitality. He was excited to see us and got quite animated. Suddenly he grabbed a pick and started to break open the wall of his house. When the hole was big enough, he retrieved a pile of bedlinen to make comfortable beds for us. These were placed there to prevent the Russians finding them. I didn't use the slightly damp bedlinen but chose to sleep in a tent in the garden. We promptly left the next day for Panowice via Dryszozow. On the way, we saw a mass exodus of people fleeing with an endless line of carriages loaded with all kinds of stuff. We saw everything imaginable being transported, even a piano! By the time we got into the village, it was full of soldiers. We learned that the Russians stopped again, this time in the Zlota Lipa valley. An open camp was established by the company in the forest, next to Panowice. The Headquarters of the brigade was set up here. By July 19th we moved into houses because of rainy weather.

The positions were rather close to each other, the river dividing the opposing forces. Our task was to dig trenches, erect barricades wrapped in barbed wire and build bridges. Later, we were assigned to another group, where we worked for the congenial old Austrian freedom fighter, Baon Bondy.

On July 22nd I wrote to Flórus (my wife): *The report you sent me about Laci* (my brother) *made me feel at ease. I expected to hear much worse news, as I have not received a letter nor a card from him for some time. I imagined that Lieutenant Szabó wrote to you out of consideration to you that Laci, was captured by the Russians and taken to a hospital to treat his injuries, but I imagined that we have lost poor Laci and Szabó could not bear to tell you the truth. On the other hand, he might have written it according to eyewitnesses' statements, in which case, the concern would be: how seriously is he injured? If he recovered, I would not worry for his fate as a prisoner, because he has a winning personality and a gentle face, so he will get along well with his captors. After a few weeks, which would be certainly a long time for all of us, we might receive some news. If he did end up in a hospital, we should receive news sooner. If we do not hear anything for two months, we should try enquiring through the Red Cross. We should discuss how to do that. After getting my letter, do not fret, because as you may suspect, war is fraught with danger; it is just the lucky ones who return home in one piece! Laci's example shows my exceptional fortune; he got injured after just a few weeks of military service but that's better than the alternative.*

These days our work began at nightfall. Our troops pursued the enemy, until they reached the most forward prepared trenches.

We could not know for sure in advance, where the enemy was, though we had an idea where they might be. A strong indication was their exertion of greater resistance. Our tired, pursuing troops eventually gave up. These lines were pre-built positions where firing trenches were strategically made by the enemy from which they could fire at the besieging troops successfully. Adapting to the enemy's lines our troops also built trenches, which had barbed wire structures for extra protection. We kept busy by digging other trenches as well, like the ones used for access. We built roads further back; huts were built for protection against shelling and general maintenance of this temporary infrastructure was done. Our challenging task began after these works were completed. At nightfall we built up the positions. Previously, in daytime we oriented ourselves, and then as darkness fell, our people went to work. Then we took some cover, where we could be safe from potential hostile fire. The degree of danger of work depended on the proximity of the enemy or in the case of a gunfight, how much of the area could be strafed by the enemy.

Last time we had worked comfortably in a big forest, but now we were exposed, situated in big fields of wheat, potato, and corn. Luckily for us, these fields were between smaller and larger patches of forests. Unfortunately, the Russians were on the hill on the other side of the valley in a wooded area and had command of the valley below. We had to descend into this valley bottom, away from the protection of trees every night to construct trenches. We did our delicate work in six nights with feverish haste, straining all our strength.

One day we had a particularly sticky situation. This is what happened: Our artillery, located in a wooded area on the hill opposite the Russians, shelled the opposite side heavily. My men were below but in front of our shelling, between the Russians and our artillery. We were waiting in the forest for nightfall and the cover of darkness when we could continue our work in the open valley below.

Reporters, with much better skills than I, day after day wrote in the newspapers, graphically describing the horrors of this type of operation. During our heavy daytime artillery fire, my men simply waited for the darkness to construct our trenches, while our "gifts of love" (ed: *Liebesgab*, shelling) were flying overhead with a terrible squeal, onto the necks of the poor Russkies across the valley. We suspected that this night the enemy would be more engaged than usual because of our daytime shelling. We could do nothing till dark set in, even though the work was urgent. Our poor soldiers had to hide in holes hollowed into the earth, until we could prepare the comfortable firing trenches, and the approach trenches. The gunfire abated as darkness came, the landscape blurred increasingly and finally darkness came at last, enabling us to step out from the forest. Moving downwards on the slope we reached the place, where we had stopped work the previous night. According to our plan I laid out the zigzag pattern of the trenches to be dug, punching in stakes according to the requirement of correct firing or other principles of trench warfare. Then I set the distance for the barbed wire barriers. I sent workers to do the job so the work could be started. I retreated up to the forest edge. My officers supervised the neat and fast work. The men did not need much encouragement to work fast; they were already aware that they had to hurry with the trenches to have a place to hide in case of enemy fire. The silence at night was not only disturbed by owl's hooting and chattering of quails; an exciting life began behind the entire enemy lines and behind our front too. Cars were rattling on the roads. A field canteen was brought to feed our troops, since there were occasions, when the fighters could eat only at night. They crawled out of their embankments by sections, and eagerly started eating – no wonder, the last time they were given food was the night before.

Naturally, they received suitable portions; they were supplied with bread, tobacco, enough for the entire day, even got wine or brandy occasionally. The enemy did not sit by idly either; they were heavily beating the stakes into the ground for the wire fence, sometimes with loud chit chat. Occasionally the odd guard grew bored with the proximity to the enemy, so they, or we, fired into the enormous darkness. These sporadic shootings were program like, nobody would be upset. Then a more restless camp guard shot out a flare pistol, so daytime light lit up the whole area. All banging, digging, and clanging stopped, and the workers threw themselves to the ground. Meanwhile on the edge of the forest I was studying the situation under the light of the flares. I have excellent orientation, so I could size up the situation myself in pitch black darkness, without getting lost. I also took it into account what I could do if battle erupted. I was never caught nor unprepared by any surprises. The approach trenches were leading me to the hilltop. I laid down on a small clearing myself, when two or three shots were fired towards the opposite Russian trenches, which met with a quick response. I stayed calmly in place for a bit, but as the shooting increased, I retreated into the trench. The enemy bullets were already knocking frequently on the trees of the small forest. I ordered the workers to march across the trench, and I made my way up to the top of the hill; however, not all the approach trenches had been built and my next trench was still about 100 steps away. I barely made twenty-five steps in the forest - the shooting was already roaring like a hurricane across the valley – I felt a strong shock on my backside. I threw myself to the ground, convinced that I had been shot. I tapped it with my hand and felt that my pants were ripped. Hello, I thought to myself, you can go to the hospital, and I waited for the warm blood to begin to flow. But I did not feel the blood. Meanwhile the bullets whistled by me so loudly, that I quickly scanned the area for a better shelter under the light of a flare. About five steps away from me, at the base of a thicker tree I saw a little pit; I got there with a few jumps. After not much fussing, I cut myself in. I stuffed the blanket I had just picked up under me and I snuggled myself into the sweet motherland. After a brief time, I was struck by some offensive scents. It was the unpleasant smell of an exploded shell and shrapnel that warned me of the impending danger. The rifle fire, which was now quietening down, picked up again with more shelling as well. Though I knew that if the Russians attacked, they would not shoot with cannons, still I carefully searched the illuminated area. The fire exchange lasted for ¾ hour. Then it died down with sporadic shots only.

Gathering my belongings, I headed to the rendezvous point. On my way, I remembered my wound again. I began to examine my leg with understandable curiosity, and I realized that I had been merely struck by a branch that had fallen from a tree or snagged as I went through the forest! So apart from a small swelling and two rips in my trousers, no harm came to me. I began to worry about my people, who were even more exposed to danger, but it turned out I need not have worried. By the time I got to our meeting place, they were already smoking pipes there, and were sharing stories of the battle. My two officer partners also turned up; only Lányi's lad was hit by bullets, extremely fortunately it was only a flesh wound on his back.

Such minor injuries later became the object of amusement. Not so on the front line. My comrade, Pálfy, was the only one of the old battalions, who did not get a position with working squads, and was now assigned to the troops. True, he did not get to the front line for a month, but one evening, as I was leading up my workers, there he was, to my great delight. He was standing there with his company just waiting for the relief. He arrived just that day to work on the trenches in the night. He was unaware that the attack was planned for the next night. Next night we worked only until one o'clock. The advance began at 2 AM, after the artillery fire ended. I was worried about him; he was the youngest of us, and so I waited anxiously, hoping to see him again. I learned that some companies advanced too far ahead of the front line. I saw these soldiers retreating in terrible condition. They crossed in front of me, the brave Hungarian soldiers bringing with them their dead and their wounded. To my infinite pleasure I recognized Pálfi's voice, who was just commanding his people. I hurried to him, and he described his experiences as follows: "We received the news of the dawn advance on the previous evening. As good soldiers, we were so preoccupied and focused on planning that we couldn't think of anything else. But as soon as we finished, our artillery began to fire. The order came to attack. The battle was on. Now they were in a shower of bullets trying to run to the road in the valley in front of them. The enemy artillery came to life and responded with heavy fire to our artillery. We had to advance, otherwise we would have been lost. We suffered considerable losses. Under an overwhelming shower of bullets, and shelling, we at last reached the target village and there, amongst the houses, we could find some protection. Still the battle continued for some three hours and then it subsided to sporadic shots until late in the evening, when the retreat order was given. We returned hungry, thirsty and tired, but proud and happy. The difference between the two battles appeared to be insignificant, but alas now you can stop worrying about me."

1915 July 17th I left to attend a court-martial in the HQ in Halicz, where I was to testify in the case of that Jewish guy, whom I caught in Rykowo. I had an opportunity to talk with some Hungarian officers, who told me that you will meet very few Hungarian officers in such military offices. Instead, these higher-level military meetings were usually full of Czech officers. The Hungarian officers predicted that this proceeding would not end well.

Galamb also travelled with me. I have fond memories of travelling with my dear friend on such trips. After the interrogation, we travelled to Stanislau. Here I met my relative Géza Speidl, who had carved out a good lifestyle living there.

We moved from Panowice to the village of Toustobaby. We were happy to leave Panowice, as the regulations against the spread of cholera were getting quite strict, which in turn meant that the epidemic was spreading. The situation was not much better in Toustobaby either. We found whitewashed gates here with "Achtung Cholera" written across gates. Here we were much closer to our next assignment, which was another reason for our relocation.

The work was more perilous here, than at our previous place. The plan was to attack from a system of trenches built in the following fashion: when we arrived at the place where the trenches were to be built, the regular troops climbed out from the existing trenches and silently and cautiously crawled ahead, maintaining a set distance of separation, where they lied down, until the others got there. At this point, we began to work, digging an approach trench forward. When the soldiers arrived, we dug approach trenches for them to the right and to the left. Feverish activity was going on; we had much work to do on the first night, because we knew that in the morning the Russians would see our advance, and we would be hampered in our work by their gun and cannon fire.

Next night, they began shooting early. Bullets were whistling in every direction. There were more injuries, so we had to dig approach trenches everywhere. We got about two hundred steps closer to the Russians with our new trenches. Our next task was to improve these positions. We made many two to three meters long trestles, wrapped them in barbed wire and took them to the front line.

One day, on a day-time inspection of the trenches, near the front line, one Battalion Commander, near the edge of his section, warned me not to go much further, but instead, go around in the approaching trenches. He told me that on the opposite side there were sharpshooters and not a day goes by without one or two soldiers getting shot in the head through our shoddily built embrasures. I might have even smiled at his well-intentioned warning and answered that I am not going around since it is my duty to inspect the trenches. Well, I almost paid with my life for my courage and lack of caution. After getting through the tricky spot, I stopped at the next embrasure to watch the Russian positions with my binoculars. Not even half a minute had passed, a bullet whizzed over my head, missing me by no more than the width of my hand! I turned pale and my dispatch runner, also visibly shaken, thought that I had been shot.

It was very unpleasant to work at night due to the perpetual rattle of guns and shelling. It made us all nervous and uneasy. If they kept shooting too long, we asked our artillery to shell the Russians so we could do our work. Sometimes we could hear the Russians yelping as they were getting injured, but at least we got some peace for a while.

They left us alone in the village; little was shelled. In Korzowa we were working on a spit of land extending between Russian positions. It was unpleasant and delicate work. In Toustobaby I was down with the flu for a few days; I was worried about it as several cases of cholera had occurred in the village. In fact, there was also a death reported in the room next to Squad Commander Fülőp's apartment. One of my infantrymen was also found dead in a barn, where he lived. His name was Zegreán, but he was diagnosed with other health issues by the doctors.

On August 25th I went to Nosow to replace Galamb in the 129th brigade. The troops were preparing a plan for a general attack. I spent a few pleasant days with the engineer officers Kopeczky and Jesko. During the day we made the barricades wrapped in barbed wire and at night we placed them in front of the front trenches.

The Russians did not anticipate our planned attack. Our carefully planned attack was launched at dawn with heavy artillery. Our troops rushed the Russian positions with only the rear-guard held back. There were many casualties as result of this action. The Russians retreated to the location of the first attack. After the battle, we were engaged in building bridges together with the engineers (sappers) but first, I took a tour of the battlefield. It was still in the morning. There were many dead and wailing, injured soldiers lying scattered across the battlefield. As I observed them from a distance, I began to realize that the medics and others on the scene did not come for the wounded, but they were looting the dead! Several of them searched among the Russian dead soldiers. Just when I started to chase them away, the Russians sent about 6 shells towards us as a parting good-bye, but they did not reach where we were. Our return fire was enough to scare them, and they scattered away, leaving the wounded soldiers there. I was totally disgusted at these people's action. I saw this type of behaviour later as well.

Next day everyone disappeared from the horizon again, and I was left without an order. I decided to pursue the Russians with my troops, which was not received well by the other working squads because they were forced to follow us. That day we got to Gablonowka. I still had no orders from HQ, so the men tried to persuade me to remain here until we do receive orders. Instead, on August 29th, I decided to march through Uchrinow to Podhajce, or more precisely to Halicz, a suburb of Podhajce. with my company and Galamb's company. This is where the Hoffmann headquarters were stationed.

As I mentioned before, two squads were formed from our previous battalion, one was called "Militärarbeiter Abteilung (military squad) I/32, the other was II/32. The first was Galamb's, of which I was in charge currently while he was away. We stopped near the Jewish cemetery. At this point, I went to present myself at the Geniestab. I was greeted here with immense joy., and I was immediately ordered to go to Folwark Debiki with my company. I inquired about the local situation but the only thing they could tell me was that the Russians had stopped at Strypa, and they were staying there for one or two days.

Folwark Debiki isn't far from the Strypa valley and getting there was possible only on totally flat terrain, which was not an ideal circumstance. On August 30th we started toward Michalowka. In gloomy weather, our small troop was marching along depressed through the unpopulated barren fields. We didn't meet anyone. I went ahead so that I could be informed about the situation in good time. Michalowka was eerily silent and deserted. There I met my old acquaintance Captain Osztoics, and I informed him of our plans. He cautioned me to be careful because the Russians just now shelled Folwark Debiki. I marked on my map the best way to get to the camp. After the whole company arrived, we turned off the road and went around a bend for a short distance, then I stopped my soldiers in a small low-lying area. I asked them to stay in a bunch and not to wander about, otherwise they could be shot. I walked towards the farm ahead with a lad and two messengers.

Page 79.

The people here were almost motionless I found the commander sitting on a bench, reclining against the wall of a huge barn. Staff Officer Captain Beregi stood beside him. My appearance was a total surprise. I briefly explained why I was there, but I hardly finished my report, when the Commander asked me, how I could possibly get there and who was that idiot who sent me there. When I said that it was the Corps Command, and my men were around the bend near us, he was visibly annoyed and ordered me to leave one of my messengers there; you can't work here day or night. It was hardly a quarter of an hour ago that the farm received 20 grenades. One of the grenades has taken the map holder from Captain Beregi's side and he showed us the hanging straps. He instructed me that my men should not move before evening came. He promised me to send a message by that time, and then we had to move with extreme care, so that only one person may leave at a time, and when he got to the haystack 2000 steps away, the second may start, and the third only after a good time. I went third, and when I reached the haystack, a shell landed not far from me. Some of my men ran to me, they have found the shrapnel that fell near me. It was so hot, that they couldn't hold it in their hands; they had to toss it from one hand to the other. Reaching my men, I ordered them to dig themselves in. I showed them which direction to dig the trenches. They went to work in a hurry, but soon my messenger and another soldier brought the order from the headquarters to return immediately and very carefully to Podhajce. Few orders have been taken so willingly. We snuck out from the pit in groups of five and late in the evening arrived back to Podhajce. Going from Jaklonowka to Debiki, then to Podhajce was a nice little walk for one day.

I presented myself at the headquarters to Major Krausz, who commended me for going after the Russian troops without orders. We were the only labor group that pursued the Russians. He congratulated me on carrying out the task entrusted to me with such precision. As a reward, he entrusted me with the construction of three bridges, which had been burnt by the Russians.

The same day we marched to Wierzbow, where we scored excellent accommodations since all military personnel have left town. The people were well disposed towards us, for they were glad that the Russians had withdrawn. Also, because they were in a hurry, they had done them no harm. We were working there until Sept. 5th. These few days were spent with demanding work. The material for the three bridges had to be located and then carried to the workplace. And it was raining the whole time! After the work was finished, my new orders were to march to Bielekiernica. By that time the working quads in the Hoffmann corps were headed by Captain Babka of the Czech Republic. It would be hard to tell you how much villainy this man has committed. It would be even harder to unravel what he has stolen. Not to mention his lifestyle; his wife even sent the lady's dresses back to the Czech Republic. He always took a large house. He frequently put on large dinner parties, where guests were served delicious food. The voice of authority was of course always carried by the loafing around Czech officers. Captain Fábry, who was my Battalion Commander, was only a subordinate, without any real authority, next to the Czech Captain. Of course, Fábry lacked any ambition to do or to arrange anything.

This role perfectly suited his personality. He drank through some months with a kicked-out Deputy Sheriff named Rác, here in Podhajce. He was promoted to Major for his excellent work on Sept. 2nd. Finally, Fábry was recalled to Hungary, based on a reprimand dating back to a time in Bukovina, for which he spent nearly one year in Marosvásárhely on quasi-remand, until the verdict was reached, when he received a ten-day barracks lockup. Such is Military Justice! We marched from Bielokiernica to Sosnow, arriving in the evening. That night my men relieved the engineers and worked all night building the bridge that had been burnt by the Russians. We worked through the night with the help of torches. Also, that night, I fell in the river and had to change clothes. I continued working and at dawn we marched on, in pursuit of the Russians through Pantalida to Tiutkow.

In the comforting belief that the Russians had totally run out of artillery ammunition, and that they would continue their retreat, getting to the front did not cause any concern. As we saw, this thinking later caused a bitter disappointment. The people of the village did not suffer from the war up to then. In 1914 the Russian troops only marched through the village, without battles and they have been living in peace under Russian rule ever since. The village was also full of farm animals, pigs, and poultry in abundance. I immediately bought three fat pigs for the company, one of them was killed and we made a splendid meal of it, and the other two I left to the care of two Romanian soldiers.

We were part of the first infantry regiment, whose companies were spread out over a several km long line. The commander was Lieutenant Frauendorf. The Russians were about 2 km from here on the opposite bank of the river Szeret. First night my men dug makeshift trenches. We were supposed to work on September 8th in the morning, but meanwhile the Russians became very lively. Their infantry came closer to our positions and sometimes opened fire. Towards noon, they started a grenade assault. At the regimental headquarters, I was sent to Battalion Commander Polgári, who was stationed in Darachow, and my workers will be executing the work he ordered that evening. I went straight to Darachow to discuss the evening's work. On the way, I was caught in some shelling; a grenade exploded about 50 paces from me. Reaching the battalion headquarters, I entered the room and I saw everybody having a wonderful time playing poker. They did not care about the shelling outside at all! Instead, they invited me to join in the fun. I said that I was keen to work but I was told that I would not be needed day or night, and then I was simply ignored. I heard the opinion expressed that we would have to retreat soon anyway.

The next day the Russians again launched a heavy artillery attack. Remembering the comments last night about retreating, I put my company on standby and I waited for orders. The shelling always became more intense towards noon. I sensed that the whole village was becoming more uneasy and restless. At noon I gave orders to start the cars and to move out while I hurried to the headquarters. On the way, a messenger was running towards me with orders to come to the regimental headquarters immediately. I instantly sent a message to the company to move in the opposite direction into Sokolow, and I went to the regimental headquarters. I found the packing up at the HQ was already in full swing, and Captain Beregi just said briefly: "Retreat to Sokolow".

We were not even 2 km away from the village, when it came under heavy Russian shelling. Had I not been alert enough, we would have been caught in it as well. We witnessed the retreating artillery subjected to heavy shelling, but they were able to extricate themselves without much loss, galloping forward. The villagers were also escaping. It was heart-breaking to see their pain, but sadly we were not able to help them.

We arrived at Sokolow on the afternoon of September 8th. Since it lies on the eastern side of the Strypa, we crossed the river, and we camped about 1½ km east of the river in the drizzling rain.

When we left Tiukow, I left our two live pigs in the care of the Romanians with the order to drive them into Sokolow. They arrived towards the evening at our field, but with only one pig in tow. In Sokolow, one of the pigs laid down and refused to move on. Frankly, I was amazed at the fat pig's arrival in Sokolow, but nevertheless I ordered the two soldiers to go back to the bridge immediately and get the other pig. Well, they went there early next morning and came back with five pigs! The explanation of this was that everybody escaped from Sokolow, and the farm animals were left to fend for themselves!

Behind the Strypa, on a hillside, our workers built underground shelters for the Brigade Headquarters. In the evening, we took barbed wire barriers to the front line.

The Russians did not follow us immediately, which was a blessing, because they could have gone all the way to Pest, since we had no reserves behind us. Meanwhile, the headquarters moved into Folwark Waga, where Sapper (Ed: engineer) Captain Kovacsics led the technical work. On the evening of September 9th, we went to Chatki with the company, and we slept there. In the night I woke up to frantic shouting: the house in front of us was on fire! It was soon extinguished, and we went back to sleep. A huge haystack behind the house was set on fire by the Russians. A Cavalry Lieutenant from the corps headquarters rode out there in the morning to inspect the fire, this was the last remnant of his estate there. He told me that he had two estates besides this one, there was one on the Italian border; both of his properties ended up on the military front. Both of his castles were burnt down. In the coming days our task was to build bases along the river Strypa between the villages of Burkanow-Hajworronka and Wisniowczyk.

The Russians completely looted a beautiful castle in Hajworonka. In the garden there was a piano, gorgeous silk covered furniture, sheet music and expensive books scattered about. The Ruthenians were walking around in a daze and in silence; you could tell they favoured the Russians. No information could be obtained from them. On September 12th, the infantry was already helping in building our positions; the work went on with a feverish pace. The Russians were already attacking our positions at Sosnow. Here, toward Trembowla, there was a huge aspen alley, a hundred steps long. This landmark served as a directional point for the troops, even at night. A bridgehead was built here, where Captain Zachár stayed with his company. The glorious days and bravery of Captain Zachár and his Hungarian patriots are linked to this bridgehead. Our tired and weak troops were demoralized and there was no sign of relief troops coming. We felt that we might not withstand another strong Russian attack. This turn of events was particularly worrisome for me.

Page 82.

In addition, currently I was to go on my first leave. I had submitted my application for leave, but I had little hope of it being granted.

On September 10th we stayed in Leskawki, a suburb of Sosnow. As I got up, early in the morning, the atmosphere felt like a powder keg. We were ordered to Burkanow, where I met Lieutenant Colonel Frauendorf, who was the commander of the bridgehead of Burkanow. He asked me to work diligently on the reserve positions to be built on the inner bank of the Strypa, because he felt, they could hardly be able to hold the edge of the forest if the Russians would advance and attack. He proposed to me to leave my messenger with him in case something urgent came up and he needed to notify me.

I had mixed feelings with leaving a messenger with the Lieutenant Colonel to notify me of danger and he did not make me feel at ease doing it. I knew that in general, during military action, especially after a lost battle causing retreat, it would be the last thought on his mind to notify me. With all the decisions he must make, including saving his precious self, it would not be foremost on his mind to secure the physical integrity of the workers who did not participate in the struggle of the battle.

On 1915 September 11-13th we worked hard on digging makeshift trenches along the Strypa between Burkanow, Hajworonka and Wisniowczyk.

On September 14th I sent the crew to work in full marching readiness. It was very foggy, while the Russian lines were approaching our positions, there was firing. Towards 10 o'clock there was hurricane-like fire all along the line. I left my workers there and went up the hillside to assess the situation and I ordered our cars to be behind the village, on the road, facing towards Michalowka. I examined the terrain with my binoculars. Two companies of infantry passed over the bridge and were given their weapons. They received the live ammunition for these weapons across the river on the forest edge, under heavy gunfire. Hoffmann had no other reserve; he threw these newly equipped soldiers on the front line. In the meantime, on the surrounding hillsides the Russians just poured forward in a 40-row formation. The bridgehead at Burkanow, built in a small forest, was under heavy shelling. Many wounded soldiers came back over the bridge. I saw that on the right side the Russians were already near the river, so I ordered my unarmed workers back, and we retreated to Michalowka without an order. I found nobody here, even the hospital had left. The guns went silent. No troops were coming back, only straggling, wounded soldiers trudging along the road telling each other the bleak stories about the dead and the whole bridgehead army taken prisoners. This is where the brave old Austrian warrior Bondy and his men met their end, caught in a crossfire on the forest edge. About 5,000 of our people were taken prisoners.

Since I did not want to retreat any further from Michalowka without an order, I stopped my company there. I put my rider, Mihály Theil, on my horse and sent him to Folwark Waga to ask Captain Kovacsics if I should take my troops to Podhajce or stay put in Michalowka. As time went on, I felt an increasing sense of urgency. Before Theil returned, I ordered my troops to prepare for a retreat to Podhajce. I was afraid that the Cossacks would pursue my unarmed troops on this magnificent countryside, and they could easily force us to march straight to Moscow.

I did wait for Theil, who had the order, to stay in Michalowka until further notice, but he added that the headquarter was already packing up, and Captain Kovacsics was debating with other officers whether it would be appropriate to direct us to Podhajce. So, I calmly took my men to Podhajce, where in the evening, I could hardly find any officers at the Corps Command.

At the Corps Command, they were so scared that they did not even leave a doctor behind, so when a gravely wounded soldier was brought in on a cart, screaming in pain due to his shattered right leg, I could not find anybody to bandage him. In my outrage I expressed my dismay to the Officers of the Corps Command. They hurried down to the cart and gave first aid for the wretched soldier themselves. I reported my arrival to the Sapper Commander, Captain Wlach. He told me to go to bed and have a good night's sleep and tomorrow we will hear from Division Headquarters.

On September 15ᵗʰ Galamb, returned from his leave. We spent another day in Podhajce. The leave request that I asked for was not dealt with in all the confusion. I marched into the "Militärarbeiter Abteilung" (Military Worker Branch) II/32 to Bielokiernicza.

For reasons unknown to us, the next day the Russians retreated to their previous position at Szeret, so we advanced again to Strypa. We got to Chatki and began to build the bridgehead positions at Sokolow. Captain Zachár was satisfied with the plans. Here I met my former comrade Árpád Pálfy, who was with the trainers during the battle of Burkanow. There he got an urgent order to march to Burkanow, which was already in Russian hands by then. When he advanced and approached the Burkanow woods, the Russians were just getting out of it to chase our troops. Pálfy directed his troops toward the Russians on the road and opened fire, which caused the Russians to retreat immediately. They did not move from the edge of the village for three days and then, as I said, they retreated as far as the Szeret.

My comrade Galamb fell ill, so I took over his company in Sosnow. He went to hospital in Stanislau. That same night I got my leave, I sent for Lányi, and on the morning of Sept.27, 1915, I handed over the company and started to Tessarowka to check out. From there I drove to Podhajce, where I got a car from Fábry and travelled to Halicz, then to Stanislau. From there I went to Pest by train through Delatyin to Kőrösmező. After 13 months away, I arrived home on the afternoon of September 24th.

The first hours of the journey home were a delight. While I was out working in the battlefield, I was not homesick but the closer I got to home, the more I yearned to be there. My leave flew by quickly with visiting relatives and dear friends. Later I thought they should have visited me that instead! In the end, there was not enough time to spend some quality, quiet family time together.

I had to return to service by October 5th. I traveled through Sátoraljaújhely, Delytyno, Stanislau, Halicze to Potutory. From Potutory, I traveled with Colonel Guillaume in a cattle wagon to Podhajce. On October 8th I appeared at a hearing about Fábry's disciplinary case. Galamb also arrived back from the hospital and on the 10th, we boarded our train together to travel to Sosnow. We met Captain Osztoics in Folwark Waga and he advised us to continue our journey only in the dark because the Russians were attacking Sosnow with their cannons. We could see their shrapnel gleaming and flashing above Sosnow and Rakowiecz. It was raining. After my lovely holiday with my family, I find myself in a depressing situation.

We reached Sosnow in the dark. We found Galamb's battalion in an upheaval. Russian cannons had been attacking them all day long. Fülöp was escaping to Rakowiecz from the cannon fire. I was supposed to go to Rakowiecz too but before leaving, I dropped in to see the sappers. While with them, I received an order: I had to start immediately with the battalion to Rakowiecz where Major Birtha required that a necessary new position be established during the coming night. I walked over to Rakowiecz in pitch dark. Heavy rifle fire accompanied my walk like a musical background and there was something unsettling in the air.

I found Fülöp having supper with the officers and waiting for the order to leave. They were happy to see me and informed me that the Russian offense had already started with full force and that we would be working on the defense line. Neither Lányi nor Fülöp had a good sense of direction so after supper, I guided the whole battalion to our destination. We were getting close to Rakowiecz where there was an artillery post. Just then, the Russians felt like sending cannon fire in our direction. We were forced to stop. The men were tired and lay down on the ground which was drenched with water from the constant rain over the past few days. In the meantime, I looked up Major Birtha in his "underground palace" and signed up for service. Even these underground shacks lacked comfort after the continuous rain and the officers who lived there suffered terribly from the damp conditions. Several working troops had been sent here. In the darkness, men from the various troops got mixed up and by the time orders were being given, it was impossible to identify and sort the men according to their respective groups. Our battalion stood in the distance and we could start immediately. Luckily the cannon fire had stopped by then.

Our order consisted in reinforcing the Rakowiecz post (possibly using sandbags). Later, during the bloody fights, we benefited from the reinforcement. We worked up until 5 a.m. in the morning and later we settled down in the shallow valley of Studynka. I slept in a miserable straw hut. By noon we received another order to move to the forest where Captain Nakrap's brave soldiers were holding the front. In the midst of strong cannon fire, we weren't able to work and we went back to our quarters.

During the night we worked in the same trench as before till 4 o'clock in the morning. On October 11th, Colonel Birtha sent us to the line of defense. We had to dig trenches that would run between the second and the third lines toward the neighboring troops, and then survey the terrain. The next night we would have to work on these connecting trenches. I established a rendezvous with my workers after nightfall at the stone cross further up the main road. They did arrive but from the line we received a signal that they were expecting an attack during the night. We had to start working diligently.

Polish soldiers were lying dead in the first lines.

Soon the attack hit, first with cannon fire. I was standing in the first line and from there I got myself up to the road where my men were working. By the time I reached my men, grenades and shrapnel were exploding left and right. The first posts in the valley were under a barrage of gunfire. The connecting trenches were not done yet but because they were badly needed in battle, we continued working under the hellish circumstances. We worked as hard as humanly possible. If the cannon attack would spread to the second line, we would need the connecting line for an escape.

While the men were working, I had a moment to be dazzled by the light of the flares and I marveled at these wild and bloody fireworks. The flares gave out a light as bright as daylight. Suddenly, we heard a terrible roaring sound coming from thousands of throats and then the sound of crackling gunshots as the Russian's attacked us. The cannon fires stopped, but the crackling of gun fire, the wails of the wounded, and the light of the flares continued, and our nerves reached their breaking point. We were worried about our colleagues in the lines.

The working stopped and we had to assess the aftermath of the attack. The running trenches got crowded, the wounded were screaming, with horror on their faces and retreating toward the dressing station. People were carrying ammunition to the firing lines. Messengers were running around asking questions. The gun fire subsided and we guessed that the Russian attack had been pushed back so we picked up our work again but the enemy reengaged their cannon fire and the whole rigmarole started all over again. The Russians were aiming at the first line which was about 200 meters away from us and we also got some of their bullets.

The Russians exercised three attacks during the night. The brave Polish soldiers pushed them back each time and we dug all the necessary lines during that terrible night.

I had to go to the headquarters at Folwark Waga. By the time I got back, we had to leave our camp because the Russians were shooting behind the lines, believing that there were reserves occupying the area, even though there weren't. The Russians had this impression because the working troops were moving around the camp more freely than they should have. The next morning a Russian plane flew over us. Our new order was to dig trenches for the reserves at the closer side of the Studynka valley. We set up camp a little bit further behind the working site and marched every night from our camp to our working site. We worked there for two nights. Cold wind sprung up and, because our camp was on an open terrain, we moved into houses on the lowland further from our working site.

Later, when the Russians had had enough of the staggering losses they had suffered, they became silent. We worked during the daytime hours from 5 am till 7 pm on the second line beside Studynka. It was my job to mark the new posts on the several km-long line. I walked back and forth all day long. On October 23rd, we got another detachment with lieutenant Straslisker as commander. I occasionally visited Podhajce and in the meantime, I visited my friend Galamb at Skinderowka. He lived with his Company and worked in neighbouring posts at Sosnow.

The battle activities had not subsided altogether as we were occasionally "honored" by visits of the Russians' cannonballs, though they didn't hurt anybody or damage anything.

Our men, who were put up in a barn, were suffering from the cold. On October 26th, we had our first snowfall. The Russians were planning further attacks. Cannon fire became more frequent affecting us. A grenade hit the ground near where two of our men were working and buried them. Luckily, we could get them out and all they suffered was a bad fright. Our 4 cannons were stationed behind the Rakowiecz forest and diligently answered the Russians assaults that heavily targeted our cannon posts with their artillery, all be it unsuccessfully. Our cannons were relentless, however, resulting in a true cannon duel and we admired our artilleryman's valiant work.

Finally, the infantry attack began on October 31st. The Germans were stationed at Siemikowce. The near bank of the lake that bordered the village had a steep rock wall that fell straight into the water and the Germans did not defend this part of the lakeshore. During the night, the Russians crossed the lake in thick fog with pontoons and from the side entrapped the neighbouring battalions. The sly plan was preceded by heavy artillery preparations. We found out about these events during the night from the fleeing soldiers. We were packed and waited for orders. In the meantime, our patrols observed the situation. On the firing line there was an ongoing battle. Lieutenant Fülöp did not bother with the front, he had a very important task to deal with. In the house where he was boarding, was holding a Christening. The family got together and they were baking and cooking. Fülöp was cooking too, since cooking was his passion. The Ruthenians are not the cleanest people, even in the best of times, one can imagine how grimy they were under the present circumstances. Many people were crammed into one room. One can imagine what terrible smells were swaying around: the terrible cigarette smoke, and release of human gasses, created an atmosphere, which made an incoming person gag, from the putrid smell. Fülöp was in his element. He was eating and drinking with them. He told us that when everybody was drunk, they were lying on the floor everywhere. He was lying on a bench and he even got a pretty Ruthenian girl.

We were waiting for orders, all prepared to leave, till the morning, but none had arrived. We received alarming news from several directions. Since the frontal break-through was exactly in our way, we decided to move a little to the right, and started moving toward Skienderowka. When we reached Malowody, we tried to contact Captain Kovacsics. We received an order from him to mark new positions from Malowody to Sosnow. We had to work on highly dangerous areas, the broken though parts of the front. It was characteristic that in those parts where the Russians crossed the Strypes and occupied a several kilometers wide area on our first lines; we didn't have a military presence behind the front. The Russians didn't have a chance to widen the occupied lines, because the 309 and 310 regiment stopped them at the edge of the Rakowicz Forest. The Russians were up on the top, left and right, from Siemikowce.

We were working all day on the side posts. Our two cannons were active by our side, led by a young officer. We were familiar with the situation from the stories told us by the fugitives. We have been watching the posts since the morning. We had an undisturbed view from our location, and we could determine the real situation on the posts. Suddenly our two cannons began firing, and to our greatest surprise they hit our own posts. I quickly sent my men to inform them of the mistake. They adjusted the cannons and from there on they were shooting to the right direction.

We were just about to depart to Malowody for the evening to have some rest when we received a new order. Both battalions had to go immediately to headquarters. They were located parallel to the edge of the Rakowiecy forest in Niederung. We received an order to clean up the areas which were regained by our counterattacks from the Russians. We departed in pitch dark, passing by Sosnow on the side of Studynka, in thick mud to the appointed location, where we arrived at midnight.

After several days of heavy fights, the men were exhausted and were fast asleep. We only found our always calm and cheerful captain awake in his underground shelter. We were right behind our first lines. Even though the men were familiar with the Russians' continuous attack policy, and despite the fact that the Russians' breakthrough happened some time ago, and they were in an unstable, dangerous situation, they were able to sleep. The captain explained to me clearly that we had no idea of the measure of exhaustion the troops were in. When the Hungarian soldier and officer couldn't care less whether they got shot or captured by the enemy, that meant their exhaustion was at such a high level that nothing could help anymore. Since there were no troops available for relief purposes, the existing troops had to stand until complete exhaustion.

We introduced ourselves and informed the captain the purpose of our appointment. The captain shouted back in a rough voice that we should get rid of the Russians first and do the cleanup afterwards, and he also told us to get the hell out of there quickly, because the Russians are preparing another attack during the night. He didn't have to say that to us twice; Galamb immediately turned around and went back to Skinderowka via Susnowa, while we crossed the closest bridge on the way to Malowody. The bridge was under gunfire which wasn't too dangerous in the dark, but it wasn't too comfortable either. However, we were way too tired to pay much attention to the whistling bullets around us and took a shorter trail to our camp. We walked a few kilometers. The bullets were subsiding, and we slowed down, and by the time we got home it was late at night. To our great surprise our location was jam-packed with German troops. We had no intention to complain to them. The poor souls had hard days ahead of them. We turned around and headed to Malowody. Luckily we found acceptable boarding there, and finally we went to sleep in the morning.

To get back the areas we lost, we went into counterattacks on November 2nd. There was huge traffic in the depression of Studynka Niederung. The mud was deep and thick, and that made getting ahead very difficult. They were bringing Russian prisoners with hundreds of cars and wagons, troops going to the posts or coming from the posts. All this traffic on the narrow road in pitch dark was fraught with difficulties. Fülöp tripped and couldn't walk anymore. We were in rotation with each other, now I had to do everything by myself.

We had to deal with the bridge again. We started in the afternoon so that we could get there on time. The bridge was under cannon fire. I went ahead with my errand boy. When we got close to the bride we heard the sound of cannon detonations. We wouldn't be able to get through the bridge before the cannon ball would hit the bridge. Every step brought us closer to the explosion, but we decided to stop and turned our back to the cannon balls, and we said here goes nothing. We could hear the whistle of the cannon ball. The thoughts crossed in our minds with the speed of light. What is going to happen with us? In one moment, I saw myself in the hospital, which is the better outcome. What would be the feeling of getting a bullet in my head, or chest, in my arm, or in my leg?

I imagined feeling the injury... Wouldn't it be practical to lie down on our stomach? But if they were shooting with shrapnel, we would give them a larger surface. We decided to stay standing. About ten steps from us there was a ditch, shouldn't we run there? The brigade could see us. I wasn't going to run about, it was already too late, we wouldn't get there on time. About 50 meters from us, a cannonball had hit the swamp with a terribly loud crash. Shrapnel rumbled through the air. All that happened in a flash. After that we ran through the bridge to the other side on the high banks of the river, and we stopped in front of the entrance of the brigade's headquarters. From the left, two riders were getting closer to the bridge. We recognized Captain Kovacsics, and three other officers. We are waving to them to hurry up, because another attack was due. They are about 5 steps from the bridge, and right in front of them a shrapnel exploded. That spooked the horses. The riders instinctively spurred their horses. This caused the riders to be thrown from their mounts, falling into the barbed wire mesh. The horses bolted across the bridge. We barely got through this incident, when a crazy coachman got close to the bridge on the near bank. He strikes the horses, but a shrapnel explodes above his head. Both of his horses fell, and the coachman slowly fell on his side and then to the ground. Men were running from the dressing station with a stretcher and took him away. On this side of the bridge, a soldier stood, patrolling the bridge. He turned into stone seeing the horrifying sight. We only noticed him now. About a hundred of us were standing there without noticing him before. We ran to headquarters and were pleading to relieve this soldier from his post, and from a certain death. They drew him in immediately.

10 cannons were working non-stop beside us on the upper part of the bank. They were roaring incessantly. They were shooting toward Siemianowice. We inquired about their aim. They explained how the Russian's resistance was cracking, and now the artillery is blocking their way of retreat. Their effort had good results. The Russian's 6000 men got trapped on the near bank of the Strypa, and they

surrendered, and they were coming in in long lines. We are marching out, and finally beginning the clean-up of the previously occupied posts.

After the recent battles we saw a horrible incident. A wagon was bringing in a well-built but fully bandaged wounded officer, who was screaming at the top of his voice: "Come on boys! Charge!!". His dreadful voice carried a long way on this dark night.

As I was turning into the running trenches, which were dug by our men, I shined my flashlight on a bleeding man, who was from our troops. On his face a mixture of suffering and happiness was visible. He could hardly talk, and he asked for water in Romanian. Somebody gave him bread, but he asked for water, and didn't take any bread. One of my men gave him a camping flask with coffee. He gulped it down and another flask too and a third one too! Now he was able to start talking. On October 31st he was left wounded in the trench, and Russians came and he stayed with them. They didn't take him as a prisoner. They gave him food, but they didn't have water. In the relentless shooting, he got three more injuries from us, and he almost died of thirst.

Page 89.

Today the Russians left, and he just dragged himself through dead bodies, and asked us to take him to the dressing station. Two of my men supported him, he could hardly walk. He was grateful to God for his escape from a hopeless situation.

Going along in a runner trench we came across a corpse. At this point, the Russian injured soldier could not go any further; he fell and died on the spot. We lifted him from the trench. We had to do this several times to the corpses we found in order to keep the traffic flowing in the trench. These dead soldiers had to be buried later. Some corpses were trampled into the mud during the battle so much that it made it very hard to remove them from the trenches. In one corner, we found a soldier sitting. He was leaning back, his face was white, his eyes were closed, I thought he was dead. My men were trying to lift him out too, but he was woken up. He fell asleep at that corner, because of complete exhaustion. He had no idea what was happening around him, and he was very happy to hear that the fighting was over, and that the Russians were pushed back from our posts. He also had to be taken to receive medical attention, since he could hardly stand on his feet.

When we arrived, we began in earnest to clean the trenches. In some places we found so many telephone wires crisscrossing that the only way we could move forward was to cut the wires in several places, and then collect them. We also found huge amounts of weapons, both ours and Russians', hand grenades, thousands of cartridges, clothes, canteens (drinking cups) etc.

On November 5th, Lieutenant Lányi arrived back from his holiday. He was a lucky man to escape the dirty work, while enjoying the comfort of his home and his warm bed. I was happy he was back, because now we can rotate the job, I was doing by myself on the posts. Now, I could have some rest, which felt so very good.

Captain Kovacsics always held his meetings at the bridge. We didn't like the idea, since the bridge was always under fire, but we couldn't say anything. When he also got the taste of an attack on the bridge, he transferred our meetings to Antoszowka. We joined with Lányi to Antoszowka to meet Kovacsics. I guided him to the posts, showed him what had to be done, familiarized him with the situation. The sappers and the pontoniers, who learned from their past experiences with crossing the Studynka, built 4 long bridges. During attacks, it was very difficult to cross these marshy areas, and the situation frequently became almost fatal for our troops. We also benefited from these bridges since we didn't have to walk a long way to cross from one side to the other to reach the location of our work. We always worked at night to repair the first line, and we were also preparing for the coming winter.

On November 13th, Major Fábry traveled back to Hungary. We scolded him often, and we didn't respect him because he was an alcoholic, but we accompanied him together with Galamb, and said goodbye to him. We returned the same day, and by the evening, we were working at our posts. This evening, we received the news of Serbia's capitulation.

On November 18th, we found ourselves in a snowstorm that I have never experienced before. Strong winds from the west blowing across Galicia made the snowfall even more miserable. At noon I was called to the telephone. It took me half an hour to struggle through the village to get to the telephone. The order I received was that I had to dig out the kitchen wagons on the way to the posts, since were stuck in the snow drifts. I started off with 100 men. We got heavily dressed, even wearing snow hats. We left in the afternoon at 1 pm. Visibility was very poor. I could never see more than 5 people out of a hundred in the blizzard. We had to shout to each other to be heard over the howling wind. We found the kitchen wagons at the appointed place.

Page 90.

Ten wagons were completely buried in the snow. We dug them out and took a long time until we got to the top with the half-frozen horses, who had to be dragged all the way to the top. The constant shoveling along the way in front of the cavalcade slowed us down. The hurricane blew the snow away on the top so we progressed in a faster pace. We went over the bridge and reached our troops. Our arrival was received with a surprise in the brigade's headquarters. They didn't expect us to arrive so soon during the terrible storm. They were offering schnapps to us, and wished us a safe trip back to our camp.

Silence reigned on the front. Though our men didn't enjoy the storm, they welcomed the peace and quiet. We arrived in pitch dark to Malowody. We brought with us a Hussar, whom we found on the side of a haystack half frozen, he lost his way and couldn't go any further with his horse. For two days, we had to clear all the roads from the high snow, and then we reached the posts, which were covered in 2-meter-high snowdrifts. For the winter we prepared covered posts, however they had their drawbacks. When the Russians crossed at Siemikowce, they could attack us from behind the covered posts, and we couldn't defend ourselves against that. That was the reason why the Russians could occupy a wide range of our posts. However, there was an advantage to the covered posts. When we had the snowstorm, our troops were well protected from the storm. Following the snowstorm, they shoveled themselves out of the huge amount of snow.

On November 21st, we were ordered to the Siemikowce bridgehead. The order was a surprise, because during the attacks it wasn't possible to work there. The Russians were lying in primitive trenches on the other side of the Strypa. They didn't have running trenches, their posts were buried under the snow, so they couldn't move around, their food supplies were inadequate, and they had to withdraw two-three km. One can imagine how great this news was for our troops, who were under constant fire weeks on end from the Russians. The

Russians' huge loss of blood was in vain, their purpose was shattered by a higher power.

We crossed on the splendid, English Made, pontoon bridge, on which the Russians came through at the time of their nightly breakthrough during the night, but on which they couldn't go back. Around the bridge 50-60 dead bodies were lying in the snow. Pioneers, with spades in their hands, were lying dead everywhere. Our cannons wreaked havoc on their lines. Further on the shore the Russian's dead were lying in a row, and they wanted to bury them. Further down amongst the wire netting, there were more dead bodies. Their attack on us, ended with terrible bloodshed for them.

After the fierce and bloody fights, of which Hofer remembered with reports, the defense takes a deep sigh of relief, and rest. Who knows for how long.

We were walking through the Russians' posts. Simple trenches, they didn't pay too much attention to the comfort, the wellbeing, and the health of their soldiers. They had hardly any running trenches. We immediately started working on the development of the bridgehead on the other side of Strypa. We didn't want to let the Russians again get too close to our posts. We were making plans for the bridgehead's structure. We wanted to be prepared to obstruct the enemy's possible advancement again. We were having a shortage of building material. We went into Siemikowce and Bieniawa and dismantled the beautiful houses of the villages and took the lumber to our posts.

Page 91.

In front of us lies the endless plane, covered with snow as far as Szeret. Nobody disturbed our work, which normally wouldn't be advisable day or night on this vast open plane. One can see long distances and bullets could fly very far. We worked without any danger this time, and that lifted the troops' spirits. We were progressing with repairing and improving the posts. We were moving closer to Rakowiec, very close to the lines. On November 29th, on a bitter cold day, we moved out from Malowody, where we had comfortable apartments. At our new stop, all the windows and doors had been removed already from the houses and were taken to the posts. We spent the night in houses without heat, doors, and windows. Next day we got doors and windows from Sosnow, but only late evening, which meant spending another night in unheated rooms. In the meantime, our men fixed up the furnace, and on the third day our apartments were fit and comfortable.

We were working from 6 a.m. till 4 p.m. non-stop. On December 6th General Blum charged me with building a bridgehead, located just before Bieniawa. This post was supposed to connect the areas between Siemikowce and Sosnow.

On December 7th, I got wonderful news. I got a telegram from my Flórus. She informed me that she was on her way to Stanislau, and we could meet there. I immediately took Lieutenant Lányi to the posts, and pointed out to him what should be accomplished in the next few days. I drove to Podhajce, where I received permission to leave. I asked for another car and drove through Halicon and I reached Panovic, where I rested and the following day, on the Dec. 8th at 5am finally reached Stanisla, and found my dear wife in Hotel Europe, who I haven't seen for a long time. We spent three unforgettable days there. Later, this beautiful hotel WAS burnt down by the Russians. On December 11th, I sent the car back, and together with Flórus we travelled to Stry. We got there at 6 a.m. From Stry, at 9 a.m. Flórus left the express train to Budapest. I left on the following day and traveled through Potutor to Podhajce. From Podhajce in a lovely snowfall I drove back by car to Rakovicz.

The Bienilaw bridgehead turned out very well. General Blum looked at our work often and expressed his satisfaction with our job. The weather turned mild, which made the ground very soft, which made our work very hard. We almost disappeared in the deep mud, and the posts were under the threat of collapsing. The water got into the tunnels of mice and shrews, and many of our tranches collapsed one after the other. To stop the destruction, we brought springs, suitable for braiding, from a 30-40 km distant forest. With the braided springs we supported the walls of the trenches. This was a slow process, but the Russians were quiet, and we could work undisturbed.

We brought forward the Siemikowce bridgehead, so it will be in line with the other two. To build these posts gave us an inexhaustible amount of work. Major Birtha and Captain Nekrep came to discuss the ongoing work. We were working together with the yellow patched Austrian detachment of Lieutenant Neumann's Austrian. Neuman was a big moused Check jewish officer. He said he was German, and he didn't try to conceal his hatred toward Hungarians, but in face to face he was obliging, and polite. His Company lived well on his savings. He was buying all sorts of things, and he got a gramophone. From Lemberg he got a bronze lion desk decoration. He was never present at work.

(Ed: **Pages 92 and 93** are missing.)

Page 94.

(Ed: Most of **Page 94** is missing. We pick up at the tail end of a story of a card game that was played on Christmas Eve, 1915.)

When he said that his official money is coming to an end, we lost all the money we won before. Lányi was left with 60 krown of winning. Then we had enough amusement for the night, and on the quiet Christmas night, we slowly walked home among the destroyed village.

A Transylvanian volunteer from the Sosnow troops wrote a poem for Christmas night.

CHRISTMAS POEM

For the holiday of holly Christmas day
Your heart be covered with calming peace
Heavenly peace, heavenly love, heavenly light
Because the redeemer was born tonight.

God sent his only son to Earth to us
To fill up our heart with love and light,
Listen now the holy teaching tonight
As Jesus taught us, love each other all the time.

Come, come to this humble little tree
You, whose heart offers love and beauty,
Be together in love and belief
That God can love you every night.

Come all of you with pure loving spirit
Because who is not able to love, not even alive
In whom still hatred lies
To them Jesus was never born.
Rest those, who are tired,

Those whose only wish is tranquility.
And my God Almighty give us blessing to our prayer.
Give peace and happiness to our beautiful homeland, Hungary!

Page 95.

We didn't work during the holiday, the brigade headquarters sent brandy to the officers and cigarettes to the troops. On Sunday we started working again. I stayed home with a mild throat ache.

In the afternoon my old officer friends visited me: Galamb, Pálffy and his comrades, Erdély, and Frőlich. Pálffy came, because his heart brought him back to us, and as usual, quickly had a glass too many, talked a lot, and gave us speeches. He was rude, but he amused us with his witty remarks, and we had a wonderful time.

On December 28th, the Russians tried to attack us from the South at Burkanow, from the Mogila Hill, occupying it overnight, but the following day we recaptured it. We captured 860 Russian troops. The front has been revived again. Artillery has arrived, the infantry was reinforced. A battle was going on at Burkanow. Major Nietse and Captain Smeu came from headquarters to examine our works at the posts. Later, we worked closer to Sosnow on the connecting posts. More exciting days were ahead. I reciprocated my friend Galamb's Christmas visit on New Year's Eve at his place.

1916

In 2015 November, they renamed our detachment and so currently our name is:

Landsturm Arbeiter Abteilung Me. 68/u.V. and the other: 69/u.V.
Of these posts the following units were standing:

Gruppe Gm. Blum:

Gruppen Kommando
Art. Gruppen Kmdo.
K.u.Inf.Rt.No.310
Ukrainische Schützen
L.I. Rgt. 35
K.u.K. I. Rgt.103
K.u.honvéd Rgt.308
Gruppen San.Anst.
Zahnarztl. - Amb.
Mil.Arb.Abt. Gruppe
2/4 Pionir Komp.

Page 97.

K. K. 131 Ldw. Inf. Brigade:
Brigade Kommando
Brigade San. Anst.
Art. Gruppe
K.u.K. I. Rgt. 81 and 88
Detachment: Götz, Farkas.
Sapper Komp. 3-12.

K. u. K. 132 Inf. Brigade:
Brigade Kommando
Brigade San. Anst.
K.u.K. I. Rgt. 81 and 88
Detachment: Götz, Farkas.
Sapper Komp. 3/12.

And to all above the following working regiments were standing:

K.u.K. Baukomp. 8/43 Res. Oblt. Oskar Peikert Studynka
Militar Arb. Abt. 5/43 Res. Oblt. Max Szenes Studinka
K.K.Ldst.Arb.Abt.205/Ldst.31.Ing.Lt.Jandaus Wenzl Skinderwka
K.u.Ldst.Arb.Abt.68/u.V.Oblt.i.d.E. Fülöp Ferenc Rakowiec
K.u.Ldst.Arb.abt.69/u.V.Oblt.i.d.E. Galamb Gyula Sosnow
K.K.Baukomp.1/Lw. 19 Oblt. Johann Madlo Sokolow
K.K.Baukomp.3/41 Res.Oblt. Josef Neumann Sokolow
K.K.Ldst.Arb.abt. 52/Ldst.19 Oblt.i.d.E. Anton Kankofer Burkanow
Mil.Arb.Abt.119/Lw.1.Oblt.i.d.Res. Vértes Dezső Bielokiernica.
K.K.Ldst.Arb.Abt.254-Ldst.2ö Hpt.i.d.Res. Babka Zahajce
K.K.Ldst.Arb.Abt.254-Ldst.35 Oblt. Thamm Podhajce

The whole month was spent on fortification works. The benefit of these works was that the Russians later couldn't attack on these lines. They were attacking all the more on the South and on the North from us. They were removing their troops, one after the other, from our front. Toward the end of the month the fight intensified, and enemy

197

planes were visiting us. German fighter planes were stationed with us. Their aerial battles kept the enemy planes in check.

At the end of the month, we moved to Sosnow. All these movements caused a substantial change for us, usually not a pleasant one. Neither that time. They started to reorganize the working troops, and as a result, I was assigned to Galamb's Company, to L.A.A.69/u.V. I should have been happy to be with my good, and thoughtful friend, but I didn't know why this happened. We had to solve new problems. We had to build a military camp railway from Podhajce to Sosnow. We also had two railway regiment detachments assigned to us:

K.u.K.Eisenbahn-Rgt. No. 3. Kadett i.d.R. Johann Fuka
K.u.K.Eisenbahn-Rgt. No. 6. Lt.i.d.Res. Burka.

Having work, the days are going fast. In the meantime, they gave permission to the troops and the officers to go for a holiday, and they were going home in groups all along the line for a few days. My own request somehow got lost, the second one was accepted on February 20th, and on the 24th I hurried home.

Page 98.

My second holiday went by the usual way, visiting friends and family. There was no time or opportunity left for resting. On March 13th, I already wrote home from Oderberg. I am on my way to the war in my home country, Galicia.

Upon my arrival, I had to replace Lieutenant Cincibuch, the Commander of K.K. Baukomp.103/14 Feldpost 213, and I said goodbye to Galamb. We are working at Strypa on the front line around Burkanow. I got in with an Austrian group, where the conversation was mostly German but some of the men were conversing in Cech in my presence, which made me rather apprehensive. This uncertainty got hold of me when I got together with my Austrian colleagues. They were spiked with Cechs. They themselves kept saying how uncomfortable their closeness was. On March 28th, I moved back to Galamb. We worked on building the military camp railway with great enthusiasm and commitment.

Slowly the weather turned to Spring. The work in muddy conditions on plowed land was very challenging. We just about finished the rail line, and it is already lengthened as far as Rakowiec. That was the place where I set up camp, the same elevation as the Rakowiec forest at Studynka Niederung. There, on the high banks, I was digging my "palace" into the ground.

My apartment was built and it contained: my room, the next room belonged to my man, then the kitchen, after that my stableman's and the stable. Great creation! My window was overlooking the valley of Studynka Niederung. The valley was wide, swampy, full of reeds and wildlife. Storks, wild ducks, and lots of little birds lived in the marsh. Life was very lively there. The top of my "palace" was covered with a thick layer of earth. At the side of it was a little garden. I planted flowers on the roof and in the garden. I was asking for seeds from home. The trains on our repaired railway line were already running on schedule. Trains left Dolina at 5:30am arriving at the end of the line in Studinka at 8:30am, and turning back at 9am, back again in

Dolina at 11:30am. The afternoon run was leaving at 12:30 pm and arrived back at 6:30pm. The wagons were pulled by horses. The troops on the line were very interested in the railway. To replenish food, munition, clothing etc. were much faster and easier with the newly built railway. I met on the line with the 129th brigade, 35th Infantry, 130th brigade, and the Hungarian 308th regiment with the following officers:

The army postal distribution were the following:
Feldpost 17: Kps. Kmdo, /Korpstrain, ausbildungsgruppen, Off.Asp. Kurs./
Feldpost 213: 54 Inf.Tr. Dion. /131-132 Brigaden/
Feldpost 350: 55 Inf.Tr. Dion. /129-130 Brigaden/

There was plenty of work, we could hardly keep up with arranging our people; so many were needed in so many places. Running the railway itself needed people like brakeman, driver, loading man, and the maintenance of the rail line needed: gravelers, diggers, rail platelayers, screw-appliers, railway tie-layers, the gravel mine, the quarry, etc.

As the railway regiment left, we started to repair the deficiencies left on the railway line. These experts treated our railway line as it was a regular railway line. There were many curves on the line, and the horse driven, well laden wagon, repeatedly jumped the line, and had to be lifted back on the tracks. We cut off the curves. We didn't pay attention to the occasional change of grade.

We worked, from morning to night, non-stop. We kept our men well, we didn't economize. In Galicia, we could spend all the money, which was earmarked for the crew.

We didn't like the general arrangements. How long are we going to stay here? Although nobody answered this question, the question itself made us very sad. I was occasionally inpatient, even though I should have been very satisfied with my lot. Everything was quiet on the front and almost nothing was happening in the posts but in front of us, the officers were giving each other parties and life went by happily. The soldiers though were working all the time and did quality work. Their work was not in vain; later on in their life they benefited from skills all learned in the army.

The quiet front draws high ranking visitors from the Hinterland. They were also visiting us. First came the Minister of National Defense Hazai Samu, who held an inspection and a ceremonial procession behind the forest. That was just what the Hungarians needed! Different kinds of celebrations were on daily, until the Russians had enough of the merriment and sent some shrapnel our way. The troops felt that we were asking for it for putting on such a show right in front of the Russians! That put an end to the high-ranking visits, and everybody disappeared as if they have never been there.

I had a telephone in my apartment. If I wasn't home, I had to sit somebody next to the phone, because it would not stop ringing. Either the troops were requesting something, I was receiving orders, or people were inquiring about the railway schedule. What I would have liked to do most was to sit my wife next to the phone, but that would have meant that I am at home. Nobody lived close by my place for quite some time. Later on, however, I did get a pleasant neighbour, "Entlausungs Anstal" whose commander was a pleasant young Austrian named Fähnrich, whom I befriended. We had good chats, played chess, and the long evenings went by more pleasantly.

Galamb, with his working men, had made a handsome, two-wheeled carriage for me. In 1916 May 10th, we harnessed Bella, my riding horse, in front of the carriage Galamb had made for me. Bella behaved well on my first trip, which took me to Galamb. I wanted to thank him for his unparalleled attention. We were continuously working on perfecting the railway line and opened a quarry, to strengthen the line. Unfortunately, in this area, we could only find white limestone, which is very soft, but it was better than nothing. Planes took note of our new rail lines. Because of the white limestones, the rail lines were highly visible which was not an advantage from our point of view. I sprayed the white stones with black mud, but the frequent rains washed them snow white again. That made me downhearted, our efforts were in vain, and we gave up spraying the limestones. The Russians paid quite a of attention to our rail line going almost as far as the front; they bombed it from their planes. This is very uncomfortable for me, since my apartment is on the riverbank, right next to the railway tracks, and they could hit me accidently. I still must heat my place occasionally. The weather is colder here than in Hungary, probably because we were further North.

Pgs. 100 & 101 missing.

Page 102.

I got an assignment to build an extension to the railway line as far as Rosochowaciec. Sooner or later at Sosnow, I had to make the railway go through a hill toward the first line. That was a difficult challenge because we lacked measuring instruments. We could hardly solve the problem of turning on the hill without the survey instruments. I was working with a simple level, and after lots of measuring, finally I found the right angle, and could build the line to Sosnow. Before noon I was at Sosnow, by the afternoon in Rosochowaciec. I had great use of my two wheeled carriage since I had to move around long distances. The Russians didn't rest, and their bombs injured two of our men. The regiments on the front were unsettled, they were helping the railway workers: Colonel Hodula at Sosnow, Colonel Altman at Siemikowce, and Colonel Birtha at Rakowiec. There were also German troops stationed at Rakowiec.

Toward the end of May, from the direction of Bohatkowce, we could hear strong cannon fire, but otherwise it was quiet on the line. The weather turned warmer in June. I visited Galamb several times. On one occasion, a Russian plane descended close to us and dropped a small bomb. We ran to the place of the explosion and we found a dead mouse killed by the bomb. The mouse's body was still warm when I picked it up.

On June 5th, the Russians attacked Sosnow. The positions, which we recently gained were bombed first then an infantry followed, but it was all for naught. The Russians didn't achieve anything. South from us, some distance away, we could hear strong cannon fire. Rumor had it that our troops were beaten at Buczacz. We often discussed the strategies with Galamb. On June 10th, we received an order that on a signal, we must destroy the rail line. The sound of heavy fighting could be heard from the direction of Bukarnow and Sokolow. Continuous cannon fire, gun fires, heavy smoke, like evil omen filled the air and our heart. It looked as if we were preparing for withdrawal on the line. On the stations huge amounts of clothing, tools were stockpiled, waiting for return transport. It was impossible to transport all the stuff with the occasional runs, even though we were trying very hard to transport as much as humanly possible to a safe place. We were also packed up and ready on our wagons and were waiting for the order for departure. We got up early the following morning. We had to transport ammunition to the posts. Around noon huge rain clouds were gathering then came thunder, lightning, warm rain, and suddenly the sun came out, the wind stayed with us, and the renewed barrage of gun fire from the full width of the front line. It was Pentecost Sunday. The battle was on with full force at Bourkanow, despite the holiday and we were transporting ammunition backwards. I had a bad premonition. They had already moved regiment 309 away. And regiment 308 went after them too. We followed them in our thoughts, and with anguished hearts on their dangerous road, and onto bloody fights. We heard later that regiment 309 suffered great losses before Burkanow and Podhajce. Their battles in this area resulted in the Russian attacks being successful, and they already crossed the Strypa. On Pentecost Monday and the following day, the cannon fight was unrelenting.

On June 13th, I received an order to move immediately to Uwsie. We got there in the evening in heavy rain and got soaking wet. Next day, at Rygalich, we worked on building up Post III. Galamb was posted far back at Tenace. We arrived in pouring rain at Uwsie in pitch dark, and witnessed a group of village people on wagons, moving away to the unknown, who were evacuated from their village, because they were too close to the front. I had never seen a sadder or more heart wrenching sight before in this war, and a more destitute, and homeless refugees on the run.

We were making new posts in an open country. I couldn't imagine the infantry could hold itself any length of time under these circumstances. On this flat land, cannon fire could chase out every living soul within a few hours. On June 15th, there was a battle at Gnylovody, but the neighbouring parts were quiet. Next day we could see 3 German battalions moving forward. Equipped with cannons, the battalions were moving toward the posts. These developments gave me hope and more confidence for the future. I talked to the Germans, at Warna they were transported in wagons like cattle, toward Saloniki. At Warna, they were waiting for the attacks of the Rumanians in vain. During their transport they were directed here. Help came from the Bulgarian border. I thought we couldn't get much help from there, and I started to worry again. "We will beat the Russians" the Germans said with natural conviction. And we had to believe in them, as we watched them marching and singing. I imagined them as iron rolling-mills when they begin to move, nothing can stop them: cannon fire or gun fire won't stop them. They just march on without the chance of anything or anybody stopping them.

They were very angry about the Chechs, rumor said that a Chech regiment gave themselves up somewhere on this front. They announced shooting them after the war. When the time comes the show-down will be terrible and the retaliation horrible, because of their heinous deed.

We received some good news from the division, the hospital where I lived, was ordered back to Uwsie. The sappers were going forward again. The Germans left for Podhajce. It looked like there was trouble brewing here. We had a battle in the evening, and we repelled a Russian attack. We were further away from the front, and we couldn't get reliable news. We were out of danger, which made us work even more diligently on the new posts, believing the possibility that we might need these posts in the near future.

According to the order of Captain Smeu, I had to report what was the situation between the Malowody and Kozova posts and had to revise whether they are acceptable for further use. Smeu spared the Rumanians, he was Rumanian too. I couldn't understand why he was still on the front at that time. I was checking the posts with my handcart all day long, and I got home in the evening.

On this beautiful, sunny June 18th, the fighting subsided. It looked as if the Russians gave up their attack. We heard we might return to our old occupation, building railways. That really means that the Russians, despite their great losses, didn't achieve anything. In any case, our front was pushed in from Burkanow to Hajworonka. We noticed that the Russians were preparing to correct their loss. Indeed, we marched back on the 20th to our railway building, I moved into my "palace" again. My flower garden was completely intact, only from my vegetable garden the hungry soldiers took away the radishes. I wished them well. Galamb also went back to F. Nagra. We rejoiced. Around this time, I felt the first sciatica pains in my leg. I was bed ridden and had anxiety listening to the Russians cannon fight from the direction of Burkanow. It lasted from 2am to 9:30 am. They told me that it might have been us who attacked, however from my bed I couldn't get reliable information. In the afternoon another barrage, the rumor was that we pushed back four Russian attacks.

The 35 Ruthenian regiment front was silent. They were Only doing reconnoitering patrols.

That kind of patrol was led by Skiwa, and in the process he succeeded in surrounding a Russian camp, capturing and imprisoning them. Unfortunately, shortly after this incident, he succumbed with a bullet to his heart.

We considered it bad news that the army corps of the headquarters were planning to move from Podhajce to Kozova. That meant that in the South we were not doing too well, with Podhajce seemingly in possible danger. That would mean that Galamb in Waga was getting too close to the front. Again, we were making a superhuman effort building the Rosochowaciec rail line. The new circumstances on the front made this rail line top priority. We were cornered, which meant, no matter which wing the Russians broke through, our escape would be very risky.

On June 25th we had to leave my "palace" again, and moved over to Rsochowaciec, because the latest news about the Russians' movements made it advisable. On the other hand, it might have served us better to deceive the enemy or to threaten them. In any case, there was something in the air, and that wasn't reassuring. We were alert and on guard, and we were trying to avoid surprises. Lieutenant-colonel Graf Corp. technician expressed his appreciation to us for the job well done.

On July 4th, I am back to my "palace". The roof is full of flowers. The railway worked again, but we didn't get too much joy from it, since cannon fires could be heard left and right daily, only our stretch of the front was quiet. We were trying to express our gratitude for that by working till we dropped. We didn't have to give orders to the troops, everybody was working silently with utmost effort.

My legs were healing slowly, now my teeth were hurting at the worst possible time. I got four of my teeth filled in a dental clinic for 11 crowns at Malowody.

The 310th foot regiment's 3rd reserve battalion was moved to Chatki, and a battery also went with them. The 35th infantry /K.K.Landwehr J.R./ Ruthenia's two regiments were coming back from Burkanow to the Sosnow posts, since, obviously, they weren't reliable. The 308 Hungarian regiment replaced them and went into that hellish battle. The 35th regiment took over the posts, which were excellently built up by the Hungarian regiment during winter conditions. That same Hungarian regiment was taken up to the North to build posts for Bohatkowce, and they were giving help at the Hajworonka break ins. The 310th regiment was ruined, and their 35th detachment was only in reserve, and never was placed in battle. These arrangements could explain why the Hungarian losses were so great. These laggard, unreliable soldiers avoided death. Mostly Austrian officers in higher ranks kept their own kind out of harms way and they always used the Hungarians in battles and to do the most difficult jobs.

In Tudynk the sappers were the center of society; many went to them to have a good time. They were welcoming and not overly exuberant. People liked to spend cheerful times with them. Lieutenant Lorbeer, Second Lieutenant Hart, Second Lieutenant Borowsky, Dr. Colonel Taussing, Second Lieutenant Krombholz, Second Lieutenant Szántó were all our good friends.

It was raining all the time and a cold wind was blowing. There was relative silence on the front; Trombitás Gyula was staying in Tudynka on the banks - he came with new cannons. He told us, he was on full alert, which we, half of us civilians, interpreted as bad news.

When the weather cleared, Russian planes appeared in the sky. On July 24th a huge Sikorsky plane was visiting us. We all ran out for the large hum buzz and we were watching what direction it took. He came about 5-6 km from us, flying high. A German fighter plane, who stayed at Folwark Waga, flew up and took after the heavy Russian plane. Our defense weapons, and cannons were heavily shooting at the plane with shrapnel, but the Russian plane ignored all that, and he turned toward our lines, and most likely, he took photographs of our lines. Most likely he didn't notice the approaching German fighter jet, who flew above the Russian plane, and we could hear their machine gun's rattle. The large plane turned on its side and glided away, and was trying to escape, but the German was fast on its track and fired again. The Russian plane caught on fire, and the plane spiraled down to the plough-land in flames. The pilot, who flew the plane, was Stebskapitan Beridge Boris, he burnt to death in the plane, his comrade jumped out and died as he hit the ground. They buried them in Wagan, the cross on their grave was the propeller from their plane.

Galamb lived in Rosochwaciec, where a Sikorsky plane dropped five bombs near his apartment. Until August 10th, our railway ran regularly, and the works was on schedule. We had a quarry, and we also did lime burning for a while. In the meantime, I was having a good time with the sappers, and enjoying the latest news. On August 10th they got orders to march to Sloboda Zlota, and I hurried home. At home the order was already waiting for me to be ready for tomorrow 's departure. For the third time we had to leave our quiet and peaceful home, but we felt that it was to be the last time.

During the night the traffic was busy on the road, and we sadly concluded that we are giving up the front. Where we will all this stop? On 1916 August 11th we started from our "palace" of Studinka Niederung. We could not foresee the difficult times that lay ahead of us. At Rosochwaciec we were informed that our withdrawal was beginning that day. We couldn't even pick dismantle our beautiful railway, nor time to destroy it. We marched through Sloboda Zlota, to Wiktorow. Galamb stayed with the battalion, and I was going ahead or rather back to Sybalin, where I found the sappers. Galamb arrived at half past one during the night.

The poor villagers are in an upheaval; they had good reason for it. That pleasant little village was turned in rubble a few days later. The work was guided by the sappers, on the following day on the Western part of the village, on the hill of Lysonia, where we built posts. The sappers conducted the works with a kind of indifference. They were giving us superficial and incomplete instructions, it felt that they were not sure if we could hold these posts, but our brave troops were holding it. If the sappers would have suspected, how furious, nonstop battles will happen far into middle of the next year, and how ten thousand men will breathe their heroic last breath, then from the start they would have put their very best skills and strength from the start and created safe shelters and perfect posts to the troops. We were used to carrying out the orders in the best possible way. Nobody could have known, what scale it would be needed.

Page 106.

Our men worked at their full capacity, although the general mood turned for the worst, because of the bad condition I dedicated every minute of my time to study the area and the situation. Even today, I can remember it in detail the events of that day. The first posts were built on the edge of the forest and the side of the village, correctly just traced, so the workers can immediately start, and not be at the wrong place, in a wrong firing position. The continuation of this clearing divided this forest from the Lysonia forest, otherwise connected it, and then continued in the forest. The forest stretched to the bottom of the valley. The first posts were indeed done here, and our troops were holding it for a long time. That post was later the site's most horrible action.

The work we did on the new posts, especially after the withdrawal, left me with a sinking heart. I saw our troops arriving tired at the half-done trenches, I saw how their instinct for life made them look desperately looking for a proper refuge, that they will be able to defend themselves. I felt the anxiety in their soul, I felt their fear of death and exhaustion. This made it twice as hard to do as much as possible and doing as good of a job as possible.

At Sybalin, all through the night, and the whole day, there were flowing people, wagons rolling by and cannons going by. This was a great opportunity for lurking people who like to fish in troubled waters. They can be recognized by an experienced eye. Their faces were sheepish, evil, shifty. They could lean on a tree for hours, two or three got together. This was important to warn each other where they shouldn't go. They were the best informed.

The village ended up being between two lines; it wasn't possible to help the population. The strategic line was drawn on the map and the village had to fall on the battlefield. They lived happily yesterday, even if the head of the family was in the war, the stock, the garden, the land all stayed home. The family members who stayed were happy to take care of everything, the elderly, the women, the children, for the reason that they can show the head of the family that while he was at war they were not idle. Today, they had to leave: the warm hearth, barn, everything, and they had to leave behind if they treasured their life. What a mind-blowing thought to leave the family's beloved cow. Those who didn't have anything else then their cow and their wine: no wagon, no horse or anything else. Where to? Even hopeless despair was pointless. When the gunfire started and even the soldiers started to leave the village, there was no mercy, they had to leave for the unknown.

The battles in Galicia start a new chapter, which will contain the heroic battles of Brzezany.

BRZEZANY

1916 August 11 – 1918 December 14.

Our troops stopped the advancing Russian army at Brzezany. Next to Brzezany at Poturory the line became entrenched because South of here the enemy advanced as far as Narajowka. This strategic position, which was attacked from the east and south by the Russians became the key to the entire technical front, and we had to hold it at all costs. It became the scene of a great battle. Przezany, Lysonie & Höfer were names involved in the command, which indicates the importance of the place where the battles were fought.

Sybalin was expected to be too warm for sleeping at night so we decided to march to Posuhow. Galamb accompanied the carts through Potutory while I chose to march straight through the forest in the bright moonlight. We spent the next day constructing trenches and preparing a new defensive position. On the ridge some locations offered an excellent view of our earlier trenches as far as Tudynka.
Our forces began to retreat Southward at midday. Clouds of heavy smoke were visible over our former location as buildings and other structures were set on fire as the troops were leaving. I wondered about the wisdom of this order. Would we not need these upon return? Did we plan to return?

Posuhow sustained major scars of former battles. Many houses were severely burned. The odds were that further destruction was likely.
The infantry rapidly progressed on 12th August to finish the trenches. On the hillside I was particularly interested in the progress of the left rear guard. Around noon they started shooting at us with their smaller cannons. We changed locations but the Russkies also followed us, and Captain Altmann stopped us. We resumed the work when our artillery intervened. We stopped at 9.30 p.m. We had to pay close attention to the welfare of the men as they worked without arms and ammunition and an armed attack could have been risky.

Somehow during these days of awaiting an attack at any time I always slept soundly. I guess this was so because I knew well that sleeping is a luxury, you might as well enjoy it while you can.

Next day I travelled by cart at dawn to Adamowka, a suburb of Brzezany. I enquired about the plan of work. The men were unfamiliar with the location and felt that it might be advisable to spend the morning further improving the trenches at Potutory. At Potutory young Ukrainians were waiting for orders. Galamb stayed at his quarters; I thought he may have been planning to work with his men during the night. At Posuhow we crossed a bridge and entered a partly dug trench. We were under the impression that on open ground they could see us clearly. The day before we were attacked from the left and plenty of shrapnel came our way. We were able to use the trenches to reach the defensive and relatively safe locations where we could see the Russians. The Officers were the target. Naturally the men cheered up and quickly resumed their task.

Page 119.

The "relative peace and quiet" did not last. Our rearguard was engaged with the enemy while they were advancing. Their artillery opened up with six smaller guns, attacking our trenches. It was impossible to continue any work. We also noticed the sudden and total disappearance of our brave Ukrainian troops. I had no idea how they could disappear so quickly! I did not know where they were heading and how they would get there. We found a somewhat safe location in the trenches and awaited the developments. The events took place on a hillside and we had a grandstand view of the battle. In my opinion the rearguard was lead poorly and lost ground. At midday they abandoned the hill and the woods across from us. This opened up the fields between us. I was in total disbelief. Why did they allow the Russians to displace them from their trenches and the protection of the woods? Instead of having a plan to defend the troops they were running away from the enemy, presenting a perfect target which was a gift to the Russians, who accepted this gift and used machine guns in addition to rifles. I saw many of our men mowed down. This was both an interesting and tragic observation. My concentration was momentarily distracted from my men by this display. My first duty was looking after my men, as remnants of the rearguard approached, trying to hide in the fairly tall grass. Since we had no firearms or ammunition, we had to think of escaping. The Ukrainians vanished and our guns were inactive at a time when a few artillery shells would have made a huge difference. The artillery was silent.

I jumped out of the trench. Running away was shameful but useful under these circumstances. So, I rushed to the hilltop and down the other side. I heard the six Russian guns fire and knew they were meant for me and my men. With one hundred men running, it was a worthwhile target. Their aim was accurate. One shell landed and exploded just a couple of furrows from me. It only took a few seconds, but these were some of the **longest seconds** of my life! Since it takes time to reload a gun, we resumed running to the highway. Here machine guns greeted us. I was hiding behind a tree and most of the men hid in a small depression and escaped one by one. I reached the bridge and Posuhow. We saw numerous casualties. The first aid locations were not well marked. One of my men sustained a leg injury but with support he got back to town. I contacted Galamb about evacuating from the village as the Russkies were bound to come and follow their offensive. Without orders, Galamb was unwilling to act. I went to see 1st Lieutenant Krumbholz who could be persuaded to see Brigadier Baukovac to get permission to move the men to Brzezany, since they were already quartered there and would have the ability to receive as well as act on orders without delay. The Brigadier was incredibly supportive. I doubt a Hungarian officer would have been so agreeable.

I told Galamb that we will not be working during the night in vain. He left at sunset, and I got our belongings and in the dark of the night we went with our carts to Adamowka, a suburb of Brzezany. I hurried to talk with the sappers. To my astonishment, all the officers were there having supper and in an excellent mood. I wondered what the reason was for such relaxed atmosphere. When I tried to elicit information, they sidestepped the issues. They appeared to feel that under such constantly changing circumstances it was best to stay home. Once again, I explained that Galamb went to work at night with his Company; they thought it was funny. The sappers were enjoying this. Much to my surprise Galamb appeared ten minutes later.

The previous night Galamb and his company reached the last viaduct without incident. However, some shooting was going on. They took shelter in the viaduct. While waiting for the shooting to lessen another group came upon them. It was a unit attempting to push the Russians back. It was fortunate that no friendly fire broke out. The second group was to retake the ground which was lost the day before.

In the meantime, the news in Posuhow was that the Russians, currently occupying our former trenches, will occupy the village. This resulted in general upheaval. There were people escaping. The highway was dangerous to walk on. Galamb, on the other hand, was happy. He could rest in Adamowka. After all the excitement we could sleep well in this dilapidated house, deserted and ready to collapse. The sound of the music of guns and rifles was present but not too loud.

Next morning, we installed barbed wire in front of the regained trenches. The regained territory also allowed us to move and properly bury our dead. Coming home the skies opened up and we got soaked to the skin. We got temporary relief in the culvert, but the water level increased, and we had to get out of our flooding shelter. We reached Adamowka wet but otherwise unscathed.

During the following days we worked in the Lysonia woods, to establish a secondary defensive line. This was about 100 feet behind the former line and under the watchful eye of Sapper Lieutenant Zborowski. Some of the refugees escaped Sybalin and were staying here. There were peasants with their wives and children and their livestock. Some were praying, some crying, the livestock bellowing as there was no food. It was a miserable situation further complicated by our inability to help as we expected the Russian reserves to attack at any time. I never found out what happened to that sorry crowd.

We worked all day in spite of the Russian shrapnel causing concern and the occasional casualties. Sybalin and Potutory burned for days. It was too dangerous to attempt putting out fires during the day. The "music of war" disturbed our days and nights. We did not find a suitable house anywhere.

Page 112.

The Russkies were slowly moving their heavy guns and were gradually reinforcing their trenches in preparation for attacking Brzezany. Opposing them were the "Deutsche Südarmee" and the Turks but this opposition cost them dearly. The so-called Deutsche Südarmee had a significant percentage of Austrians and Hungarians. On the King's birthday the sappers prepared a great meal. We were also invited. After lunch we had excellent black coffee and liqueurs. The atmosphere was wonderful. All of a sudden there were four explosions very near us indicating a Russian artillery attack after which was normally followed by an infantry attack. The gathering was jolted back a reality that we were actually at war, not a birthday party. The mood accordingly changed. Galamb returned to our old place but I was looking for a new place. They were planning to install a Howitzer in the vicinity of the house in which we celebrated the King's birthday. After installation, once the Howitzer is used, the area will become a focal point for destruction by the Russians. Since these attacks do not take place with pinpoint accuracy, so it's wise to keep a safe distance. This is exactly what happened. I found a lovely unoccupied house behind the church. Galamb remained in the old house which I considered unsafe. He eventually moved but at high risk. I chose the smallest room.

During those days we worked on the Lysonia day and night. Several of my men were wounded but in spite of that, the work proceeded day and night. The Romanians entered the fight as they felt it was time to attack an already suffering force. They had no idea that they would be recipients of unfair treatment by their allies. The matter was too depressing to mull over. We did not expect a significant loss of territory. We were mistaken.

The beginning of September saw fighting which resulted in heavy losses on both sides. The Russians would start their now-familiar introduction to battle by firing their heavy guns. The first, usually heavy attacks yielded gains for them and this would result my men and the sappers moving to higher ground between Raj and Brzezany to avoid injuries. In the woods we would fabricate *Spanish Trestles* [a wooden obstacle which could be readily moved] and placed them ahead of our second trench lines. There was considerable anxiety mostly because of the uncertainty of war. This problem was magnified by the knowledge that we had no reserves. We received many orders, several of which were contradictory. On 3rd September we started the battle with our artillery and followed up with an infantry attack. Despite a vigorous Russian counterattack, we held on to our gains. Eventually we were ordered to march to Basowka to our rear, near our trenches at Lipa. I went ahead and Galamb was to bring the companies. He was not as careful as he should have been and the Russians lobbed a few grenades but luckily caused no injuries. We could not complain about our new orders. Brzezany was in a cauldron under constant rifle and gun fire.

Only one highway led to our rear. This meant that a retreat could only take place in that direction. This would be troublesome for the laborers who got used to an easy life in the army. Their work that was required was not unsafe but retreat would have been both dangerous and tiring. The "easy life" did not last long. On 8th February we were all transported to Lesniki by car. From Lesniki we marched to Raj. In Raj I got my orders in the Potocky Castle by the General in person. The task was to build defensive structures on an urgent basis, leading from Adamowka to Raj. This location was likely to become the front. We had three rows of defensive lines, since we were so far behind the front that if the front reached us maintaining the safety zone would have been difficult. Sapper Lieutenant Hart worked with us every day. The General allowed ten days for the project. With much effort we met his estimate for the completion of the reinforced defensive structure.

Galamb went on leave. This made me happy for two reasons: first of all, he was tired and needed a break. Probably more importantly this left me in charge. This was important for many reasons. Whereas Galamb was very careful to avoid dangerous but unnecessary situations and was usually smart enough to recognize and avoid these, this was not always so and put our men in harm's way. Worse, he was not willing to change his mind when these risks were explained. For example, when we marched from Lesniki to Raj he insisted on the risky route through Brzezany and spent the night with his Company in Brzezany, even though he already experienced such a risky move just recently. I was sure his men would prefer the route which would have been two hours longer but much safer. It was never a good idea to stay in the vicinity of the Headquarters. One reason for this was that everybody felt justified to give us orders, often conflicting and at times criminally stupid. We had such an experience in the past, following one terrible order just to be reprimanded later for doing so. It was just so on this occasion. I presented a very strongly worded argument against us staying in Brzezany and succeeded in getting a very nice ten-day assignment, not at the front.

Following this we became popular. Other work crews quickly caught on that when they had an easy and safe job they should stretch it out much longer than necessary. This caused the appreciation of our work and I was given two large crews with two officers: Lieutenant Colonel Hartnant Puchen and Lieutenant Kankofer. They were pleasant and hard-working officers. At first, I had to report to Staff Major Marcikény, then Lieutenant Colonel Graf accompanied me visiting the trenches. We constructed one line of trenches after another. As time progressed more and more doubt rose about this construction being of value.

At first the Russians attacked the Dzikie-Lany hills, where in turn the Turks, then Germans, then Landwehr and Hungarian troops fought bloody battles in the trenches we built. While constructing the trenches we also built a bomb-proof shelter underground, also called *Corps Gefechtstand,* which turned out to be very useful. Colonel Hart was assigned to me. We were requested to construct trenches through Adenowka between houses. This was unpleasant work mostly because the Russkies did not spare their artillery harassing us. I met with civilian leaders about the need for dismantling some houses and what reparations would be fair to the town of Adenowka.

We were digging trenches in three different directions. Because of constant rifle and gun fire we could only move by walking through the trenches. I got very tired.

I traveled by cart to Straty on 27th September to see Captain Babka, a Czech, who was head of the work squads. In the Hofmann army corps, only Czechs could be officers. Then I traveled to Strya. By the time I reached Potutory a major battle had developed. Three of my men were casualties. By early October we were losing ground and we were forced into the second trench row. During the night our task was to build barbed wire obstacles in the trenches and place them in front of the trenches. In similar positions higher on the mountain the Russians already occupied our former trenches. During the cover of night, we used the highway to move with less difficulty. We were constantly under rifle fire, both across and along the highway. They were aiming too high and we had no casualties. We reached the trenches where the sappers were located near a culvert under the highway. To our right was a small stream and Dzikie Lany, to our left was the stone quarry at Lysonia. We found the sappers there, planning to blow up the highway at several locations to prevent the use of the road by armored vehicles. Sapper Lieutenant Zborowsky wanted to blow up the desired locations prior to our installation of the barbed wire obstacles. We knew we had a difficult task. Upon the explosions destroying the road, the Russians would know that we were planning something which was not beneficial to them. They would start firing rifles, and step it up to machine guns fire as well. The explosions destroying the highway were successful. After a while the intensity of rifle and machine gun fire abated, and we went to work. The Russian trenches were 200 to 300 feet from us. After such a long delay they were anxious to complete their task. The rush caused unintended noise, which alerted the Russians' strategy. They started firing and my men ran back to the safety of the trenches, which in turn woke up the sleeping infantry, who were frightened by this, and many left the trenches. It took me some time to reestablish order. When everything became calmer, we resumed placing the barbed wire obstacles. Our task was also slowed by the large number of dead still lying on the ground. The continuous live fire in the battle did not allow time to bury them. We arrived in Adamowka at 4 a.m. and went on to Raj.

The main Russian attack was aimed at Potutory and Dzikie-Lany. Later they added Lysonia to the list. For a while they would advance. The strong artillery support and the large troop size would allow gains, then we would attack and repel the gains. One night, once again, we were assembling the barbed wire barriers in the woods above Brzezany, then went through Posuhow and a small stream finally reaching the trenches and placing the barriers in front of them.

On 3rd October at 10 a.m. I received an order from Headquarters. I was told that since I was considered most knowledgeable about the overall *status quo* around Lysonia, they would transfer me from the 139th brigade to the 293rd brigade. This was like getting a passport directly to Hell!

Page 115.

We got in the middle of an unbelievably awful situation. The stroll from Brzezany to the edge of the woods in Lysonia was far from ideal. The shrapnel and grenades flew around like flocks of sparrows. The guns caused the soil to appear as if it had been plowed recently. In the woods we were walking in silence, each of us preoccupied with our thoughts. The guns kept firing, rifles and machine guns trying to do their best to disturb the peace. In the woods the dead were covered by sheets and in protected areas were rows of freshly dug graves. At the first aid stations it was sad to see crying injured soldiers in various degrees of severity. At Headquarters serious and fatigued faces met me. I was to organize the replacement of German soldiers by Hungarian soldiers. The Officers' safety refuge was sturdy. A grenade hit the side of the structure, which caused a slight tremor but the main structure remained intact. Everywhere around us we were surrounded by craters and even the trees appeared severely trimmed. It was obvious that the Russkies were all around us. They did not spare rifle or gun ammunition.

Daylight was gradually fading. We led two companies into the trenches without being aware of the location of the German troops. We thought they might be near the stone quarry. We walked into a clearing between two sections of the forest at Lysonia. The Officers led, followed by the Companies and the laborers brought up the rear, with Lance Sergeant Legeze, who was a teacher during peacetime. There was little talking. Most of us thought how lucky we would be to get off Lysonia alive.

In the woods our progress was considerably slowed by pitch darkness. Using any light would have invited a quick departure from the land of the living! Upturned carts, cadavers and trees leaning in unnatural ways attested to the battles which were fought here. We walked through the ugly horrors of war. We reached the spine of a small hill exactly at the stone quarry. We walked along the edge of the woods. The Russians kept lobbing shells in our direction but they kept exploding to our left. When they exploded the ground shook. By this time there was enough light that we could see the dead and avoid tripping and falling over the corpses. We knew we were near the enemy. We stopped the soldiers and Lieutenant Láng and I went ahead to reconnoiter our route prior to placing the soldiers in harm's way. I had to find the defensive trenches we dug recently and locate the Germans. I had a good feeling that we were doing well. Then we found the trenches. Our work in the near past was not in vain. Not only did these trenches provide safety but they also stopped the Russian advance. I imagined myself being in the trenches, with the aim of killing as many of the enemy as possible. The love of our homeland and the need for defending it as well as defending the troops in the trenches motivated us.

The trenches were unoccupied. Later, from the direction of the highway, we met the first German Officer. He talked in low tones because the Russian trenches were only about 50 to 60 steps away. He led Lieutenant Láng to the highway. The second Company also moved along the trench and the workers remained. A Russian was trying to shoot me, but the bullet passed over my head. We were awaiting the orders for the work to be done. Sergeant Legeze approached and whispered enquiring whether I thought the Russians, still firing, were advancing toward us. I was uncertain but soon realized that he was correct. The bullets from the rifles were accompanied by brighter illumination which further supported the suspected Russian advance.

I spent about an hour here. Afterwards I went to see my Hungarians, downhill, towards the paved highway. Since this was between two enemy lines, due caution and care were essential. I learned of the real risks we took three hours later, when I reached our trenches. These were leading to the ravine. I asked Lance Sergeant Legeza to locate the troops and advise them of my arrival. Since it was near daybreak, there was no time for us to do any work.

Next day, 4th October 1916, I presented myself at Headquarters in the morning. I saw General Blum, an old acquaintance, who returned from leave and was accompanied by Galamb, who also just returned from his leave. General Staff Captain Jahn ordered our workers to resume work at 4:30 p.m. There was little likelihood of us getting any relief and it made sense to move from Raj back to Brzezany. We got to our command center and we left the woods at 7 p.m. carrying the assembled wooden obstacles (Ed: to which barbed wire could be attached) to the ravine. Major Wiblinger was there on the line. The sappers were with us, as was Dr. Rottmann with the 52/19 work division. I led a group to their work location and after that I led the sappers to the rock quarry. My men were in the middle and Rottmann was on my left. Here the unfortunate soldiers lay in a poorly constructed trench with inadequate protection. The well-built trenches we constructed were now in Russian hands.

The entire line was unsettled. The Russians were 200-300 steps from us, having conquered our trenches the day before. They kept up firing and lobbing hand grenades. The soldiers were begging us to leave the connecting trenches alone and instead make the main trenches deeper and safer. My men really liked this sensible request and immediately started digging. The spades hitting rocks caused the Russians to increase the firing. Trying to find my way back made me realize how shallow the transverse trenches were; while I supervised the main trenches, which were much improved, the transverse trenches were neglected, and I found it very difficult to find the Company Commander. When I found him, I discussed the dangers this could cause. I told him that both of us were responsible for the safety of the troops. We joined forces and these traversing trenches were dug deeper and to our mutual approval.

In the same trench in which I met with the Company Commander, I also met Sapper Lieutenant Cimponeriu. I simply could not understand how he got there before me. I led him to the stone quarry. It was impossible to do any work without making noise in that rocky ground. Any such effort increased Russian countermeasures. The men worked diligently, disregarding the bullets flying over their heads. I preferred lying a bit nearer the rear. It was impossible to stand without risk, yet soldiers were moving around in silence and I soon realized what they were doing: searching the dead and removing anything valuable.

First aid men reported that they heard people moaning in front of the front lines. I sent two soldiers to investigate. They returned with an injured Russian. He was a tall, imposing man. He was also heavy; it took **five** men to bring him in. He only began to believe that he was going to survive the ordeal when a doctor examined him and an interpreter provided details.

Page 117.

Through the interpreter further details came to light. This Russian was injured and was lying between the trenches for five days. During that time, he suffered further injuries. He heard the Germans but did not dare to seek attention. He was afraid he would be shot dead. Only when he heard Hungarians did he seek help. The poor man was crying as he told his story. The sappers brought in two more in similar circumstances.

From time to time, I left my place to supervise the work. I had to walk above the trenches with bullets whistling by and I was envious of the soldiers and workers in the safety of the trenches. As a rule, the Russians attacked early, therefore we tried to move the workers away at 2 a.m. Some were so tired they would have preferred some sleep. The usual dance began early that day also. We had hardly reached Brzezany when the guns started firing. This was on the 5^{th of} October 5th, the beginning of a sustained and brutal Russian attack. They were absolutely determined to break through our lines, come what may. By this time, I shared Galamb's house, because my former abode in Brzezany was now occupied by Germans, who were dangerous companions. They stole everything they could steal. The house Galamb occupied was on the highway to Raj, on a hill by the edge of the town. The very loud sound of guns made us realize the seriousness of the offensive and from a short section of the highway we could watch the entire battlefield. The assault began from the direction of Potutory and the woods at Lysonia. The guns were aimed at the area we had recently worked on and their roar was frightening. The Russian infantry attacked in very large numbers from the South. At this point our artillery began with the force of a tornado well aimed at the amassed Russian infantry. The result was an immediate and severe loss of Russian soldiers, with some survivors running around like chickens with their heads severed. Within minutes most of the infantry were dead or injured. The sight was horrible. Hundreds and hundreds of guns were firing. When the firing subsided, the remnants of the Russian infantry gathered, presenting yet another perfect target for our heavy guns. The result was as before.

The guns gradually ceased firing on both sides. The entire valley was filled with the smoke of spent gunpowder. The smoke gradually lifted as if a higher power wanted us to see the devastation that both we and the enemy caused. By the elevated railway track there was a long line of injured waiting for first aid. Their cries sounded like a distant murmur from our position. We realized that there were very many more too badly injured to walk just lying on the battlefield, alone and suffering terribly.

I returned to my place in a profoundly sad and depressed mood. I could still see, in my mind's eye, the dead and injured. I was wondering what could justify this? Even in those who survived the injuries often caused lifelong suffering. How could this fighting amongst nations be beneficial to either side? Any strong nationalistic sentiment appears unjustified in supporting such atrocity!

I awoke to the sound of intense gunfire. I went back to my previous observation post. Now, once again, the Russians were aiming their guns at us.

Our guns responded, anemic at first, then with full force. In a way it resembled a giant concert, at one time one side louder than the other, then variations followed, somewhat like a large orchestra, with children marching happily in front of a military band.

The Russian guns were suddenly silent. The infantry prepared to attack. In response our artillery opened fire with vengeance. The Russians attacked with concentrated infantry. As before, the poor, wretched infantry was mowed down as if they had been rabbits. Once again silence and the smoke from the guns, followed by horror, as if an unseen killer decided to rest overnight only to continue the killing next day. The Russians made five major attacks during the morning. The hospitals were filled with our wounded troops.

During the night Galamb was on duty to take a Company to the woods. He was to leave at 3.30 p.m. He shook my hand and said a warm farewell. During a lull in fighting, he left. The enemy fire intensified and was directed at him and his Company but no injuries were sustained. He reached his destination. Meanwhile there was intense rifle action around the Turks. Galamb did not receive permission to approach his final location where reinforcements were needed in the trenches.

The top of the hill, at 327 meters, was occupied by the Russians. Not far away, Dr. Rottmann lost a man during the night. Galamb returned four men short. Three of these made it home but an entertaining event happened to the fourth. When his Company left, he was so asleep that, by the time he woke up, he had to stay concealed in the trenches for the rest of the day and the night.

The 6th October saw further vigorous fighting, both sides aiming to take Lysonia. Brzezany also received shells and shrapnel. During the day's fighting I hired an 80-year-old Polish Jew (who had a very long beard) to make me a shirt for 44 *korona*. I noted that several German Companies were marching toward Raj, indicating that they viewed the battle as "over and done with" in our area. With the Turkish lines all was not well at the Dzikie-Lany line. The fortunes of war changed rapidly at the stone quarry of Lysonia. Our lines were disrupted several times, only to be reclaimed. Eventually we regained and held (most) of the contested ground. During the night I was repairing the first trench while under light machine gun fire.

It was my turn to work on 7th October. The sky was overcast. Mortar firing was present, and our house shook. Uncharacteristically the Russians did not react. Galamb went to Krag, and I left for the trenches. On the way we received shrapnel, but no injuries resulted. In the woods activities were much livelier. The Russkies were at work, their guns aimed along our entire front line. This prevented us from doing our job. Our infantry managed to clear out the trenches so that we could do repairs. We had just left the woods at 10 p.m., when shrapnel hit us.

Page 119.

The shrapnel killed infantryman Csipkés and injured infantryman Trohan. Another man was buried by a grenade explodingbut he was quickly dug out and apart from fright suffered no consequences. The guns seemed to come to life and then some! By the time we reached the ravine, the guns produced a regular concert to entertain the nighttime wanderers in the woods! I spent a long time looking for a medic, but Csipkés was beyond help. Trohan was taken to the hospital. It seemed the Russians were particularly keen to attack the ravine. The shrapnel and shells hardly stopped. When these were taking a bit of a break, we left the ravine and climbed in order to reach the Potutory ridge. We needed to place a permanent barrier across the trenches since the Russians now occupied a portion of "our" trench. Once again this proved to be easier said than done. The Russians used hand grenades and rifles to prevent us proceeding with our work. A grenade injured the shoulder of Lukanics, one of my men. He had to be carried to a first aid station an hour away. Then we reached the peak and were alone. Defending the peak was impossible. Below the peak was a circle of defensive trenches. Half occupied by us; the other half occupied by the Russians. Our trenches were vulnerable from three directions necessitating the utmost care while repairing and reinforcing them. My men were in two places. The trenches were confusing and when I left one group at 2.30 a.m., I got lost. I got out of the trenches and made a beeline downhill and got home.

The same morning the Russians rushed our trenches on the hillside and reoccupied them. We were fortunate to get out when we did! The Russians used many different caliber firearms. The talk in Brzezany was that the Russians were planning to bring in reinforcements of two army corps. If so, we were in for a long fight. In the 33rd field hospital they treated 5,000 injured, of whom 120 died. I wonder how many more lay hidden in the fields and on the forest floor.

By midday we were assembling more barbed wire obstacles in the forest. Galamb will oversee placing them in their final locations. We buried our friend Csipkés in the Brzezany cemetery. We even had a clergyman do the burial ceremony. Galamb had an eventful night. The trenches were full of soldiers. At one location where they worked an incident took place. The Russians kept lobbing hand grenades and we replied in kind. Just to get some variety and flavor to the mix the Russians provided heavy guns, which were also directed toward our trenches.

On 9th October 1916 Colonel Siegl formed a unit and I was assigned to the force. The sappers were also assigned to our group. They were armed, thus adding to our safety. When they tried to get my men to place the barriers in their final locations I objected. Under our variable conditions it did not appear justifiable to send unarmed men into harm's way. We were redirected to continue repairs and improvements of the trenches.

Next morning was overcast but warmer. Generally, the front was quiet along its entirety. Since the sappers had no difficulty placing the obstacles in front of the trenches, I asked Galamb to direct that chore. The front was quiet and the soldiers were exhausted. They deserved a break which we could provide.

There is no page 120 in the Napló.
Page 121.

If the situation worsened, the final decision to leave the area was Galamb's. While we worked there, we became familiar with Russian tactics. We recognized that with arrival of reinforcements the Russians would attack soon. We finished our task and did not waste a moment to get out of danger's way. None too soon! The Russian guns opened up with vengeance. Our area received about 50 shells. The Germans were suffering the worst losses. I counted seven dead; many more were lying on the highway with injuries.

Finally, the Russians ceased the gun fire, and the Germans resumed their march. We took shelter behind a church. It was cold and I did not order the removal of the topcoats. The bombshells were still falling, and it appeared advisable to wait longer. I asked for a volunteer to bring my topcoat. Once I got my coat the shivering stopped.

I was aware of the daring courage of the German troops but very much disagreed with their attitude. They lost between 20 and 30 troops marching to Raj, instead I would have chosen a route perhaps 15 minutes longer but without any injuries or deaths.

Since our house was hit by a shell, the roof was open to the elements and was no longer habitable, Galamb and I were looking for another place. We found another house uninhabited nearer the town center.

We were assigned to the 35th regiment located East of Posuhow. During the day we assembled the barbed wire obstacles in the forest and at night we placed these in front of the trenches. That night one of our men was injured. The reserve soldiers of the 35th regiment were assigned to assist in placing the obstacles under the cover of night. They had no appetite to do that job and simply disappeared. We had the same orders next day. However, we made it clear ahead of time that the workers were to be followed and protected by armed soldiers. It all turned out very well.

Since operating at the front is difficult and the Russian losses were heavy there was a lull in fighting. It allowed for the resumption of granting leave. The quota allowed was 5% for Officers and 3% for troops. With our Company there were two Officers. How were we to select 5% of two Officers? I requested a leave from Sapper Captain Smeu, under whom we served.

The following night we worked with the 35th regiment again. Their trenches were located on a downhill section of Lysonia. I was given infantry support but locating them was a challenge and I found them only after a long walk. Headquarters did not know the precise location of the Companies. For me this was a problem. I knew the area well. Eventually they were located and we took the obstacles to the point where the valley and the highway intersected. They called a protruding rock formation the "Nase". We could have reached it by climbing above the rock quarry and along the ridge to the Nase. Here the Lysonia's peak dropped down to the flat land around Potutory. This was the earlier mentioned Hell's Entrance. It was considered to be the key to the occupation of Brzezany.

Page 122.

This gentle valley was the undoing of the Russian attacks. The opposing forces were near each other. The slightest sound resulted in rifle shots. The trenches were well built, including frequent and well-designed connectors at slightly less than 90 degrees to the trenches. The wood supports were assembled and taken to the desired locations and barbed wire was attached to these supports to serve as an obstacle. I am reluctant to repeat the same litany but that was exactly what we were doing. It was important to do a thorough job of connecting the barbed wire as the Russians were not above stealing our supports to use them for themselves. The guards gave one warning shot on opposing sides which often resulted both sides shooting. Anyone on foot outside the trenches was at risk of getting shot. Yet our job required us to do just that: work on the barbed wire **between** the safety of the trenches. That night three of my men became casualties: Kola, Popoweniuk and Zagreán. This was despite observing the silence and slow, careful movement we demanded. I was actually observing a couple of my men traversing the trench on a wooden platform when a bullet hit one of them, and he fell into the trench. The next pair of men crossed the same trench without hesitation. This reinforced my previous observation that my Romanian troops were reliable and trustworthy. This night made me appreciate my troops even more.

A stray bullet hit one of our guards who fell into the trench with a loud scream. I went to check on his condition. Judging by the force of the cry one might have expected to see someone at death's door. I found a small injury on the shoulder of this gypsy soldier. Others envied him. Having an injury meant he could return to his home. By The Officers of our division were not overjoyed with their posting. There were not enough foremen to oversee that work progressed appropriately and lacked quality control. The result was shoddy workmanship and a less reliable product.

Next day I went to see the Headquarters of the 35th regiment. My concern was that the repeated abandonment by the infantry and the consequent shortcomings of the work would reflect on me personally. I did not wish to blame others or to be viewed as an informant. I did not wish to lodge a complaint. In reality, the men on the line were under constant threat and I was not. They met me without any kindness at Headquarters. Furthermore, when I met with others in the Commander's waiting room (which was underground) I met the Officer whose troops vanished and he accused my men for not completing their work. His untrue allegations, largely based on his belief that I, like him, was never present in that vicinity and he assumed that I would remain silent. I felt angered about his insinuations and expressed my views with uncharacteristic strength bordering on rudeness.

This placed the Regiment's Officers in a dilemma. Now there was proof that all I said was true and another Officer from the line vouched validated my statement. The Regiment's Commander's deputy immediately walked into the Commander's room. I was invited to see the Commander immediately. I was told that my men displayed exemplary work and asked me to name some of them for medals in appreciation of that. That night he personally observed the infantry properly attach the barbed wire to the wood supports in "no man's land".

In the afternoon we received some Russian shelling but otherwise the front was stable. The sound of battle from Zlota-Lipa and the area surrounding Lipa was much worse. The Turks fought to prevent a Russian attempt to break through the line. Even in our vicinity the intensity of rifle fire increased. By the time we arrived at our allotted location it was clear that we were facing a challenging night.

We dug a long communication trench along the Potutory highway and connecting trenches between this and the trench dug for the reserves. I tried to see how the communication trench would function. It was not deep enough to use, so I asked Artillery Lieutenant Schramm, who made his base in the viaduct, to do what he could so that our men would be able to deepen the communication trench. Our artillery got going and the Russians slackened. Deepening the trenches was done. Throughout the night the alternating sounds of machine guns entertained us.

Eventually quiet descended on both sides. Really, the Russians were in a situation similar to ours; they also had to place their barriers just as we did. We spent the night with rifle shots, machine guns and guns firing shells for company. After a long night we were happy to return to Brzezany. Galamb returned home. It was an unusual relationship: I was relieved when he returned daily, and it was just like that with me too. Every day we parted we said our goodbyes with a joke, yet we both knew there was nothing funny about it.

Back in the trenches my Romanian troops did well under demanding conditions. The Officers in charge of providing our food and others working with sanitation were the sources of news about the world outside our narrow vision of the fighting. We even heard new jokes. The regiments' physician also visited us.

On 17th October I had news. My leave was approved and Galamb was to take care of my men. I was asked to take letters to Budapest by several Officers. I left the same night. Löwe came with me; his destination was Transylvania. He was to return to the front on 6th November.

We returned on 6th November, arriving in Lemberg at 7 p.m. Our next stop was Wolkow, where Galamb's letter awaited me. He was informing me that new orders directed me to travel to Hinowice, where I was to take the place of 1st Lieutenant Stepan, who directed a railway work project.

The ammunition and food were to be transported by train and cars (modified to run on railway tracks) from Hinowice to Chatki. Chatki was above Brzezany and the railway line was under constant fire, therefore it was used at night with the loaded wagons quickly uncoupled and the empty ones returned as quickly as possible to Chatki. The area had heavy army presence. Here the station was under the 54th Division under Captain Holinka. I met Galamb that night. He told me that Lieutenant Colonels Smeut and Graf were transferred from the Deutsche Südarmee [German Southern Army] to the 54th Division; Galamb was to work also in the rear. Vértes and Fülöp and their Companies were to go to Lemberg. Of the original friends only Galamb and I remained on this front. I did not think this was so because they disliked us. As I learned later on many units were sent from here to the Italian front, including Fülöp and Vértes and their Companies.

I went back to Hinowice, expecting to lodge with 1st Lieutenant Stepan only to find a fine looking *Verflegs Assistent* Tipow announce that he needed an office and regretted that he could not share it with me. I did not object but instead I engaged him with pleasant discussion about several topics. After this he offered to share his place. He said the former talk was just a pretense; he was afraid he might get an unpleasant, disagreeable person who could make his life difficult. We had time on our hands and discussed various aspects of life in general, interesting stories and experiences. I spent several most enjoyable weeks with Tipow. He was well educated, had a pleasant demeanor and an honest and kind disposition. We played a lot of chess and shared a love of photography. With plenty of time on our hands we probably enjoyed our long discussions on a wide range of topics the most. After two years on or in the vicinity of the front lines this was Eldorado! As for experiencing events of importance relating to the war, I must admit there was nothing. One event is worth mentioning. It happened in Chatki. I took a train from Hinowice to Chatki and immediately returned to Hinowice riding the locomotive. The cars left behind had their brakes on, filled with ammunition and food. From Chatki to Brzezany Station the track is on a downhill path, which includes a sharp curve. The station is within reach of the Russian guns at Potutory. To protect the station, they removed a 2-meter section of the train track (on one side) and near the station the placement of many sleepers provided an obstacle across the tracks. In addition, the viaduct before the station was mined so that destruction of the viaduct would have been an easy matter. I had hardly arrived back in Hinowice when I received a telephone call. Apparently an 18-freight car train (without a locomotive) had improperly applied brakes. It got loose, rapidly gained speed downhill successfully crossing the (mined) viaduct and the section with the removed rail. The wooden obstacles stopped the runaway train at Brzezany. It took two locomotives and to bring them to Chatki. Miraculously this worked! The train went through the area where the rails were removed (and not replaced) and the wheels got back onto the rails! However, it took us all night to get back to Chatki. This was a dangerous job. Probably the most risk was with having to do repairs within the range of Russian guns. The risk was even more with the two locomotives puffing and making noise. This area was a favorite area to bomb with shells, some of which landed in the lake taking with them fish which survived the earlier "fishing" by soldiers using hand grenades!

Page 126.

When I was in Hiwonice I went for my physical examination in Stry and travelled to Musterung on 14th November. I was 38 years old. I was examined by the same physician and was found fit for service on the front. The same fate awaited 1st Lieutenant Neumann and 2nd Lieutenant Czurkowsky.

Captain Osztoics was also there, angling to get Galamb and his men assigned under his command at the front lines. He was unaware of Galamb's current position behind the front lines. I did my best to discourage Osztoics from this idea. Being in the rear was much safer for Galamb.

King Ferenc József died on 20th Nov. 1916. Millions of funny stories and speculation took off. Stepán fhgy. will arrive from his vacation on the 30th. I will join Galamb, who was still in Brzezany at that time. The active combat action was limited to some local attempts by the Russians. We were doing some work in the rear, at Div. Proviant Amt above Lesniki and we were also building roads.

There were disturbing rumors about the Turks. They had no mercy for the enemy. The prisoners of war were killed and they killed the injured with their bayonets.

The 81st regiment found an Officer and 80 Russian soldiers unarmed, on their way to Russia. The 32nd Hunter Regiment confiscated whatever arms they had. The leader of the labor companies was increasingly concerned about dead or injured men of both sides having their valuables stolen on the battlefield. When he gave generous gifts to many Officers, we understood they were bribes. The Officers were mainly Czechs. Lieutenant Colonel Graf showed me the fancy boots he received. Questionable parcels adding up to a tidy sum were sent as gifts to the military leadership. Under my command

and the command of my fellow officers events like this were very rare.

We were transferred from the German Southern Army to the Army Over Command under 1st Lieutenant Szesztay's Engineering (Building) and this will be described my experiences in Galicia. That is the next chapter: "Road Construction".

ROAD CONSTRUCTION

14th December 1916 - 24th February 1918.

As usual, newcomers were assigned work nearest to the front. In war we did not choose whether we might prefer a good, a moderate or downright dangerous assignment. We also had no choice whether we got deployed at the front or away from the front. We never expected an easy task but knowing what was expected of us was a relief. We worked on the highway, which was hard work, but there was advantage to this work. The weather was getting colder but the work kept us warm and looking at the bright side nobody was shooting at us. This meant that our thoughts did not dwell on the risk of, or at times the desire for, dying. We could imagine returning home alive! While in Brzezany we went to work away from the front. After my travels I got diarrhea and moved to Pawlow with 50 men on 14th December 1916. Galamb worked elsewhere and stayed in Brzezany. This was our Christmas.

During the afternoon and evening Galamb was with me and we enjoyed each other's company on Christmas Day. The well-to-do and smart homeowner and his family were photographed. Galamb came over again when a pig was slaughtered, and we had a very nice meal. While having a wonderful meal, I received an order which marred the pleasant atmosphere. I was assigned to a new position. The time I was to report was shortly after lunch, so I said my goodbyes. My new location was Demnia, under Lieutenant Ivanovich, who had disagreements with 1st Lieutenant Szesztay and they parted company. Departing from Galamb was particularly difficult; we shared company since the war broke out. There was some advantage: I became my own master, which was just fine. I had to join the new unit on December 27 at Domnia. By that time my unit was working in Olchowiecz in a stone quarry. My position is with 1st Lieutenant Szesztay, who is based in Podwisoki. Alongside me worked Lieutenant Békeffy, a pleasant, well-mannered man with a kind disposition. The clergyman for the camp was Bálint. The entire group was a fine, cohesive unit. I spent New Year's Eve in Lesniki with Galamb. He and his men moved from Brzezany to Lesniki, where his men built barracks. The odd shrapnel still reached them but there were no injuries. Later on, they moved to Pawlow to be near work.
My squad was transferred to Lieutenant Kriekl, an Austrian, who will take my place while I met my Flora in Lemberg. I got my leave 14th January, 1917 to return and was wonderful to find this oasis of plenty. Our days there were unforgettable! Upon my return I found myself in charge; Engineering Lieutenant Sigismund Federsky was my predecessor. We worked at the rock quarry above Lopusna. I moved back to Demnia.

The Russians at the front appeared to be more active. The rumor is that Daichy-Lany is in Russian hands. However, another rumor was that they were repelled successfully. Meanwhile we are working at the quarry and on the road. Not much excitement, hard work but safe.

The work was on the road from Pukow to Podwisolki. It suffered major hits and badly needed repair. We moved Prezalski near Pukow. Somehow it is considered as part of Rohatyn. There was a rock quarry in the hills nearby. That is where we worked. In Przelasky I lodged with Anna Sandura, a fine village woman. Basalt was brought by train. Civilians by the hundreds and reserve infantry were involved crushing rock which was placed on the road surface and road rollers compressed the surface. Usually, life was peaceful. Békeffy moved to nearby Danilce with his men and his wife. He bought a peasant house and converted it into a veritable castle! He had outdoor water tanks, several hens, beautiful flowers, even a gym set! This must have cost a lot of money and sweat and toil. The only thing he did not possess was commonsense. Despite all his shortcomings I liked him. Unlike him, I bought my own clothes and paid for clothes I had tailor made.

The Commandant at Pukow was 1st Lieutenant Hajós. I had a pleasant relationship with him both on the official and personal level. I left on leave on 10th   133 returned to Pukow on 2nd April.

Page 134 is a photo.

Page 135.

Before I left, I had some painful problems with my right middle finger. I had Dr. Schöller examine it in Budapest. His diagnosis was "infection in the nail" and wanted to operate. I had insufficient time and I saw Dr. Vas, the regimental physician, who removed the nail under local anesthetic. Next day I was able to travel to Szesztay in Podwisokie for a game of tarokk [Ed: Tarokk was and still is a popular card game in Hungary].

Until the weather remained cold, we could transport the rocks by carts pulled by oxen. When it got warmer, the roads turned to mud and were unusable. To overcome this, I had to find or design a practical solution. I planned to use a cable supporting a container so that the containers loaded with stone could safely travel from the quarry to a much lower level where loading the carts would have been much less complicated. I showed my idea of a pulley system carrying the rocks down the cable at the same time pulling the empty boxes up for reloading. We were searching for suitable [heavy duty] cable only to find that all such cables were sent to the Italian front. I got all the men likely to understand the requirements and the task at hand together. There were Silesian Germans and Czechs mostly. They designed the cable made of soft steel twined in a manner suitable to support the heavy weight. Woodworkers designed the carts and the wood guides to control the downhill path of the loaded and dangerous carts if the descent was uncontrolled. Brakes were designed in a circular form, like a wheel and lined with steel. With inadequate brakes tragedy would result. As expected, during the trial phase problems arose and were rapidly solved. For example, the brakes lined with steel overheated and set the whole braking mechanism on fire. With the steel removed the problem was solved. This modified cable car design was so successful that the carts which were to move the rocks to their destination could not keep up with the quantity of rocks removed from the quarry.

I was given a new task. I was to plan a road to be constructed if retreat was planned. This was across plowed fields. It required enormous amount of rock, trucks and personnel. I was given large number of trucks and cars. The project advanced beautifully, but Szesztay was afraid his name might be tarnished at any failure and did not inspect the cable car design we came up with. Lieutenant Prykryl copied my design in secret and drew a diagram as well. He copied the design, but his challenging factors were a longer and steeper downhill path. Since he was an engineer (and I was not) I assumed that he would take those two important factors into the design of his "cable car". I think I overestimated the engineering advantage he possessed. Had he asked for help I would have been happy to advise him. As it was, he did not ask me. In their version the trial run the container accelerated uncontrollably, the cable broke and – since there was no brake – accelerated and the container, loaded with rocks, and crossed the highway at high speed narrowly missing a collision with men and equipment. He spent much time improving the design. Eventually he succeeded and had a photograph taken to prove it. He made sure the Commandant knew about his success. His plan did not work so well; by the time he completed it the tempo of the required speed of rock production for the road planned increased by a larger amount that was planned because withdrawal of our forces became more imminent. A consultant from the *Deutsche Südarmme Technische Ref* [the technical advisory unit] arrived to inspect the "cable car for rocks design". He was a young Officer who inquired how I was able to produce so much rock. He examined my setup and I explained how I built and modified it. He congratulated me for a fine design and drew a picture of it. By the time Szesztay came into the picture the entire High Command was already fully informed.

Szesztay's attitude was typical of his command. Senior Officers openly talked about him in the least endearing way. Basically, he was a coward, afraid of rifle or gun fire. He was in the good books of Colonel Olschak and he sent regular packages of the "fruits of war", as I mentioned earlier, to his home in Graz. To be quite honest I did not think this was honorable although some might disagree.

Page 136.

I did not send any such gifts home. I never took funds that did not belong to me. Even clothing, footwear and underwear was bought by Flórus and sent to me.

In Pukow they rearranged the distribution of my men. Of 100, 53 were sent to the front.

During my leave a Jewish man, Colonel Rottmann, took my place. On my return I received the Company's funds. I did not inspect it at that time. It was part of a bulky set of documents. Since we had to pay for over 100 laborers and civil contractors as well as the carts with their owners and drivers, we always had a large amount of cash on hand. When I got around to thoroughly examine all the packages almost all had a small discrepancy, altogether totaling a deficit of 160 *korona*. [Ed.: This was a small sum at that time, perhaps the cost of three pairs of boots].

Assisting me with the motorized component of my unit was an engineer, Krycki. In our vicinity there were several others. 1st Lieutenant Kankofer, sanitation head Föhnrich, Neumann and Galamb. From time to time, we got together when work allowed it. We could talk about our families and life before the war.

At this time, they started a new source of revenue to support the war effort. Depending on the size of the purchase of these war bonds. 5000 *korona* would allow a three-day leave. Although I did not have the money but I desperately needed a leave, I signed a promissory note and left for three days. During my visit I saw my older sister's adopted son, Ignác Elő, for the last time. Upon finishing high school, he volunteered for army service and was assigned to the infantry. He was on the Eastern front and during the first attack he sustained a bullet through his heart.

Galamb told me that he was reassigned to help with the harvest along with his Battalion. Temporarily he was losing his rank, obviously someone else had more pull at Headquarters.

Here some men have their families in our area. Ensign Kanozsay has his two daughters nearby. They came from Esztergom.

During mid-June 1917, we heard rumors of a forthcoming Russian attack. We were issued gas masks, which I suspect were ordered by the division in charge of moving the military. The road completion for retreat became yet more urgent. We were working on the road from Lipica Dolna to Pukow. The road had to withstand the very heavy artillery weight.

In Stryj they arranged a course for the workers on the road. Since activity at the front increased, Szesztay immediately volunteered to stay at the course according to 1st Lieutenant Lessner. In fact, he was so worried that he kept Lessner awake with his concerns. Orders specified that I was to take that position. Szesztay objected and someone else was named to deal with matters at the front. I would have been happy to take that instead of the classroom chores.

Vigorous gunfire was heard and Szesztay was considering a move to Pukow, which is further from the approaching front. He was especially afraid after an air attack on Demnian, a neighboring village. He was especially worried about yet another matter: near Podwisoki, another neighboring village, an observation balloon was set up by the Russians. Szesznay is unwell according to Lessner, who is sharing accommodation with him.

In the meantime, the Turkish Army Corps were about to depart. After the snow melt, generalized and more intense fighting necessitated the delay in the Turkish departure.

Galamb arrived from Lesniki, which was within range of the enemy guns. He was working in a stone quarry while I worked on the highway. I had a German engineer from Leitmeritz: Lieutenant Vogt. We became friends very soon after his arrival. The bond strengthened as the months progressed. We agreed on how to solve problems. Our friendship provided a stress free, peaceful time for both of us. A rare relief from the uncertainties and unknown aspects which were part of the war.

Several troops of German soldiers arrived from Pukow. They were transported to the front by cars. The battle continued and the cars returning from the front carried injured German and Turkish troops. Podwisokie also received some shelling, much to the discomfort of 1st Lieutenant Szesztay, who escaped to Pukow, leaving behind his Company, because he was unable to bear the stress of being anywhere near a battle. His Battalion was moved near his new neighborhood to Chesniki, where the Headquarters were Turkish. After the war many of us felt that the statue of the "Unknown Expert of Hiding, the Real Drückenberger" (Ed: obviously referring to an uncomplimentary statue I do not recognize, perhaps a fictitious name for a future statute) should be modeled after Szesztay in Budapest. I must make a special note of his behavior after the war. Whereas most of us survivors were happy to have survived the war and the short period of communism in Hungary felt it more appropriate to remove our uniforms, place our medals in some drawer and remember those events with bitterness of losing the war as well as a large part of our Country, Szesztay was different. We remembered the awful battles, men injured and dead but here was Szesztay, marching around with three or four young men, bedecked with his medals, appearing as if he had been a mastermind of the best men who ever served in the war! I preferred seldom thinking about him. I will attempt to avoid the topic altogether.

1st Lieutenant Galamb and his squad were placed with the 55th Division on 3rd July, 1917. They were in Martinow-Wigalka under

Captain Szvoboda. We were facing major changes. We received scores of orders. The work on the Zolcsov highway was abandoned. We received a short period of rest which was more like recuperation. We were told to become active at very short notice. The Genie-Park was divided, and Captain Schuster was left without a job. This Officer had a cushy assignment. He lived in peace and comfort; now finding himself afraid, with an unknown future. He was searching for a suitable alternative such as being desired for being the most senior Officer. The reason was that my men were largely Austrian, and I was Hungarian. He thought he was the obvious choice for that position. He was mistaken.

Our attack in Zborow yielded good results. The news of Russian retreat reached us on 21st July. Our win was of very great significance. The wildest stories became a reality. On that day we were taken by car to follow the Russians. The highway was packed with vehicles and soldiers marching with their faces showing the concerns of what their future might be. Then there are some delighted faces, enjoying the increasingly rare moments of pleasure in wartime.

During our advance one of the most interesting events were visiting our former trenches where we fought the Russians. We visited fields where thousands perished. Walking in the bright sunshine we were deep in thought. The memory of those days seemed permanent, impossible to erase from memory. I revisited Lysonia where we dug most of the trenches. I saw the forest, at least what remained of it and the fields which were ripped by the shells. Many bodies still littered the ground, hands and feet sticking out of the ground. I left deeply moved by this sad sight.

We belonged to the 55th Division and our primary assignment was to make telephone poles. We were moving North destroying woods near Byszki and Koniuchy. We set up camp in Urmán. The systematically raised edges of the Russian trenches were interesting and deserved further investigation. Our trenches situated against theirs were manned by the 88th Division. They were well constructed yet were badly damaged during the fighting. The Russians used heavy concrete blocks around the machine guns and I suspected the damage our trenches were caused by these guns. In addition, they constructed exceptionally well-made passageways. Along their lines the fighting left terrible aftermaths. In one case a shell landed on a reinforced safe room. The ceiling did not support the force of the shell and it collapsed on the occupants. All we saw were eight pairs of feet sticking out. In the village ruins were all around. An old woman sat in front of her house on a stool, behind her were the remnants of the walls. It seemed she was at peace with the knowledge that there was nothing more to lose. The Russians were in a rush to retreat and they left behind a lot of *war materiel.*

Once again, we were reassigned to the *Deutsche Südarmee* under Captain Schröder who gave us his orders. It appeared we became specialized in making telephone poles as once again such were our orders. We marched toward Monastersyska. Along the way the devastation was vast following the Russian retreat, with hundreds of vehicles by the roadside burned and otherwise destroyed. Some appeared perfectly fit for use. By the roadside were thousands of discarded boxes, many filled with ammunition and food. We really had to revise the situation to a major win and some of us secretly hoped for an early end of the war.

I sent 14 men from my group through Muzsilow to Podhajce. I remembered Podhajce from my earlier days during the fighting at Strypa, when it was the center of the Hoffmann Army Corps and the labor division. The field railway to Sosnow and later to Rosochowaciec originated here. As a departing gift the Russians destroyed most of the town. The town previously had a particularly lovely Town Square, now burned to ashes. We had a very well-appointed field hospital. It was fully supplied with fine English instruments, much of it intact but some expensive equipment was sacrificed in the fire. It would have been smart for us to dismantle the train tracks prior to our departure, whether it was an oversight or rapid Russian advance that prevented it remains a mystery. At least the railway should have been detonated at a number of places. That did not take place either. We handed the Russians a railway in full working order. Naturally they made full use of it. The terminal station at Podhajce I saw boxes and boxes of new Japanese handguns and rifles, also food for horses, thousands of bags of flour were left behind. They tried to burn these and largely succeeded. Civilians also rummaged through the remnants. We had food problems. I left behind two carts carrying the kitchenware and the food. I sent a message requesting that these should be well packed and sent to me. They either forgot the name of the village or there was a misunderstanding and my worthy cooks went in the direction of Tarnopol, so we waited in vain.

Page 143.

With rapid advance and no telephone lines such misunderstandings were commonplace. Eventually we heard from them five days later from Zlotniky, near Burkanow.

From Urmán to Pomorce we travelled on 28th July 1917. The Company covered a huge distance. Pomorce is South of Buczacz. My orders were to go to Buczacz. The Russkies left behind a very large amount of cooking oil and the people in the village made fast use of this gift.

We guessed that this probably was an attractive town in a delightful setting before the war. By the time we saw the town the ravages of war were obvious and the ruins covered formerly stored edibles now getting ruined, much to please the local rat population, which had a feast!

I set about locating forests, preferably pine, for the telephone poles. The locals told me that such forests were in the Trybuchowce and Pomorce areas. We went to Pomorce. The villages on our way were not happy to see us. In Podhajce the inhabitants provided bread for the Russkies for a full year. When they were retreating, they asked for yet more but the inhabitants would rather pour the flour into the river. They still had some grain. The Russians left behind barrels of salt fish which these folks did not eat.

The forester in Pomorce told me some interesting stories. He thought he was spared the Russian looting. Unfortunately, he was mistaken. In the retreating army there were twenty Tartars, who robbed him blind. Anything that could be moved were placed on their horses when they left. Footwear, clothing, bedroom curtains, sheets were all gone. They blew up the beehives and enjoyed the honey. When they heard of our approach, they mounted their horses with their hands still covered with honey.

In the next village, Repince, they had a sawmill. Although the Russians set fire to it, much heavy lumber remained mostly intact. In Buczacz I met Alexi, who was my colleague in Moktár, my Merchant Bank in Budapest. He had the build of an athlete; he had a great disposition and was a fine soldier. I heard no recent news which troubled me. I heard that the Russians fought successfully but stopped at the Hungarian border at Zbrucz (Ed: About 60km southwest of Ternopil, Ukraine.). The Commandant moved to Czortkow (Ed: About 55km South of Ternopil, now known as Chortkiv.) Just one week prior, someone suggested the possibility, serious mental problems were suspected. The Germans attempted to dislodge the Russians from their trenches. They were repelled but at considerable cost to both sides. The town was not damaged by the Russians. The hospital was full of injured Russians and Germans.

I spoke with Captain Krüger, a German, who was in Czortkow. He was unable to provide vehicles, even the replacements he received did not meet his needs. We had to march from Muzsylow to Pomorce (Ed: now Pomirtsi, distance 56km.) Colonel Vogt led the men while I travelled in a cart to seek new orders. Lack of food became a problem as our kitchen and food did not reach us. In the smaller towns we could purchase food at reasonable cost. All sorts of motorized equipment were lying by the roadside. One of these was an American steamroller. It was identified as "The Gaar Scott Tiger Line, Manufactured by M. Rumely & Co., Richmond, U.S.A."

Another road roller was identified as Munktelle Mekaniska Verstads Aktiebolag, Eskilstuna, made in Sweden.

Pomorce is the property of the Count Wolinsky. The forester with whom I stayed was in the Count's employ for 44 years, beyond the forest watching the trees grow to maturity and watched their beauty unfold. The Russians cut the best oak trees while the forester watched, heartbroken. Though damaged, the forest was not lost. We requested 150 pines for which we issued a receipt. The trees were chosen with the forester's approval. Staying with the forester and his family for 3 days was a pleasure. The residence of Count Wolinsky was not far, located in Trybuchowce, where he had his castle. I travelled there but I wished I had not done so. The once beautiful old castle was destroyed beyond repair. The frescos were covered by paint, everything broken. Simple German soldiers were wondering around acting like vandals, stealing anything of value. Items which could have been restored were now beyond hope.

I was looking for Captain Reibiger, a German, who lived in Buczacz. He issued our orders promptly, he also cared. On 8th August the Company were to depart for Biezloboznica by car and marching to Siemikowce. The river Szeret winds along a valley with villages on both sides. The Russians did not hurt them. These villages appeared as if in peacetime, even when I was there.

In Siemkowce I stayed with a lady teacher. Two women teachers lived in the same house. They had no problems with the Russians. One of them was two months pregnant when her husband enlisted. He became a Russian prisoner of war. Since then, she gave birth to a wonderful girl who was by now 2 ½ years old.

They told us about discipline in the Russian army was disintegrating. A few days ago, a General and his adjutant arrived at their door, extremely fatigued. They asked the women to guard their horses, because any unguarded horse was likely to be stolen by the infantry.

No sooner they laid down the women noticed that soldiers were trying to steal the horses and they woke up the Officers who tried to prevent the theft. The interaction was short: the infantrymen gave them two choices; they could keep their horses and join them or they would take the horses. The Officers left with the soldiers.

I went to Chortkow on a cart to get money. By this time the advancing army had all functions operating normally. Despite the longer distances in this larger area, the telephone lines worked very well. We did have difficulties with getting supplies because the bridges were blown up and trains could not operate as before. A large amount of our supplies arrived by cars and carts. I did not receive the money in Chortkow. They sent me to Kolendzany via Szmankowicziky to the Army Corps Treasury, where I received 8,000 *korona*. Near Chortkow I saw a defensive fence consisting of three rows of barbed wire, erected, but not used, by the Russians. Apart from the railway bridge, which was blown up, the town was spared of any harm. The streets were untouched by the war. The shops were well stocked with the necessities, even with luxury items such as French and English goods, expensive wines and spirits and delicacies at unbelievably low prices. Everybody was buying. The men bought all they needed. It only took five days for all the goods to disappear. Naturally the law of supply and demand caused ever increasing prices and lack of available goods. This happened likewise in Stanyslau, Stry and Lemberg.

Page 145. **[The forester's saga]**

I was discussing the matter of storing freshly cut lumber with Mr. Kendlik, the forester, who had stories to tell fit for a novel! To a lesser extent the same was true for many inhabitants of the town. At first there were no battles in the area. Advance guards of opposing sides had minor skirmishes. These were of no significance. In the fertile river bottom land of Galicia, the Russian occupation was peaceful. An occasion arose when a Russian advance guard was provided with enough wine to render them drunk by Mr. Kendlik, who notified us, and the Russians were easily arrested. Soon after this, the forester was guiding our advance guard, led by a Hussar, through the woods where the Russians were also advancing. Someone told the Russians about the forester, who was duly arrested. At first, he tried to appear sick and mentally deficient. He was physically unable to march, and they took him on a cart, accompanied by 14 Cossacks. He asked whether it might be a good idea to bring along a heavy gun. The Cossacks thought this was funny. His situation became more serious later. He became a prisoner of war and was under strict supervision. The advance guard was taken seriously and shared much the same fate. They were taken to Czernowicz and later to Sadagora. The forester, along with others were unaware of the value of the Officer amongst them. They regarded the forester as unimportant. He got on well with his armed guard and even managed to convince the guard to hand over his firearm to him. For a few seconds the forester considered shooting his guard, but he quickly realized this would be futile. He hoped one day the jailer would forget to lock his door. That happened. Afterwards he was questioned in one town after another, but he remained on the loose. After several months of wandering, he was questioned by many authorities one judge sentenced him to death. This was despite his claim that his memory was very poor, and he could recall little of his past. Besides, he claimed his old age rendered him of no value. His claim was reconsidered. His sentence was reduced to life in prison. Then the Czar was deposed, and he was freed. He returned home. In his absence his wife contracted measles and his house was robbed. The return home, expected to be a joyful occasion turned out to be a

period of poverty and bitterness. He had to start anew. He started selling wood to the Russians, who wanted to give him receipts instead of money. He realized he was not going to get any cash so he circumvented the Officer and dealt with another "officer", explaining in secret that he was not going to give the money to the owner but he was willing to share the money with this "officer". The man suddenly found ample cash shared equally. He was unable to count and was shortchanged, but this he never realized.
[End of the forester's story.]

Our orders were to march toward Podhajce. We reached Bielohoznica that day. We camped in the open on 11th August 1917 when it was warm. An order arrived with daybreak canceling the Podhajce destination to Kopyczince. We were to report to a German Captain Krueger, who lived in Czortkow.

I went to meet him. He gave me a car to help me get around. I drove to Puczacz to locate my kitchen and cooks and ordered them to turn around and proceed in our direction. Vogt and the Company was provided a truck and planned to meet us at Knyczynce. The town was full of Germans. We set up our camp in a lovely pine forest. In my travels this area was notable that it was spared the ravages and uninterrupted farm work continued, unlike the rest of the region where we saw elsewhere. The towns and villages remained unharmed and peaceful. There was no sign that battles were caused by the behavior and appearance of the population and there was a welcome absence of suffering.

Initially we felt a warm welcome in the villages. With the ever-increasing number of vehicles and men this changed. With the increased demands of the army at times reimbursing the providers well, sometimes adequately and sometimes without any reimbursement the feelings changed. Later, the draft commenced. From 1914 to the time of our arrival there was no draft here and men lived in peace, working the land, getting married, starting families. Suddenly they were taken to war. The happy faces soured, and the sadness became palpable. Men attempted to stay out of sight with the hope of somehow avoiding the draft. They were aware that they were better off while the Russians were there.

The Jewish shopkeepers were not unhappy. It did not matter to them whether the money was Austrian or Russian.

Our food came from Smankowcy, the distance was 15 km as a bird flies. We were making telephone poles in the woods. I needed to cover long distances to Czortkow, Oryszkowce, Jablonowka in the heat and the dusty roads. Not my idea of a joyride! Galamb and Békefy also worked in the country. The Germans gave me a car in Chortow to enable me to survey yet more distant woods in search of pine trees. I found such forests in Baron Lenckoronsky's beautiful forest. Then I drove through Jezierzanyn to Bilczeb to see the forest of Paul Sapiche Würst. I drove on to Glenhoczek and Jezierzanyn to Czortkow to meet Captain Kruger and discuss future plans. My next port of call was Oryskowce, where I met Galamb, I slept there because the plans for the following day were daunting. I took my Company to the above-mentioned forests and cut trees for the telephone poles.

In the Lenckoronsky forest we met Johann Wakalski, the forester, and made plans. The Company was placed in the middle of the forest. The weather turned much cooler, and we returned to Zalesie. Békefi settled in a farm near us. He had 30 men with him; the men cleared all the areas we left untidy. The area was previously occupied by Russians, who were not too troubled with tidiness.

We cut several thousand poles in this wonderful forest. The trees were 40 to 50 years old. The roads were wide. There were still many pheasants. The trees were around 20 meters high. I felt as if I had been transported into a magnificent cathedral! For a while I forgot about the war. 1st Lieutenant Klaus, an Austrian, was the commander of the forestry division. Later on, I inherited his Company.

Page 147.

We went to Bilce and thinned out Count Sapiche's forest. The Count was staying at his castle when I tried to make his acquaintance. He was flying around. His properties encompassed 16 villages. The inhabitants wore clean clothes during the week but on Sunday they were dressed in colorful traditional clothes which would have made very pleasing painting. We were received with kindness and cooperation. It seemed that the Southern part of Galicia was living with more funds, education than their Northern neighbors.

I met the Count's forester, Zdislaus Giernczynsky at my place. His face did not appear notable and his rigid desire to keep the interaction a purely business matter did made me uneasy. I suspected that he was not capable of fulfilling the responsibilities such a large area needed. When he requested money for the Count and himself, I lost any remaining trust I may have had in this man. His unwarranted and crude comments about the Government were the last straw. He realized that I was tired of his company and he departed.

On 3rd September 1917 we marched through Glenboczek to Pienky. This small village was at the Southern edge of Count Lanckorosky's forest. Next day I drove to see Colonel Olschak in Chortkow to request my leave which I was due to receive. A letter from my Flórus awaited me. My poor younger brother, Náci, died in battle. When we last met, I had a strong premonition which I was unable to shake, and my soul was crushed. His face kept appearing and I was unable to erase it. He always smiled, even when going to battle. He was in the shock troops. My mind played games with me. I would have loved to protect him and save him from certain death. He moved to a new address. Not long before his death we resumed writing to each other. I felt a special bond with him and myself.

I received my fifth leave on 5th September 1917. There was a hitch. How could I get someone to take me to the nearest railway station 75 km away? Perhaps a miracle could help. I met 1st Lieutenant Thaler who oversaw the telephone service and therefore had cars. I asked him if he could help, perhaps I could go with someone who is heading that way. 1st Lieutenant Knizsek, whom I didn't know, overheard my plea! He said he would be glad to help; he had a truck going to Brzezany and he also gave the necessary pass for me and two of my men to get on board. The truck was to depart at 4 a.m. I was fortunate to find a room, thanks to a friend, in the Podolsky Hotel, where I slept soundly until 3 a.m.

We squeezed ourselves in the truck, the driver, Lieutenant Schönberger and me in the front, others in the back. To my delight, the truck departed at 4 a.m. and I hoped there would **not** be an order redirecting the truck! We departed in darkness and daylight gradually materialized. We passed through Podhajce and from then on, I was on familiar ground. I remembered the tragic events with all its bad memories in this area all too well. The uncertainty of the future came to mind again. But the autumn sunshine and the happy thoughts of getting home allowed us to enjoy the moment.

Page 148.

We were approaching Litiatyn. This was the area where the Russian troops were, near Zlota Lipa River. We observed the evidence by what was the left behind: blown up ammunition, thousands of destroyed tin cans and all kinds of buildings burnt or ruined was seen next to the highway.

Just before Litiatyn, our truck stopped suddenly and we came back to reality from our thoughts, what happened? The driver gets out of the truck and scratches his head: the rear wheel was found broken. Somehow it was patched up and we limped into Litiatyn but no further. So, we stood on the highway and tried our luck hitchhiking. Along came an artilleryman with his ten kitchens. We hop on and get as far as the Potutory blown up viaduct. We start walking towards the railway station, 4km away, but luck was with us when a German car caught up with us and he takes us to the railway station.

The stationmaster, Lieutenant Scheffer, informs us that the next train will arrive at noon tomorrow. Well, this did not make us very happy but we had to accept the inevitable and wait. Szesztay's camp was in the nearby village of Sarancuky so I again hopped on the German car and visited him. This area was close to the front recently and was left bare and in ruins. That night we drank champagne about which I felt very uncomfortable under the circumstances, all in the elegant setting of Szesztay's home. Next day, he took me back to the railway station. I found Captains Osztoics and Pintér, both of whom were on their way home like me. They also got here by a circuitous route. Their horses stepped on nails and they changed them with small village horses. As it got dark, a car took them to Monastersyska and from there another car bought them here.

Time went by but there was no sign of a train. We learned that the train was stopped and the operators arrested. But the Gods came to the fore and we spotted steam rising on the horizon. The twenty or thirty holiday bound greeted the train with a boisterous hurray! On arrival the locomotive operators announced that they have been they have been working for the last three days **and** nights and they are unable to work anymore. After a serious meeting of all present and collecting 60 korona, they decided to take the train to Podwysokie, provided that it was understood that they take no responsibility if anything bad happens due to them being exhausted. Scheffer called ahead so our connection would wait for all of us.

After we successfully negotiated a few obstacles like mined rail lines, which were temporarily fixed and a bridge that was ready to be blown up, we arrived in Podwysokie, where our train was waiting for us, all set to go. We quickly changed to the next train and we were on our way flying home. By 6 PM we were in Chodorow. We should have been with our happy family by this time, but we were pleased to make it this far. (Ed: Chodorow, now called Khodoriv, is 550km from Budapest.) It was dark by the time we arrived in Stryj. I was sad that we will be travelling over the Carpathians at night.

I arrived home on 1917 September 7. I sent Löwö on vacation right away. According to my wife, the next day we will be spending visiting people here and there and the following day doing the same. I would have been just as happy to

Page 149.

be able to rest my head in my wife's lap and enjoy the quiet joy instead! Around this time, a message arrived from Sassnitz that my brother, László (Laci), was injured and was on his way home on a train with other injured soldiers. We were watching the trains and went from one office to the next to locate his train's arrival but without success. Eventually Laci wrote from Brüx (Ed: Now Most, in the Czech Republic), telling us that he was quarantined. I decided that on my way back I would visit him.

I traveled to Brüx on 19th September, where I met Laci. The meeting was joyful. He told me his story. Our army left Lamberg, chasing the Russians. His group advanced too far. They were not notified when their forces retreated and were left behind. They kept fighting until they ran out of ammunition. They started retreating. They hardly left when he suffered a rifle wound to his left thigh, shattering the femur. For three days he lay in a field of rye. Several Russian soldiers found him but apart from stealing his valuables did not hurt him. Eventually two Russians found him, and he was taken for medical evaluation. When he was found, he was in and out of consciousness. Eventually he went through Kiev, Saratow and Czerdin, where he was in a camp for prisoners of war. He was taken to Brüx under a wounded prisoner exchange agreement.

We traveled together to Vienna along with other wounded Officers. They were all subdued and sad. Many had given up the hope that they would ever see their homeland again. They were afraid of the reception upon their return. They feared that returning may cause a nervous breakdown. My presence was a welcome relief: they could talk in Hungarian, and I was familiar with much of their experiences as I also experienced many of their miserable stories. I tried to reassure them and make them see not only a happy life but an even happier appreciation of a new future was possible.

They said that in Moscow the Czech Officers were allowed to leave the camp unaccompanied. Others could leave the camp with a minder. The Czechs at the gate beat Hungarians attempting to leave. The 55 injured Officers included two Czech Officers, who declined the return. They believed they would be better off in Russia. Lately in the camps, there was a real shortage of food, which resulted in the death of many, caused by scurvy and so called "cinga" (Ed: "cinga" is an old Hungarian word, not commonly used anymore, which refers to a form of being very thin, probably because of not having enough food. Basically, a form of starvation. It is also in the pejorative sense.) Rumor had it that about the same time they were building the railway line to Murmansk and 30,000 P.O.W. (Prisoners of War) and 3,000 Russians died. Particularly hair raising, awful stories circulated about the fate of the Jewish P.O.W.'s.

From the camp, some Officers were able to get civilian clothes from Russian families. They would escape during early night and return before dawn. If caught, they would be imprisoned and locked up for varying periods. There were Russian Officers locked up there also. The benefit was that these places were cleaner and for low-cost decent meals could be had.

In Vienna I bade farewell from Laci. He caught the express train to Budapest and I went to Stanislau.

Without small talk, we said goodbye. My thoughts for his future were rosy and enviable. In my view unlimited happiness awaited him. He was out of the war. He could plan for his future. His fiancé was expecting him to return and rekindle the ember of love, the forthcoming marriage and the hope of a family with children. He was imaginably fortunate to meet her when they were both children; the ongoing friendship which blossomed into love, with fanatical belief and trust in each other throughout the years is exceedingly rare. The war's merciless evil spirits spared him, his fate was not sealed with sorrow, the Almighty looked after him. Their honest, open and caring for each other and compassion for others appeared to predestine them for a good life together. I, on the other hand, remain a pawn in the chess game of life. I appear destined to see the war to the end. Until then, "Pass the pitcher of beer!" and I will face whatever eventuality future, hand in my keys and pass on to happier hunting grounds today? tomorrow? the day after? The journey to Galicia was long and it allowed (too much) time for brooding over my future. Through Lemberg I arrives at Stanislau. The town was severely burned. There was nowhere to stay, so I returned to the railway station. By this time nobody was there to announce the impending arrivals or departures of trains. The station was filled to the rim with soldiers, Officers and Jewish merchants.

Some advice or information could be gained from the military Station Commander, but his knowledge was sketchy. Freight trains arrived and departed. Occasionally a couple of regular passenger coaches were attached to the train destined to Budapest and Hatvan. The most recent coaches contained hard benches to sit on and were marked: "For use for 6 horses or 36 people". If you needed help finding your train, you could ask the Military Station Master, who usually kicked you out. There was certainty in the information given: "Warten!", which meant "Wait!" in German. This meant you had to be a horse or cow to travel! More experienced travelers knew better: ignore the big wheels and ask the staff working on each train about their destination.

The traveling soldiers understood the game and used it to their advantage. For example, when they found out that a train was heading away from their destination, they would hop on and happily travel and get off after a few hours, have their military passports franked, sometimes several times at the same station, thus "proving" the superhuman efforts they took to get back to the front as quickly as possible. After an all-night trip in a cattle wagon, at 3 a.m. I arrived at Wyganka, near Czortkow. After visiting Galamb I requested a car from Lieutenant Hause and I went to see Captain Papierka. All was well with my Company. They were contented, work went well, and everything was in good order. Exactly the opposite would have been the case in peacetime!

Once again the Company was ordered to Piensky. We marched to Kopyczince and took a train to Jezierzany and marched to Pienky. The Company was under Lieutenant Vogt's command while I discussed the matter of road rollers with Lieutenant Colonel Olaschak. We got out of serving under Szesztay and came under the *Genie-Stab*.

The road through Jagielnica-Ulaszkowce-Glebocek-Borazkov was originated by the Russians. The civilian population was made to work every day, even Sundays. The women were rounded up after church and joined the men. Jewish men were used to crush stones, the peasants were left alone because the harvest was essential for their war effort. The horses were also "borrowed" to assist the road construction. When they retreated so went the horses!

The completion of the road became our task. Had our number of men been twenty-fold, the work would have taken several **months of hard work!** The first priority was to repair the existing road after each heavy rainfall. After reviewing the forthcoming task with me, Vogt departed on leave, and he left.

Pienky was a well-to-do village. Their houses were neat and tidy, the men were well received and housed. The orchards were bearing an excellent harvest. Plums in particular did amazingly well. My men were strictly forbidden to steal any fruit and they were not to accept any without paying. The cost was very reasonable. I personally bought plums for the men, and some for myself, from my pocket.

I was due to be named a Captain. The first step was to go through the Szesztay group. Since Szesztay was younger than I was, he was afraid my advancement would delay his. Since he could not stop my request, he did his very best to delay it. Since he could not find fault with my work he tried to make me withdraw my request and make me forget about the whole issue. He failed in this endeavor. I did not care about him and avoided his company. He upped the ante and assigned much more difficult work for me and the men. He started canceling my work areas and assigned new ones. Prior to completing my last order, I wrote a long and full account of the work I was requested to do, including the fact that I was required to do work in which independence and self-reliance were essential. I also brought up the fact that I was due to receive a higher rank. So, I requested a new evaluation of my status.

Now this was an open declaration of war between Szesztay and me. I knew Szesztay would try to meet me and discuss this matter. I made myself unavailable. He went to Békefy to help him by requesting that the letter be withdrawn. This resulted in an apparently friendly discussion and agreed that both of us would be present at Headquarters at 10 a.m. next morning. Now that would have been more natural that we arrive at the same time but Szesztay arrived one hour earlier at 9 a.m. and saw Olschak. (I was not smart enough to anticipate this it.) The Colonel knew me well. Nevertheless, he wanted as little problems under his command as possible. He knew Szesztay was his court's carrier [whatever that means] and he did not want to lose either of us. His comment was that he was happy seeing two Hungarian officers at loggerheads.

From the *Geniestahl* I went to visit Galamb. I told him the welcome news about Szesztay, and we shared our distrust and dislike of Szesztay. He told me that Szesztay will soon be discharged since he worked a farm.

In the AOK, (Ed: which is **A**rmee **O**ber **K**ommando or Army High Command in English) or as the café comics nicknamed: "Alle Ohne Kopf", (Ed: Which means: "All Without A Head" i.e. brainless; both have the same acronym, AOK) ordered the nearby work crews and engineers through the *Geniestab* or Head of Engineering Services, to be part of a group serving far from the central command. In theory this would have qualified for higher remuneration, but Olschak somehow reduced this benefit.

This resulted in Olschak and one other group receiving this benefit. Not us. He was smart enough to ensure maximum benefit for himself. This resulted in a lot of uncomplimentary comments about Olschak. He was succeeded by Colonel Herrmann. Olschak's last parting moves were to give Békefy and Szesztay the German Iron Cross. I never envied others receiving decorations or medals for fine achievements. This was not the case for these gentlemen. Those, who served at or near the front line with diligence and honor should have been the recipients. Not the fake soldiers who never even saw the front lines let alone serve there!

My photographs were developed in Bilce, and I sent these to the kind hosts with whom I stayed. I asked both Löwe and Theil to get me some cigarette papers. They each got me some, but they had to do so with caution: by that time buying or selling cigarette paper was illegal. Sure enough, they were detained by Germans but they were crafty with this matter and the Germans let them go.

I received a request to go to Court in Stry. I traveled there on 3rd November, but before leaving I called my Flórus and asked her to meet me in Stry. On my way I saw the beautiful town of Stanislau burnt severely, just like Podhajce, by the retreating Russians. Flórus arrived on 5th November and left on the 7th taking the express train through Lemberg. We spent several happy hours together. I returned via Stanislau on the November. Next day I was in Hadynkowce and I went by car to Probuzna where my Company worked. It was Fall by then, the weather turned cold and foggy.

I visited Colonel Herrmann. We enjoyed each other's company. The workers will be replaced by Italian P.O.W.'s. He trusted me with the orderly transport and provided me with 2 Officers, 17 men, all armed. We left on the 15th in the evening using torchlight. Next day we spent the night in Stryj and on the third day we headed towards Budapest. I phoned ahead from Miskolc to let the family know of my whereabouts. The compartment was unheated. From Pest I travelled to Vienna, where I met my brother-in-law, Gyula Sarkady, Baby Schmidt's husband.

Sarkady was Hussar 1st Lieutenant when he enlisted. In Upper Galicia he took part in a mindless Hussar attack and suffered serious injuries. When his health improved and he assigned a desk job at the War Ministry. On the 20th I reported at the Sigmunds Herberg camp, a huge camp for P.O.W.s. About 40,000 Italian prisoners were housed there at the time.

In front of a warehouse there was a huge pile of turnips. This was meant to be the main food source for the prisoners. The prisoners begged their captors to **not** cook these, as the raw turnips were more edible. The matter of further transport was not settled. I was given leave to travel to Vienna and I departed immediately. I stayed with my uncle, Ede Dubasievics from 22nd November 1917. I lived the good life here! I received the news, that I was promoted to Captain: /P.V.B1.No 31 1918.03.01.

Page 153.

Through the intervention of Sarkady at the War Ministry I was able
to telephone Flórus and the children. I asked Flórus to come to
Vienna. She caught the Midday Express from Budapest and we
stayed at the Hotel Egerlander, simply because it was in the vicinity
of Franz Josef Station, which was the best route back to the Sigmunds
Herberg POW camp. We visited Baby and her family again. To allow
us to travel together we needed the permission of the Station
Commander, and this took time. We could not obtain lunch and got
on the train somewhat hungry. There was no room in the camp, but
we found a room: the unheated room of a train engineer, Josef Horák.
The room was attractive and clean. The *federbed* was generous and
the cold air was not a problem. The hosts were attentive and kind. I
was notified on 26th November that they had no more prisoners to
provide, and I was redirected to Matthausen another POW camp.
Flórus wanted to come with me, but I was unfamiliar with the camp,
and I sent Flórus back to Budapest. The camp had 9,000 Russian
prisoners but different units requested 23,000 and I was given
another leave. I immediately travelled to Pest.

My dear father had ever increasing problems with his second wife.
He came to visit me and discuss the available alternatives. I travelled
to Apc, where I hoped to reach a mutually amicable solution. I was
unsuccessful. There was intrigue; she lived in peace with my father
until all sorts of intrigue arose. She desired that my father give her
the ownership of the house. From then on, she became intolerable.
The children had no opposition to this plan, if my father had a
peaceful life. I suggested a divorce, but my father remained
unconvinced. He returned to Apc.

One of the relatives had a great idea. Their very good friend, General
Schnetzer, could intervene and on account of my long service at the
front could request a desk job. I went to Vienna to discuss this topic
with the General. He was attentive and kind, but he was about to
travel, and he said he hoped to do something upon his return. I
travelled back to Pest. I received an order on 16th December 1917. I

was ordered to return to Matthausen where I met Colonel Schön and his assistant, 1st Lieutenant Dr. Beer. After a short discussion I received a brief leave. I could spend the Holy Night with my family. I received an order via a telegram. I was to return immediately to Ostffy-Asszonyfa. I arrived an hour and a half late, caused by a severe snowstorm. The camp was organized well. We had a billiard table, card tables and other luxury accessories. I met 1st Lieutenant Ribiczey, who had some disagreements with the Germans and was placed on house arrest.

The matter of my reassignment was still pending, so I went to Pest and was able to be with the family on New Year's Eve. I returned to Ostfy-Asszonyfa on 4th January 1918. The same day, the first Italian POW transport left, under 1st Lieutenant Hribernigg in enclosed carriages meant for cattle, naturally unheated. Csurkowsy and Ribiczey left next day, after collecting 600 *korona*. I left on 7th January 1918 with 800 Italian POWs bound for Galicia.

Attached to the locomotive was a carriage which was from the last century. There was some heat. Flórus was waiting for me at Kőbánya, where we said our goodbyes once again. In absolutely bucketing rain, we had lunch at Hatvan. Towards Miskolc, at a slight curve, the train stopped. The operators of the locomotive, the engineers, were briefly explaining that they had insufficient steam even for the mildest slope. The prisoners were getting out of the train and largely gathered on the parallel track. I feared that another train could result in tragedy. Getting the prisoners back into the train was difficult. We stopped at Miskolc, where 1st Lieutenant Rottmann and my Officers had coffee. Captain Eperjessy was the Military Commandant and I told him about our problems on the rail line. He apologized for the problems, but he said he had to make sure that we leave immediately and promised that the train in Sátoraljaujhely would wait for us. We caught up with the train using the Express. Upon arrival we had coffee. A prisoner escaped and by the time he was recaptured he broke the mail coach window and stole several parcels.

We were approaching the Carpathian Mountains. There was ice and snow everywhere. The view was fantastic. We had to stop in a tunnel for a while and continued our way slowly. A prisoner fainted and following the example many others claimed illness. We got some food at the smaller stations, but medical attention was unavailable, so we had no other choice except to continue the journey. We continued our way at midnight, but the train stopped again at 2 a.m. Amid a snowstorm and high wind we found that our locomotive had vanished! We found a station with much difficulty. In that storm you could see 5 steps! Apparently, we were near Stryj. It took lengthy and complex calls to get a locomotive! Perhaps the High Command needed to decide. We got to Stryj at 8 a.m. So far food was provided for us but from this point on it became my responsibility.

In Stryj large kettles were installed on the snow-covered road. Coffee was served. The Officers served themselves at a nearby restaurant. At midday we were still there, serving soup, meat and coffee. The

Officers had lamb, there was nothing else. At 4 p.m. we left for Zsidacsow. After a long wait we noticed cooling of our compartment. The Germans stole our locomotive. We, the Officers, tried to warm ourselves in a small hut by the track. I shuddered to think how the prisoners fared! More telephone calls were made. We served supper; order was almost impossible to maintain. We used bayonets to keep peace. That was a hard job. We begged for and eventually snagged a locomotive and arrived in Stanislau at 10 p.m.

The railway station was badly shot up and was neglected. The restaurant was dirty. The meal was a hamburger. A far cry from the great food at home! We left for Chortkow at 3 a.m. We did not arrive there until 4 a.m. next morning. Our prisoners no food for this journey.

The food distribution did not exactly go as planned. It was a small miracle that total disappearance of order was avoided. Shots fired in the air helped to maintain some degree of control. Food consisted of a tin of food, a very small piece of bread and coffee. Complaining got us nowhere; the stores were empty. While the meagre rations were distributed it was snowing and was very hard to watch these hungry and cold men.

The station at Jezierzeny was crowded with soldiers. Nothing appeared organized. We were fortunate to retain our own belongings let alone maintain discipline and provide food. I was particularly concerned about this because the mildest man becomes a wild beast when he feels his life is on the line. The lack of food and the cold exacerbated the risk of disorder, and I was going to avoid it. I called our end station, Borszczów, from Teresin, the station before, to request food.

Along the line we saw numerous trains filled with German material. There was a rumor of a forthcoming full offensive starting on the Western front and that the Germans were to be replaced by the 25th division.

Upon arrival at Borszczów, what would be more natural than to expect no food for us? I telephoned Hauptmann Zimmer, who was amazed that we were there. He did not expect us for another 3 or 4 days. He arranged a shelter for the men in the tobacco factory. He also requested food from the Commandant.

The exhausting journey and the bitter cold conditions followed for these broken men to move into the tobacco factory. Once again, what would be more natural than having inadequate room for these men? The different heads of army units existed without any cooperation. We marched the poor souls into a music hall. If it was very cold outside somehow it was colder inside. I felt pain seeing such misery.

On the other hand, lying in the trench, hoping the next bullet was not meant for you was not ideal either!

I was staying in the Officers' quarters. I met 1st Lieutenant Dezső Egressy, who was my school mate, who openly boasted that he was able the front line until the spring of 1917 w2hen he was finally sent to this front. His job description included "fattening pigs and commerce." He was Jewish. He had no respect for my rank. I found his questionable antics avoiding service and to be proud of this feat disgusting. After the war they might erect a statue of him, alongside the statue to Szesztay.

I travelled to Sapaho on 15th January 1918 where my Company was located. I completed my travel accounts and in the severe cold I returned to Borszczów. I received an order to transport prisoners to Lanowcere to join the group of Captain Babka. I hoped to hear from 1st Lieutenant Lessmer the confirmation that I would be given the Austrian *Baukomp* leadership, currently held by Captain Claus, son of a Viennese carpenter. The Austrians were mostly kind. It was only later that I realized that there were more Czechs than Austrians.

Page 156.

Next day I took the prisoners to Folw.Teresin and placed them in barracks and I went to Lanowce, where Claus resided. In the afternoon I went through Zielince to see Babka. At the *Sőgerwerk* they kept the prisoners. Babka was not willing to accept the prisoners because they received no bread for two days. While I was returning to Teresin the warm wind melted the snow. Békefi was also there, with a number of POWs. His house was very well appointed, and he did not have any needs. He appeared to have carved out a great position for himself at the Headquarters. On the Name Day of the King Claus declared a holiday and Békefi was to deliver a speech.

Life was uneventful but we all felt that something was brewing, but there were no details.

Activity at the front virtually stopped but beyond the front, activity rose with a feverish pace. This normally was followed by reassignments, which in turn led to movement of forces. Those used to stability were anxious to retain their positions and locations. The roadbuilding, barracks construction and similar activities were continued. At the same time bad news also arrived. 1st Lieutenant Lessner, then assigned at Headquarters, requested to be reassigned at home. Instead, he was reassigned to Italy. Alexi, from Moktár, who received his pay without fail, was now advised that he will not be paid unless a relative with valid legal papers vouched for him at the Head Office. These signs as well as the increasing lack of essential food items did not bode well for the future. Most of us felt that increasingly troubled times lay ahead. There was a significant section of the population who took advantage during these times. More thorough oversight was planned. We thought the outcome of the war would hinge on economic issues. We all tried to do more with less.

I saw Captain Adler concerning the iron crosses for Károly Corps, or other awards, but I was met with complete lack of interest, and I achieved nothing. Most of us, with the exception of Szesztay, could not care less.

I received the funds for *Baukomp 3, Lst. 25,* on 22nd January. The German Crosses arrived and I called *Belobungs-Antrag* to advise. The *Deutsche Südarmee* [German Army South] was divided, the 2nd army group will take its place. Sanitation Lieutenant Mond and others were moved to new positions. Jan Nekut, a Czech; Ferenc Szamek, Czech; 1st Lieutenant Juwan, Czech; all remained with our group. The German Iron business was quickly resolved: most of them were distributed amongst the office staff. One or two even reached those fighting in the front trenches! 1st Lieutenant Lessner, who got a cross, was nevertheless aghast of hearing what took place.

I was used to swapping books with 1st Lieutenant Szántó. When I tried to return his books and collect mine, only to find empty shelves. He was reassigned to the Italian front. At that time, I met a Jewish officer, named Rottstein, who told me that he was bored with the stale Hinterland (Ed: the area behind the front, i.e. an area with no fighting). He got his wish in the fourth year of the war and action on the front lines.

My orders were to join my new unit in Jezierzany, where I lived with a Greek Orthodox priest, Leoni Korosty, in a very nice place. The army units were always changing. Two other people visited me there: 1st Lieutenant Mlcoch and Kriczkl, head of 4/4 Baukomp (building divisio). Our three segments were to request funds. I had the feeling that travelling to Italy was our future destination. The Captain was signaling the same message. In the meantime, we continued working on roads in the day and relaxing with the clergyman at night.

The atmosphere was refined, cultured and with music and discussions on multiple topics; it was relaxing.

I received my orders on 5th February 1918. My unit was to depart to the Italian front to join 11th Armee. We understood that the location was on a flat area. Personally, I would have preferred a hilly terrain. Later, they called about winter outfits, which suggested hills. Nothing was certain. We requisitioned 8 days' food. We got evicted from Jezierzany and we were sent to a Merlawa, small village. Through my intervention Captain Primavesi was able to extend our stay at *Genie Stab*. Artillery Colonel Scapinelli joined us. On 18th February we moved to Zalézia, where I got an unheated room, which was impossible to heat. I moved to a room with 2 stoves. We were to arrive at Bielo-Cortkow on 25th February, so we left Zalesia, and thus Galicia on 23rd February, after 3 years of this battlefield.

We were unable to take all our belongings and exchanged the surplus for bread and sausages. We spent the night in Czortkow in miserable, cold wind and foul weather. We boarded the train on 24th February 1918 in late afternoon.

Part 4

ON THE ITALIAN BORDER AREA

<u>1918 Februauary 24 to 1918 May 14</u>

Page 159.

We took our places on the train (Ed: in Czortkow) quite quickly. The train did not leave until 2.30 a.m., but without heat we felt miserable. Once the locomotive was connected, we got some heat. At Nizniow, one coach of the train developed a mechanical problem and had to be replaced. We passed through Kőrösmező on 26th February and went to Királyháza. From there I traveled by the regular train and arrived on the 27th of February at 7:00 am. We arranged to meet at Rákos. Here we found out that my train would be redirected to Kelenföld so I went home to visit the family. When I returned to rejoin my troops, another surprise awaited me at Kelenföld. The train would proceed through Rákos but I was unable to find transportation to that town. I telephoned the Officer at Rákos for advice. He suggested that I get on the locomotive of a freight train. This would take me to Kőbánya. The carriage's seating arrangement in the compartments was arranged without a hitch. However, since we had no locomotive, we had no source of steam, which would have provided the heating. The train finally left at 3.30 a.m. and our locomotive provided heat. They changed one carriage at Nizniew, because of mechanical defect. On February 26th, we were at Kőrösmező and arrived at Királyháza by the afternoon. I went ahead on my own with a passenger train and arrived at Pest in the morning by 7 a.m. on 27th. We planned to join up again in Rákos. I went out with Flórus, (my wife), as she wanted to see our train. When we got there, they told us that my train would arrive there at 11 p.m. at Kelenföld, in Budapest.

We went home to see the family and I made my way to Kelenföld in the evening to meet my colleagues. There was another surprise. They redirected our train, and it would pass through Rákos. I could not find any way to get to Rákos and so I could not reach them and did not even know which way they would have gone from there. I phoned Rákos and they told me that the train had not gone through there and so as a traffic officer suggested, I got on the 1st steam locomotive freight train to Kőbánya. I climbed into the cab of the steam locomotive and when I arrived at Kőbánya, I found that my train to Palota had already gone. Once again, I got onto another freight train, also riding in the cab of the locomotive, and arrived at Palota at 4 a.m., but our train was not there. The sleepy traffic officer offered us some cigarettes and then set to finding some transport. The train was stranded at Pécel, and it would take ten hours to get to us once it leaves. I lay down on a leather sofa in the well heated room and tried to make up the hours of sleep that I lost the previous night. We left Pozsonyszöllő with no heat on 1st March, going through Saint Pölten and Amstetten to Linz. We departed from Linz at 7 p.m. From Steindorff on we enjoyed the spectacular Alpine panorama. In Salzburg we had time to do some sightseeing until midday. We continued through Zell-am-See, Saalfeld and by morning, Innsbruck. Once again, the heating stopped working, but from Franzenfest on the heating was working again. We passed through the Brenner Pass and numerous tunnels. As we descended the snow seemed less and less. We saw troops. In the afternoon, around 3 p.m., we passed Bozen, in the evening Trient, arriving In Caldona at night.

We slept in the train as it was raining. We slept well in our unheated carriage, until someone woke us up for some signatures, otherwise we had a pleasant night. We reported to Captain Martinides in Levico on March 5th. He had a Sapper Group attached to the 11th Army Command. I was then referred to the Technical Referral Group, where 1st Lieutenant Hepfner, 1st Lieutenant Dr. Waschilius and Major Khistler were in charge.

Levico was a magical place before the war, a well sought-after holiday resort, which the upper crust of 10,000 enjoyed, with a new spa and all the luxury amenities. These days the Senior Military Commanders occupied this once wonderful place where they lived in luxury. These days, in this paradise, orders are issued, which will cause the demise of many a soldier. It's just not fair.

They assigned all three sections that came down from Galicia to the Third Corp, which was stationed in Vezzena. You can get there on the cableway. It is at the edge of Caldonazzo, and the first cableway stop is Rover, which is above Caldonazzo at 1,200 meters. Our train was to depart at 3 p.m., which allowed me to look around the town in the meantime. It must have been rather hot there recently; not from the sun's rays, but from thick artillery fire. Most of the town's residents have left and now the streets were filled with military personnel. The furniture in the flats were gone; the people simply took anything they could carry with them.

I never liked to stay in a place with lots of military presence; you could hardly keep the place orderly and clean. Property security was iffy at best. We went out to the cableway in the afternoon. The cable car units were made of narrow slabs of wood from bottoms of boxes and completely open!

I didn't particularly like travelling, but there were many things that soldiers didn't want to do during the war, still, they had to do it and do it willingly. Starting on the cableway was unpleasant; they to pushed this "seat", so it swung in all direction. It calmed down somewhat as we started getting further up in the air and people became ant-sized. The further we ascended, the thicker was the snow cover. It was rather frightening as these contraptions went over the places where the iron-band held the joint in the cabling: you felt like you would fly out at that moment. We had to change at Rover to get to Vezzenna, but this part of that cableway was closed, so we could only contact the headquarters by phone.

I wouldn't have been happy to travel down the way we came up, so I requested the use of a closed truck that was parked and not used and I was granted permission. My flat was in the Station Komdo in Caldonazzo; I had heating in my room. The other officers lived in one of the flats in a block; the stone staircase had collapsed and they had to use a wooden makeshift staircase to get up there. The rest of the men were in houses, but these were not very pleasant. Next day we gave in our baggage at the cableway and started walking up the mountain. We had to march for two or three days to reach Vezzena. One of the routes towards Alla-Stagna was closed due to the danger of avalanche and so we went via Carbona, which was longer. We were in good spirits walking through beautiful woods; work and enemy were a long way off. As we got higher up, there was heavier snowfall and carts got stuck; I decided to leave our carts in the small town by the name of Centa. Madoniovits chief lieutenant told us with a great gusto, that the road was completely blocked by an avalanche at a tunnel; he had few people and so I could help with my men, seeing as we couldn't continue our journey anyway. We gave our report by phone and we were working at the tunnel the next day. We were allowed two days to complete the work. During this time lieutenant Krickl was in charge – another slide came down wiping out all the work we did up to then. We worked all night with lights from torches. The following day it was my turn to go to the tunnel that was 3 ½ km away from our resting place. It was an incredible sight for us to see how the men pried loose very large rocks and let them roll down the slope. The valley was 800 m deep so these boulders broke up before reaching the bottom.

We continued our wanderings on 8th March 1918. It was hard for the carts going up on these serpentine roads. The men really felt the food shortage. I saw some soldiers sitting nearby some dead horses that had fallen; the men took out their pocketknives and they were cutting bits of meat off and packing these up in dirty cloths, that they spread out on the snow. We arrived at the cableway in Carbonare and we were promptly ushered on our way. I lay in the first greasy, snowy wooden box and I sent the chief lieutenant Krickl to be in the last one. Through Rover and Vezzena stations we wobbled along to Pusterle. This was a two-hour journey above the Alps. Somehow, we got used to all the unpleasant things during this time and if only it hadn't been so cold and damp, we could have enjoyed as the beautiful panorama went by on the right, the left and also below us. Occasionally we seemed to have a bottomless valley as we looked down.

Then we wobbled along above a sea of rocks. This Lavarone plateau is the bloody stage of King Charles' offensive.

At Monte Rover we looked down at our starting place, the royal Livicoba to Caldonazzo; there were bright lakes, white villages and dark forests in the distance in the vast valley. We arrived in Pusterle half frozen. We have quite got used to not having danger around us and so we were quite taken aback when we received the answer to our question as to why there were so few people at such a large station. They replied that the Italians often sent us messages. The sergeant sent us to division 52 in the Assa valley. /Val d'Assa/. We didn't see the Hinterland way of life as we were able to see it in Galicia, this far away from the enemy. Again, the reason was that the Italians were placed across the Val d'Assa, they could see the whole extent of the valley and they fired all the way with the main road going all along the bottom of the valley.

Monte Verena /2019 m/ is in the bend of Val d'Assa and this area is virtually impassable because of the numerous rocks and boulders in the way. On the east of this are Monte Meata /1875 m/ and Monte Internotto /1410 m/. A while ago tourists talked with pleasure when mentioning these names. The sides of these mountains had been covered with pine forests, but a lot of the trees had been cut down during the battles that were fought there.

When leaving the valley of the Assa, we arrived at the lovely village of Camporovere. Presumably, this is where the tourists rested, before they started their trek toward the exclusive Assiago. People who toured here during the war in the hills, villages and towns the names of these places bring back sad memories. To them Val d'Assa was the gate to Hell even after the battles were over.

People walked quietly, almost afraid as they were still remembering the bombing, which had taken place there. The cableway had been blown up and it hasn't been used since then. I wasn't given my orders as the person above me in the pecking order was on leave. Rushing about to find a solution, I got back to Pusterle, where captain Köhler found us a flat. The hospitable captain invited us to dinner and there he familiarized us with the situation. He mentioned the January offensive that he called a terrible story.

I went to Vezzena with Krickl on foot on the 9th to get proper orders. Major Rambausek marked my area out as from Gipbruch in the Val d'Assa to Assiago. I took over the running of 5 squads: we built and repaired roads. Köhler said that we could work only at night. On our way back we met our carts and we travelled on them to Poterle. In the meantime, Szamek found a new flat and we moved in, but as it was rather draughty, we wall-papered it with paper. In the next flat to us some officers were singing Hungarian songs until late at night. It was most entertaining. I went to see the Chief Major at squadron 52; Codor will make his decisions as to what we should do next. I met Captain Guszti Wanke, an old friend of mine. He is the elderly officer of squadron 38. They are also coming from Galicia and will take over the line from the foot squadron 52.

In the afternoon I was looking for a flat in the Val d'Assa with Krickl. All the barracks we looked at had been riddled with gunfire. They had a tough time here towards the end of January. We chose some barracks for the men and returned to fetch some building material.

This is where I met captain Gál, who is the director of the Nyiregyházi Népbank (Ed: People's Bank); his squad lies next to mine. We arrived back to our place next to Pusterle, rather tired.

There are some gas chambers at the Pusterle Lager. This was news to us. The men had to practice. They gave them these masks and sent them into the gas chambers, but they couldn't bear this for long. It turned out the masks were faulty. One would have thought that they would have brought usable masks for this job. The report had gone in to say that the practice had been done with the newly recruited people. Occasionally I had a cold and Sramek took over the building process. He was an ambitious man and he chose a Swiss style of building; he was concentrating on the officers' pavilion that we were building on the side of a steep hill. This was not to our liking, being war veterans and I asked him to make the simplest plan for the building. We had to find a caverna and we went to look for one. While on our way, a large group of Italian aeroplanes flew by above us towards Pusterle and soon we heard the defence squad's shooting and the detonation of the bombs that were thrown at the town. This group of 70 planes were the reply to our previous mission on the Italian side.

By the evening the road was full of carts carrying food and ammunition. They stopped at start of the flat area, the Assa Sperre and continued to the flat only under the cover of darkness. We were on our way to see our night-time workplace. It wasn't easy to negotiate the road with all the heavy night traffic. We risked travel in dusk in the open valley. For about 5 km there were pine branches along the road, so slight movements would not be seen. It seemed that this road had not been built properly before the war and the Italians started to build it at the plateau. Correctly shaped stones were piled by the roadside; they made walls to protect the road, but since we had chased them away, they blew these up. There was a water system from the hills: this was also blown up. We got to Camporover with our tumbril (Ed: Hungarian word is "kordé" or kordély", tumbril in English, which is a horse drawn cart or trap meant to carry people, typically prisoners.) The odd soldier just stared at us. From here we went to Assiago on foot; it was getting darker by then and the Italian flares lit up the whole valley, giant trails of light were swirling round in the air, you could almost enjoy the sight, if you didn't know their purpose. Here and there we could hear gunfire, probably as they spotted some movement and they tried to disturb them.

In Assiago there were colossal stone pieces in the middle of the road. They were parts of a blown-up church; I ordered their removal from the road. We returned to Camporover, got on the carts, but we moved very slowly, because of the traffic coming the other way. The men moved into their new quarters after they were ousted from Pusterle. It was freezing overnight in the half-ready barracks. I felt poorly, though there seemed nothing wrong with me; I was exhausted, and I didn't feel like working with the men. One night, flares lit up the skies, some shots were fired but no one got hurt. The 38th regiment took over from us. We were under colonel Treplár. He was thorough and he was a decent soldier, who didn't demand frequent reports; we just had to work properly, he knew what our men had done.

Page 163.

Once again Nekut Feldkurat appears on the horizon; they express appreciation for our work. The general belief amongst the men was that some very important event was in the offing if they gave a priest to each work squad, so he could administer the last rite to the dying presumably. Such important people who come from a long way away are bound to bring some news with them. The men on the front are realistic and they cannot think up such unbelievable news and they cannot believe them either. Nekut heard that the officers were to do whatever orders are given by the parliamentary minister of defense. It was true, that, as an enlisted man, I was not supposed to fight in foreign lands, but nobody thought of that. Neither an enlisted man, nor rebel, or an active soldier or a reserve soldier who wasn't involved in the war: everybody worked hard and did his duty defending his country. At this time the men with different ranks upheld their responsibilities. They were forever reminded of this each time they were fighting the enemy, whether they were young or old, in good health or ill, rank and file, they were all indiscriminate recipients of the enemy's bullets.

In Assiago everyone had to be in hiding during the day. A 24-member squad of men arrived one evening and took shelter in the cellar of a blown-up house. They found it very quiet there the following day and were going in and out of their place despite clear warnings. The Italians blew up the whole lot of them the following night, their bodies were lying about all over the place next to the church.

My orders arrived to inspect the roads leading to Assiago-Gallio and Assiago-Nos. While I was walking along these roads that are just behind the front, a very large bombshell fell on Assiago, the blast was echoing backwards and forwards all along the valley.

We cleared up the road from Val de'Assa to Assiago and we removed the pieces of the ruined church from the road; the Italians noticed this and on a nice day they bombed the road all the way, their offensive was much rougher than the Russians'. We had a lot of work to do to get the road in a reasonable condition and as quickly as possible for hundreds of carts to pass along it. An Italian plane plummeted down near Assiago.

If they started shooting the road in front of our barracks, the men ran to the rocks, but they weren't protected properly there either, especially from the shrapnel of the bombshells, so for them we started to construct caverns. This process was rather time-consuming. It's getting warmer during the day but still frosty at night. The warmer temperatures started the snow melt. New orders came for us to make the upper part of the road passable, the one that leads to the Garmarara valley. It would have been easier to approach this road from Assiago, but it wouldn't have been advisable, so we chose the more difficult route. This place was at least 12 km away from our place and the work was to take two days. I was planning to find a shorter distance to get across the Interotto hillside. I left with my men, unfamiliar with the conditions on the Alps. In the valley of Garmarara we took the steeper side of the hill, holding onto the creeping plants until we were exhausted. The Monte Interotto is very high up and my undertaking it was more than naïve. We turned back; if it was hard to go up, downwards it just didn't work and we sled down without sledges until we got back to the road.

The next day we made our way up with the whole squad, which take the tourists days of preparation. In places we even had to use ladders. At the top we marveled at the barracks that were built on the rocks. They were only just visible under the snow.

Clearing away the snow at night, we started on the artillery building, then, shadowed by the peak of the hill, we turned to getting the road in order. After a few phone calls we managed to find the place where our work was indeed waiting for us; there was enough to do there for a few thousand people. I left the company in the hands of Krichl and started my return journey home in the cart, which I left in the valley. On my way I met carts carrying food and ammunition. The animals pulling these carts did their work heroically for the country and fell by the wayside in their hundreds, exhausted by doing this ghastly task. I got home at daybreak with pleasant and sad memories of my journey through the Alps.

I could feel my strength draining away and my health was not so good and realized that I needed to rest. Since my return from Galicia, I worked non-stop and my nerves got so bad, that I started shaking at the least excitement. I gave in my request for time off. In the meantime, I was given further orders, despite not having finished our assignment at Interrott. The place that they were to give over to the men was given to others, and as they couldn't put down camp in the open on account of the cold conditions, they were all sent back. They arrived back at 11 o'clock. Now we must repair the road to Assiago-Stella, Assiago-Roana, and Camporovere Intorotto. Now another squad is to join mine with 1st Lieutenant Hammer in charge. Hammer was the bookkeeper of the Temesvár branch of the Hungarian bank. I gave him a flat a bit further from the banks, but he is not happy about this as it is closer to the front and he said he would complain to the lieutenant colonel. In the end he accepted the flat and he didn't say anything to the lieutenant colonel; I didn't either. Because of the orders and the load of work, they phoned me and I didn't have to go to headquarters to give in my report; each of these journeys would have been equivalent to a trip up Svábhegy. (Ed: Svábhegy is a popular day hike for Budapest folk, perhaps 5km from center of the city.)

One morning I met general Molnár, who is the leader of the 38th regiment, whom I knew from back in Galicia. He stopped to talk to me and said that, seeing that I was so young, I could easily be his deputy commander. I didn't tell him, that I didn't crave such fame anymore. They are taking away 2nd Lieutenant Sramek and ensign Popovits as well. The latter had been the leader of the 3/31 squad and he was known for drinking champagne all the time. I didn't understand this at all, as we hardly had enough to eat by this time. The administrative work of the squad and checking the work, when it was done, gave us a lot to do. Our priest, Nekut, accompanied me for my journeys.

One day, as we were working in Assiago, Lieutenant Colonel Preplar told me on the phone that he wanted to inspect all the work with me and that I should wait for him at 8 p.m. on the main road. He travelled by car for such trips and I was delighted to have the chance to go by car. I waited until 9 p.m. by the side of the road. One car went by, but it didn't stop. Later I concluded that the lieutenant colonel stayed in Assiago and returned quickly, having changed his mind, and that is why he didn't take me with him. My request for time off was granted after a long wait, and I was ready to look for a replacement, who would take my post, and so I handed in my papers to the lieutenant colonel and soon I was given permission to leave.

In the end, he came in the afternoon, took over my squad, but they didn't have enough money to pay me. Hammer helped me by lending me money and so I was able to leave the same day. We put my stuff on the cart and I started my journey at 6p.m. with Löw, my orderly, and Theil, my groom. We arrived in Vezzena in fog and total darkness. From here it was snowing, as we descended to Monte Rover. We were given good accommodation and food; even my coachman had some tea, wine and something to eat.

I didn't feel like using the cableway in the morning, so I started off on foot down to Caldonazzo; the men travelled on the cableway with my belongings. It was snowing, but soon turned to rain, but despite the weather, I felt happy among the blossoming fruit trees, next to the green grassland on my way home from these foreign lands. I got on a train at Caldonazzo. I had a continuous headache, for which I took aspirin. We had a two-hour stop at Innsbruck, then left at 7 p.m. and arrived in Vienna by 9 a.m. the following morning. I travelled towards Pest and arrived home by 1 p.m. on Thursday, 2nd April 1918. I made enquiries from home about Galamb and Korbuly, my good friends. Korbuly was working at a prisoner-of-war camp; Galamb was in an armoury factory: I visited him there. I reported in at the office and at the director general, who was surprised that I still hadn't been discharged. Legányi, who took over for me at the time had been exempt from enlisting from the beginning of the war, because he pretended to have lung disease, said that he didn't know my wartime number and because of this he couldn't deal with my request of exemption from serving in the army. It was easy for me to refute his statement that he didn't know my number and I told the director general that my wife spoke to Legányi every day as he oversaw purchases. The director general stared at him and sent him out of his room. Then he prepared an order to immediately prepare the customary order for my exemption.

Legányi was protective of his position at Moktár Bank and tried to block my return to work. He sabotaged every attempt I made to gain my discharge from military service. Several years later, his past finally caught up with him. Here's what happened. I was Director of Personnel and I received a complaint about his (Legányi's) spending habits. I was obliged to investigate the allegation and since he was the Financial Exchange Deputy, there was a potential of embezzlement. Thus, the complaint went to the Managing Director, who requested that Director Schürtz should continue the investigation. Schürtz reported a few days later that Legányi led a normal family life and there was no need for concern. However, Director Appel and I were not happy with the investigation. We decided to do a surprise spot audit at the month's end meeting. This type of audit was such a rarity, that it caught the attention of the entire department. Since I spent several years in the Exchange Department, I was given the task of leading the investigation of this audit. At first, we found no abnormalities.

The Head of Accounts told Director Appel, that on the approval of Legányi, Kálmán Horváth, Inspector of the Hungarian National Bank, was given access to funds which were managed by Legányi. Appel called me about this checking account because there was a discrepancy to the tune of 25,000 Kr. [Ed: Kr. is korona in Hungarian, the Hungarian currency at the time]. Using the most up-to-date figures we sent the bill by Registered Mail to Horváth. He called about the accounts receivable and denied owing 25,000 Kr. and he suspected an error. We invited him to discuss the matter where we showed proof of the allegation. He went to see Legányi. A heated discussion followed. Horváth paid what was demanded and left. Horváth was a personal friend and when I met him, sometime later, he said that Legányi abused his trust and stole a lot of money from the bank. Moktár arranged for Legányi's immediate forced retirement. I personally conveyed this news to him from the Board.

I was still in Pest, when my uncle Nándor Dubasievics came with the joyful news that I was to receive the József Ferenc medal (with the swords). At the war office I had myself examined, they found a few health problems, they found me fit to return to the front and they suggested I have an operation on my haemorrhoids. They looked at me at the district medical care, my old colleague from Galicia Árpád Sipos lieutenant-colonel sent me for another appointment. Dr Winternitz, university lecturer suggested that I take an 8-week thermal spa treatment, but he said I was ready for duty. They suggested an operation again, this time at the Zita hospital, but as I said before, that I was deemed fit to fight. Due to the poor state of my health, Dr. Manninger didn't think an operation was the way to go; he said that, if I was to return from the front, I should ask to go to his military hospital for admission. Moreover, Balogh staff sergeant doctor also had a look at me and said I was well enough to go back, and because my leave was over, my discharge process wasn't finished, according to the rules I should be sent back from there after they had studied all my medical papers.

In the meantime, I had to try to sort out the situation about our flat. We had let our flat in Városmajor-u to Lieutenant-colonel Kolozsvári with the proviso, that he vacate the flat on my return from the war. He didn't want to move out, therefore I sued him, so we could move into our flat.

I returned to the Valley of Assa on 2nd May 1918. I changed trains at Prgerhof and I travelled through Marburg and Franzensfest and arrived at Trient at midnight. I found good accommodation at Hotel Venezzia. The sirens went off at night, warning us of the approach of bomber-planes. The lights went out, but later the sirens went off again to indicate that no more plane attacks were imminent. I continued my journey to Caldonazzo in the morning and I went over to Levico to sign in. I found out there, that my discharge had been dealt with, but the final decision hadn't arrived yet. I left Löwö and Theil at the cableway again and I climbed up to Monte Roverre on the narrow track that was created during the war years. I went over and called in sick in the afternoon to Mayor Nagy in Pustern. I was sent for a medical examination to the military health center. The chief physician examined me and sent me to Hinterland in Pest. According to the rules, he could only suggest a treatment and send the patient to the nearest hospital. I also saw chief physician Dr Stark, but he just signed my papers, which had to be also signed by the staff doctor, (Ed. Törzsorvos in Hungarian) Dr Gebhardt. There was one more thing to do: say good-bye to the men in my squad.

The front was busy despite the rain and the fog: the Italians were shooting at the main road, using their tanks. I had to do 2 km along this road with all my papers in my hands.

Page 167.

I said good bye to the officers. They were envious and yet they parted from me amicably. There was only one exception, 2nd Lieutenant Hlava, who was a young Czech from the timber mill. He was upset, that he had to remain in the new position he was given recently.

We gathered all our stuff and they were carried down to the main road. The company's horses were useless and the few that remained were propped up with lifting belts in the stables, because they were too weak to stand up. My poor saddlehorse, Bella, paid with her life for my freedom. By the time I returned, they made a meal of her, because she had the most meat on her in the stables. The lichen and the pine branches didn't provide enough nourishment for the horses. These working horses of the squad should have had hay and straw, but they seldom had such food.

In the drizzle we walked behind the lorry carrying our things to Termine to the military hospital K.u.K. Feldspital no 311. Dr Szluka, Colonel, examined me on 7th May 1918 and he ordered a series of spa baths there and then. I found this suggestion rather amusing and asked him if he really thought that I would take baths in a wooden baroque on the top of a snowy mountain. He asked his servant to leave the room and asked me if I was an active officer, then he told me that the front is restless, they are planning an offensive and so he is not allowed to send an active officer to the back. After a friendly chat he granted me permission to continue my journey, but, again, only to the next military hospital in Vezzena. So, the next day we climbed up onto a slow lorry and made our way, sniveling, to Veszena. A 1st Lieutenant, standing at the front door of the hospital didn't even allow me to enter, he signed my papers to Rover. He said that he must have the hospital empty, because of imminent battles. They welcomed me at Rover, the food and the Hinterland atmosphere were excellent. I was put up in the sick bedroom.

The nurse brought in a thermometer. I thought this was routine, so I laid down on the bed and took my temperature. I was the only patient in this room with 8-10 beds. The nurse suggested coffee with milk; he brought black coffee, but it was good. He was busy with the thermometer. The German nurse was obviously not happy seeing 36.3 C. I must have looked frightened or rather stupid, or maybe very intelligent, because he started to rub the thermometer. When the temperature reached 38 C, he showed it to me, saying "look". I gave him a crown to show my gratitude, thinking that, although I have no need for a temperature, there might be other people who would be returning home this way, who might need a rest, even if they don't have a temperature.

Löw and Theil went down the cableway, I walked down to Caldonazzo on 8th May. It was interesting to see a mud slide. An incredibly large mass of mud was moving down the few hundred meter deep valley. We got across somehow, but we thought that in the event of more rain, the road would become impassable. A Czech doctor refused to sign my papers. His face showed unbridled hatred and I felt that from this beast I was hardly going to obtain permission to continue my journey. For this reason, I replied in a surly fashion to his question, but he just turned around and left me there. The chaplain listened to our agitated conversation. He stepped closer to me straight away and told me in Hungarian, that there was a hospital train arriving in half an hour. I shouldn't worry about the Czech doctor; I should continue my journey.

Instead, I went into the office and asked the same doctor once more if he would sign my papers. He wasn't brave enough to be so nasty again, so he allowed me to go to Pergine, the next stop. We hurried to the station, and in a few minutes, we were travelling in the hospital train. I ended up in a transformed cattle train with a group of young officers, who were playing cards. The more seriously wounded men lay on beds. After introductions they urged me not to get off in Pégin, but I did get off, and found myself face to face with the staff sergeant doctor. I introduced myself and showed him my papers. He told me in a polite and sympathetic manner, that I can go as far as Innsbruck, where everyone would have to leave the train.

We arrived at Innsbruck at 9 in the morning; we went to the Kranken sortirungs Anstalt by tram, where we could have a bath. From here we were taken to Canisium to the K.u.K. Carnisonsspital No.10.

A very kind university lecturer examined me and we had a long conversation about war and Hungary. He was to send me on to Pest on a train carrying Hungarian wounded. The hospital was clean and quiet; the food was excellent. I hadn't had such a good and uninterrupted rest for a long time.

The Hungarian Red Cross train left on 12th May and we arrived to the Déli Pályaudvar (Ed: Southern railway station in Budapest) at midday on 14th. There were many seriously and not seriously wounded on the train and they were greeted by one solitary hussar-captain. Not one civilian. Everyone was removed from the train: they were put on the ground, on bare stone. Whoever could, sat on the steps; we just stood around or sat on the steps, like the others. The captain was frantically phoning around and he felt very uncomfortable with seeing everyone's accusing look.

At last, 5 military cars arrived. First, they took the seriously wounded, then it was my turn. They took me to a Radetzki barrack on Pálfi tér. The corporal rushed to us as we got off, saying: "Why did you all come here? Every place is taken. I was exasperated: all of us returning from the front were a big burden for everyone. I sat back in the car and asked to be taken back to the station. I told the hussar captain what happened to us and that there is a place for me at the military hospital of the financial institute in the new building of the Ericson factory. That is where I am going by car, whatever plans he has for me. He was happy to give me his consent; anyway, order had changed to chaos, and everyone went where they wanted to go.

I was given a bed in the hospital in a room with 30 beds. There were only two people in the room: a one-legged flying officer and an assistant officer. They told me that everyone was staying at home and I should also go home straight away. I was to be back in time the day after at 10 a.m. for the doctors' visit. They examined me the following day and told me that I could go home and have my treatment there. Later, when they finally received a request from the financial institution, they gave me permission to leave military service. This is when I was officially discharged and this is how my war duties ended.

On the last page of the Hungarian Napló there is a handwritten note by Stolmár Géza. It says the following:

This book was typed by my daughter Ida in 1936 July, in Domonyvölgy. (Ed: Géza had a cottage in Domonyvölgy.)

Below this note is the signature of Stolmár Géza.

Appendix – Pages from the original Napló

Felrobbantott vasuti hid Stryj mellett. /Chodorowi vonal./
1915. május.

Blown up railway bridge near Stryj. Chodorowi Line 1915 May

A magyar honvédelmi miniszter Hoffmann altábornagy, hadtestparnok csapatainál. 1. Hazai Samu honv.min. 2./ gróf Lemesan vk.ezr. 3./ Blum tbk. 4./ Hodula ezr.
szemle a rakowisci erdő mögött.

Ceremonies near the front lines. National defense Minister Hoffman, Lieutenant General, Commander of the Army Corps 1. Hazai Samu, Defense Minister 2. Count Lemesan, Colonel 3. Blum, General 4. Hodula, Colonel

Brzezany. Kaszárnya.

Brzezany. Állomás épület.

109

Brzezany: barracks. and Brzezany: railway station.

311

Galamb fhxy. fogata, Ger János udvari kocsissal. Lesniky 1916 XII.

Galamb Gyula fhxy. lesniky-i palotája előtt.

125

Galamb. Chief lieutenant with stage coach driver Ger János,
Lesniky, 1916, December.
and Galamb Gyula in front of his Lesniky palace.

Slip & Railway construction.

Házigazdám és családja Demnián 1917 február.

Vacsora Demnió-ban.

171

Domestic help and family: Suppertime

314

Theil Mihály lovászom és
Löw Mihály tiszti szolgám.

Leányok przelasky-ból.

Thiel Mihály, my horseman, Löw Mihály, officers' servant
and Girls in Przelasky.

Civil munkások szállitása Pukow-ba.

Uti motorhenger Pukownál.

Transporting civilian workers in Pukow.
and Roller road compactor in Pukow.

"Asszonyok beosztása
a kőtörőkhöz.

Allotting women to rock-breaking workers.

317

Przelesky. A kőbánya csuzdája.

A pukowi kórház.

Slip from the rock mine and Pukow hospital

-A podhacci vasutállomás az oroszok visszavonulésa után.

Podhajce: aftermath when Russian retreated from there

Buczacz.

141

Buczacz

320

Monasterzyska, vasutállomás,
1917. szeptember.

Monasterzyska Railway Station, 1917 September

Monasterzyska, vasútállomás.

Monasterzyska Railway Station, 1917 September

Az oroszok visszavonulási utjáról.

What the Russians left behind after retreating.

Robbanbások az oroszok visszavonulási utján..
Buczacz.

Buczacz: What the Russians left behind after retreating.

Náci on his last vacation.

By Kopicincze 1917 August: Our home in the forest and Papierna

Voyt.

Próbi lab?-... Kop'cincze nalletb. 1917....

Papierna.

Laci (Younger brother of Stolmár Géza.) Target practice.

Sebesültszállítás.

Schranak, Békefi, Stolmár, Klaus, Kond, Halut.
Lanowce-n.

Moving the wounded by train
and Six soldiers. Faint writing: Schranak, Békefi, Stolmár, Klaus,
Kond, Halut, in Lanowce.

Drótkötélpálya Caldonazzo és Monte Rover között. 1918.márc.

Cable car in Caldonazzo

Val d'Assa, Veraloy.

Husvét vasárnapja a Val d'Assa-ban.
1918. március 31.

Easter Sunday, 1918, March 31 Val d'Assa

Estoril szerpentin ut Monte Rovernél.

Serpentine road Monte Rover.

Fábry Bertalan.

Fábry Breton

Mü kisérőim a háboru elejétől a végéig.

171

My faithful followers, from the start to the end of the War. (Ed: Stolmár Géza's family: Ida, Flóra and mom Flóra, who was often referred to as Flórus by Stolmár Géza.)

A Dubasievics iratok között talált régi arcképe
a királynak és a királynénak.

172

Found amongst the old Dubasievics documents:
pictures of the King and Queen.

Ed: Left to right
Géza on mom's knee, Flóra (mother, often called Flórus), Flóra
leaning on mom's shoulder, Ida standing, Géza (father), Jóska
(baby)

Géza and Jóska, the twin boys, were born on 1918 July 17 so this
photo was probably taken in the middle of 1919.

www.ingramcontent.com/pod-product-compliance
Lightning Source LLC
Chambersburg PA
CBHW021043090426
42738CB00006B/164